Richard C. Gillespie

Managing is Everybody's Business

Illustrated By

Dan Youra

Work/Life
MANAGEMENT SYSTEM™

Work/Life Systems International, Inc.
Everett, Washington, U.S.A.

ISBN # 0-940828-21-9

Published by Olympic Publishing, Inc.
7450 Oak Bay, Port Ludlow, Washington 98365 U.S.A.

Managing is Everybody's Business

Richard C. Gillespie
President and Founder

Work/Life
Management System™

ILLUSTRATED BY

Dan Youra

Acknowledgments

My deepest appreciation of gratitude is extended to:

My family, my wife, **JoAnn**, whose faith in God and caring for me have enriched our lives during the years we have learned to work and live together. To our twins, **Jennifer** and **Robert** for providing me with so much good information from which to develop the personal side of managing. To Mark and Donyce, the older ones, who grew up along side of me when I first began to climb this mountain.

Gerald R. Oncken, Ph.D., *Organizational Psychologist*, former partner and co-developer of the ***Work/Life Management System™***. Jerry and I worked together for six years sharing our knowledge and experiences. Jerry's efforts will always be appreciated;

Chuck Rice, President of IMPOD, consultant, seminar speaker and former IBM associate from Boulder, Colorado, for giving me valuable counsel and encouragement through the years. Also to his wife, **Kay**, whose patience with both of us during our intense sessions I will always treasure;

Lanny Osterhage, retired Weyerhaeuser corporate executive, whose 30 years of managing validated these concepts and tools in action;

A.J. "Skip" Moen, Ph.D., entrepreneur, theologian and friend who read every word and gave excellent specific advice and direction;

Larry Peterson, business manager, author, educator and futurist, who was part of the very early thinking of these ideas 20 years ago, and who continues to make a contribution by his in-depth comments.

To the board of directors of Work/Life Systems International, Inc. who are Mr. **Marvin Crumb**, chairman of the board; Mr. **Jeffrey Miles**, treasurer, and president of Miles Insurance Planning; Mrs. **JoAnn M. Gillespie**, secretary; Mr. **Gerald R. Kingen**, a premier restaurateur, founder of the Red Robin chain and president of Creative Concepts; and Mr. **Greg Hubert,** president of Zanner Hubert, Inc. I am blessed to have people with such vast experience in the business field, high ethical standards and personal commitment to the ***Work/Life*** approach to business on our Board of Directors;

Richard Allan Stull, premier executive consultant, speaker and author whose chapter on Uses of Humor is a special favor and adds value to one of my opportunities for improvement – increasing the use of valuing humor.

James Torrence, US Forest Service Regional Forester (retired), for his continuous support these last 10 years; and to **Hank Montrey**, Director, Rocky Mountain Research Station; **Jeff Sirmon**, Deputy Chief, US Forest Service; **Steve Schlobohm**, Former Director, Youth Conservation Corps Center;

Dan Youra, publisher, editor and long-standing friend of seventeen years, whose illustrations and guidance brought this book to life; and, **Pat Thompson**, who provided helpful counsel through the evolution of this book;

Special thanks are due to **Cindy Wacker, Sheila Moir, Ellen Theisen, Teddi Tolf, Jan Haliday, Cherie Osowski, Terri Ludwig, Julie Torrice** and **Terri Reitz** for transforming the original manuscript from a stack of floppy disks through many changes into a readable book.

Richard C. Gillespie

TABLE OF CONTENTS

"Let all things be done decently and in order"
– Corinthians 14:40

List of Charts viii
Preface ix

1 Introduction: Managing For Continuous Improvement 1

Part I - SOFT SIDE of Managing 27

2 Work Behavior: a Tool Toward Improving the Bottom Line 31

3 Building Trust 49

4 Working Guidelines 63

5 Giving & Receiving Valuing Feedback 83

6 Uses of Humor 97

Part II - HARD SIDE of Managing 113

7 Putting the Basics Back into Managing 119

8 Strategic Managing 149

9 Operational Managing and the Business Plan 173

10 Operational Managing: the Task of Doing the Work 185

11 The Working Agreement: A Managing Framework for Assuring Success 203

12 Making the Working Agreement Be a Vital Part of Today's Reality 221

Part III - CHANGE: Personal & Organizational Challenge 251

13 Managing Change is Everybody's Business 255

14 Work/Life Approaches to Managing Change 283

List of Charts

Organizational Effectiveness 14

Characteristics of Useful Information 20

Part I SOFT SIDE of Managing

Whole Person Model 40

Thinking Out Loud 44

Interpersonal Communication 56

Working Guidelines 67

U.A.S. 73

Validations 88

Criticism Without Blame 95

Part II HARD SIDE of Managing

Managing System Overview 116

S.E.A. 141

Managing System Matrix 172

Working Agreement Overview 214

Sorting Out and Prioritizing 234

Levels of Information 241

Part III CHANGE

Change Model 279

Preface

This book is intended for people who take seriously the notion that *Managing Is Everybody's Business*.

The information in this book has stood the test of time. In 1957, while working for IBM in a manufacturing plant, a project leader for Quality Control named George Vasilof asked me what I would like to do the most in my career at IBM. My response was "learn how to get things done".

Thirty-four years later I'm still pursuing that goal. What I have learned of value about getting things done, I share with you in this book. There are no *Mirrors, Magic,* or *Muff-Ti-Fuff.* Some people **KNOW** about the *Basics of Managing*, others **TALK** about the *Basics of Managing* some people **DO** the *Basics of Managing*, few people **KNOW, TALK,** *and* **DO** The *Basics of Managing*. The ***Work/Life*** approach to managing helps people determine where they are in the **KNOW, TALK,** And **DO** stages of the *Basics of Managing*.

I commonly find people running a business that is profitable and growing with a few glitches here and there. As the business grows beyond their personal ability to handle problems, others are brought on board. Others are included to help keep things growing and profitable. Sometimes this works well, many times it doesn't. The ***Work/Life*** approach helps both.

The ***Work/Life*** approach to managing ties the **"SOFT side of Managing" (Part I),** such as behavior, attitude, motivation, communication, feelings, spirit of intent, etc., to the **"HARD side of Managing" (Part II)** such as goals, objectives, marketing, sales, manufacturing profits, bottom lines, etc. The integration of the **SOFT** and **HARD** sides of managing completes the *Basics of Managing*.

Work/Life Systems International, Inc. is pleased to share this information with you. Many people in our business withhold useful information from the general public to protect their "seminar" business. We have a different philosophy and that is to "share our useful information" so that none will be denied the opportunity because of our selfish interests. As the Chairman of our Board has said many times "We, too, are in business to acquire wealth so that we will not be denied the additional capital to grow and prosper."

We intend to keep growing and prospering by following our Christian Beliefs and following the Corporate Beliefs I learned while at IBM for thirteen plus years—in the integrity of the individual, striving for excellence in the quality of our products and providing the best possible service to our customers.

Thank you for making the investment in our ***Work/Life*** approach to managing. Remember *the only difference in people on the job is their scope of work.* This means we all deserve to be valued, know what we are hired to do, be given the opportunity to do it and be rewarded for the results.

May the Lord continue to bless you in all your endeavors.

Richard C. Gillespie

Prologue: How To Use This Book

Why another book on managing? Usually, we think of management books as complicated guides for corporate executives wearing three piece suits on the 27th floor of tall buildings. And indeed, most managing books are written for corporate executives. This book, however, is about a lot more than concepts for corporate management.

This book is not just for the boss. It is written for everybody. Everybody is somebody's boss. As the title of the book states, *Managing is Everybody's Business*, and we mean it. This book recognizes each of us as managers – the high school service club leader, the young mother trying to manage two kids, the local government worker, the boss at the office, the church board elder, the executive in the corner office on the 27th floor, the supervisor in the high tech firm, the teacher, the coach and you.

We all manage something or somebody everyday. Whether we live and work in the same house or we commute daily from the suburbs to the headquarters, we all *manage* to get things done in one way or another. What this book provides are management *tools* that anyone can use to manage his/her own work and life better.

This is a guidebook to mere common sense. It is a reference book. You might think of it as The Boy Scout Handbook of Managing. It takes the theory of managing and shows you how to weave it into the reality of how you behave. You go to the book when you need to answer a question on *how to get something done.*

You learn how to convert ideas into practical results. Just as the Boy Scout's handbook helps you learn how to read a compass so you can find your way out of a woods, so also this guidebook helps you learn how to use tools such as the "1-to-20" scale to check out commitment levels.

It is important for you not only to *learn* but also to *use* what's in this book. This book is not about how much you *KNOW*, but rather about how much you *DO*. This book is full of tools, tools to help you solve problems, serve your customers better, value people and add a higher quality of living to the fabric of your work/life.

Here are some ways to use this book:

- Check out the Table of Contents. Find a chapter you might like and start there.
- Start reading in any chapter. You don't need to start with Chapter 1.
- You can skip around. Skip a chapter and feel good about it.
- When you run into an idea that really "fits well" for you, stop and make some notes on how that idea can be helpful to you and those around you.
- Seek out others who have a stake in what you're doing and share these particular ideas with them and develop specific ways to immediately implement these ideas to improve your personal work/life.

The reason you can start anyplace in the book is because each idea in the book can stand alone as a tool. Like all tools, they can work in any combination together. For example, we state that "the most prevalent form of organizational theft is the withholding of useful information." To help combat that problem we present a number of tools that work together to *increase* the flow of useful information and open up the decision making process.

Some of the tools you will learn are:

- *8 Working Guidelines*
- *CWB* – Criticism Without Blame
- *"1-to-20"* Commitment Scale
- *SEA* – Situation, Expectation, Action
- *UAS* – Understanding, Acceptance and Support
- *The Working Agreement*

The Working Agreement in the book is a format for integrating the *hard side* of managing and the *soft side* of managing into an effective change model. Use your own interpretation of the working agreement format, yet be true to the principle for each of the categories in the format, such as

Overview – my turf
Focus – "vital few" work
Tasks – who, what, where, how, why and cost of doing it
Visions – the energy that keeps us moving beyond the tough moments of today
Beliefs – the underpinnings for maintaining integrity for both what we do at home and what we do at work.

From the evidence we have from people who have been in our seminars we see people implementing these ideas in ways that are often far better ways than ways we had thought of. We have seen people become successful at applying these concepts in new and creative ways to achieve new directions and new rewarding results in their lives.

None of us can *create* the energy for others to change, but we can *commit our energy* to change. We can go on a treasure hunt to seek out others who are willing to commit energy to change. This commonsense approach to managing helps people who are threatened by the possibility of change to shift from viewing change as a threat to viewing change as a friend.

Our visions for the use of this book include seeing it:

- used by business people because it provides a common language for people from the Chairman of the Board to those who are closest to the point of action;
- adapted for use as a general curriculum in high school to help young people learn these ideas and avoid the pitfalls of those of us who did not have these ideas available;
- referred to by parents in helping families live together better;

- used as a central textbook for teaching;
- used as an auxiliary text book for courses.

The ultimate test of the value of all of this information is when each of us identifies a task and integrates the use of these tools to effectively "get the results" that help us to be more profitable and improve the total quality of our lives in a manner that values people.

These ideas are fundamental to work and to life. We have found that these commonsense ideas are quickly usable with what you already know. You can take these ideas and implement them, applying them in your own way.

Do it.

Chapter 1

Introduction:
Managing For Continuous Improvement

Chapter 1

Managing for Continuous Improvement

Managing is happening all over the place. Even when we're not supervising people, we are managing. And good managers seek out new and different ways of getting the *managing* portion of their work done.

What is new and different for one person may not be new and different for others. Managers, as a vital part of their work, should regularly take inventory of the managing tasks they do, and ask, "how relevant, valid, timely and reliable is my 'formal learning' about managing?"

Why?

Because most of us are managers without having a clue about *The Basics of Managing.*

And many of us supervise "on the job" development of people reporting to us, themselves managers. WE manage at the expense of those around us, because we have little formal knowledge about what it takes to manage well.

The communication era is on us. The media tout mavericks in managing as the answer for "controlling our future before it controls us."

Fear-of-not-being-on-top sets in.

Sensing the panic, advisors sneak out of the woodwork to solve that fear with video tapes, audio tapes, books, manuals, hit-and-run seminars and, above all, one-hour speakers who have the "real" answer. Speakers "pop in," "pop up" and "pop out." And many times, the 24-hour test of the meat in their presentations reveal them to be nothing but cute, sometimes dirty stories, put downs, "case histories," passionate theatrics, high price tags, and subtle anger on our part for being had.

As Wendy's Restaurant chain raised the question, "Where's the *Beef*?", all managers should raise the question, "How do we *Beef* up all our managing if we care about the consequences of our actions?"

An example of an organization that does care about the consequences of its actions is the USDA/US Forest Service. The USDA/US Forest Service mission statement is "Care for the Land. Serve the people." Routinely, we find managers who hunger to *really* care for Our Land. After all, *"your land is my land"* can be interpreted as a unique kind of "take over" *or* serious interdependence. In this case it's the latter.

We also find managers who are committed to serving the people. Typically, some are self servers, some serve selfishly and some serve *ceaselessly*. In this case we also mean the latter.

These are the managers we are proud to be associated with: those who are serious about working interdependently and who are willing to work ceaselessly to get the job done.

To help hard working managers get the job done we need to maintain continuity with the past, as we move into the future. **Being responsible and focused ensure our competency to manage the present with hope, excitement and energy.**

We need not apologize for where we are at, just as we need not wail over selling the Japanese scrap material to build a "war machine" for bombing Pearl Harbor.

We need not wail over MacArthurs' excellence in helping Japan gear up for the future of producing goods for the world.

We need not wail over the trade deficit or the budget deficit.

We do need to take charge of our opportunities to ensure the success of our belief.

We are capable of having a working climate which shouts out, by our actions, the notion that all of us are in the managing business.

Imagine the shivers up the backs of our international competitors. They have hundreds of years of benevolent dictator managing—we don't!

We can outdo our competitors with the practical *Work/Life* approach of *managing together.* With our technological genius, our financial acumen, our marketing wisdom and our visionary bent we can't lose.

Our ***Work/Life*** approach begins with an overview of the framework on which we hang the "hard" and "soft" basics of managing—as you *work.* We say *work* through these chapters. Keep in mind that you are rubbing shoulders with ideas that are proven to work and are *critical* for success in the communication era. The openness, courage, commitment, discipline and action to get things done—will all help us to grow and prosper.

We must always cast about for current useful information on how we are doing in our managing efforts in order to:

- Believe in and support the integrity of each person
- Strive for excellence in all our personal and Work/Life
- Provide the best possible service*

*three IBM beliefs

Over the past 20 years we have slowly summarized our reserves of knowledge reflected in our ***Work/Life*** approach. We have done this in a time when we need it the most. There is a crying need for people to acknowledge, and act with conviction, the idea that *"Managing is Everyone's Business."*

To oversimplify just a bit, three general principles have guided ***traditional management practice*** for decades and these can be seen as a mechanized view of managing:

1. The total work load of an organization is like a large pie that can be repeatedly subdivided until serving-sized pieces are achieved, i.e., until individual "jobs" are defined.

2. Find people who are qualified and motivated to fill each of the defined jobs. Communicate clearly to each employee what his or her job is, and establish an employer-employee relationship based on "a fair day's work for a fair day's pay."

3. Then, if everyone simply does his or her job, it all adds up and the work of the enterprise gets done.

While most managers today would acknowledge that these ideas are simplistic, many still behave as if they were true. These simple principles are appealing: they offer relief from overwhelming challenges that confront managers as a result of profound changes occurring in our society and, indeed, in our world.

Unfortunately, the relief is only temporary at best. The changes are real; they must not only be recognized and acknowledged, but also integrated skillfully into management practice. Here are some of those changes:

- **People today want more from their work experience than a paycheck to take home.** They want to be a part of something, to make a contribution, to help create something in which they can take pride and from which they experience a sense of personal achievement and growth.

- **People are no longer willing to fragment their lives.** An old notion is that employed people have two lives—their work lives and their personal lives, and that they should be kept separate. Today, this dichotomy is rapidly dying as work/life replaces yesterday's work—life.

Now, to a much greater degree than ever before, people are seeking to integrate their lives, to experience a sense of continuity in all of their endeavors. They recognize that attempts to separate their work/lives from their personal lives require a lot of energy and are largely futile anyway. The resulting stress affects every life function.

Furthermore, people are less willing to separate their spiritual lives and secular lives. The idea of being a "Sunday Christian" or having spiritual practice be a separate and private part of life is giving way to making faith and spiritual practice part of one's everyday experience. We see God working through us in our work, our family life, and everything else we do.

- **The nature of work is changing.** It is more complex than ever before. As we move more completely from an industrial economy to an information/service economy, it is more difficult to define specific jobs and to measure quality and quantity of performance. There is a quantum expansion in information which leads to more discretionary time, which in turn requires creativity on the job, not just skill repetition. The whole is no longer simply the sum of its parts; sometimes it's more, and sometimes it's less.
- **Because work is more complex, there is a greater need for really effective teamwork.** In our experience, those organizations that have really mastered teamwork, and they are still relatively rare, are far more creative and productive than those that have not.
- **With the need for improved teamwork comes the need for improved skills at communication, conflict management, and collaboration.** People need to be able to recognize signs of impending conflict and turn it into effective, creative action.
- **With more complex work comes the necessity to have flexible, organic ways to plan, manage and evaluate the work that people do.** The old "position description," while useful for job classification and salary administration purposes, simply does not handle the complexity and dynamic nature of the work people must do.
- **The environments in which many enterprises function appear to be changing more rapidly than ever before.** In many high-tech businesses, what is on the market today is already obsolete in relation to what is in development. The speed of change is increasing.

Who would have thought that the old gasoline service station would give way to the convenience store/self-service/one-stop place? (or that the small convenience store would become a gas station?)

The impact of rapidly changing environments requires a new level of nimbleness in developing and implementing strategies that keep an enterprise viable.

- **Implementing new strategies requires appropriate and effective ways of managing change.** People who are affected by change need understanding, acceptance, and support for their part in doing things differently. As we'll discuss later in the book, failure to achieve understanding, acceptance and support for decisions and/or changes is one of the greatest barriers to effectiveness in most enterprises.

- **Company strategy is no longer the exclusive purview of senior executives.** Some of the most effective and creative organizations we have experienced are those that 1) involve employees at all levels in developing and implementing strategy, and/or 2) make company strategic and operational information accessible to most or all employees.

This openness invites people to be a part of something more than just a job and a paycheck. At the same time it can also be very threatening to managers who believe that being open with vital company information diminishes their own power, influence, or value to the enterprise.

- **Even so-called "enlightened" companies are experiencing problems.** Some organizations have attempted to overcome the negative effects of large size by creating new "entrepreneurships" - small, relatively autonomous units within the company that have complete responsibility and authority for a particular aspect of the overall business. The idea is to create an entrepreneurial sense of ownership and involvement on the part of participating employees.

What has happened in some cases, however, is that while the autonomous units are effective and productive, they have become detached from the overall company strategy. The result is a collection of fragmented units not contributing in a coordinated way to the overall enterprise.

- **Technological changes have revolutionized not only how work gets done, but also what work is done.** Many of the more routine, repetitive, manual jobs have been mechanized.

Secretarial work has changed as more and more managers find it more effective to use word-processing equipment to generate and edit their own letters and other documents.

The ability to retrieve, process, store, display, and communicate information with electronic immediacy is in the hands of more and more people at all levels of organizations.

Coping with these changes requires new frameworks or ways of understanding organizations and the tools to go with them. The ***WORK/LIFE MANAGEMENT SYSTEM*** provides such a framework. It is a tool kit that puts handles on how to deal with the complexities of managing today's organization.

ORGANIZATIONS AS SYSTEMS

One of the foundations of the ***Work/Life Management System*** is the idea that **the most useful way of understanding organizations—regardless of their size, scope, or purpose—is as systems.**

People have studied systems in a variety of scientific and applied disciplines, including biological systems, mechanical systems, and the astronomical systems. While the subject of systems can become very complex, the basic principles of systems are quite straightforward, and they apply regardless of the type of system being discussed. **A system is a collection of parts organized into a whole.** Furthermore, the parts of a system are interrelated, that is, when one part of a system does something or is altered or changed, this usually affects other parts of the system.

In a family, each person is one of the parts of the system, and the family is the whole system. All of the relationships among the various members of the family help define the system.

A similar understanding applies to organizations. The individuals, departments, or other units are parts of the organizational system, and the organization itself is the whole. The relationships among the parts of an organizational system can also be very complex. For example, how well does information flow among departments or organizational levels? How do changes in pricing strategy, initiated in the marketing department, affect work in other areas such as purchasing, manufacturing, credit, product engineering, and sales?

CHARACTERISTICS OF SYSTEMS

Although different types of systems seem on the surface to be very different (e.g., organizations, termite colonies, and galaxies), there are some remarkable similarities. The following characteristics seem to be true of all systems:

1. **The whole system is not equal to the sum of its parts.** In order to understand a system, like a family or organization, it is not enough to understand each of its parts; it is also necessary to understand the relationships among the parts. For example, imagine two people who form a business to develop computer software programs for sale. Each has done so individually prior to their collaboration, and each person has a track record of producing one new software package every 90 days.

A person not thinking in system terms may expect the joint venture will produce two new software packages every 90 days. Although this is possible, it is not likely. In fact, other possibilities exist:

Their working relationship may be such that it stimulates in the partners ideas and ways of doing things that neither would have thought of alone. As a result, they produce more and higher quality software programs than they would have done individually. This relationship is characterized by synergism, in which the whole is greater than the sum of the parts.

Or, they may find that the energy and time required to maintain their relationship actually detracts from their productive energy. The resulting output is lower and perhaps of poorer quality than would have been produced by either partner working alone.

Furthermore, **there are some qualities of systems which are only attributes of the whole.** For example, you cannot measure a person's vitality by doing an autopsy on his parts. A cake has qualities different from its individual ingredients.

The idea that a system is not simply the sum total of all its parts has some rather dramatic implications for understanding and working with organizations. In diagnosing any part of the enterprise, it is not enough to focus attention only on that part.

It is also necessary to examine the ways in which that part is related to other parts of the enterprise. For example, how would changes in the marketing strategy affect other parts of the organization (e.g., sales, manufacturing, administration), and the organization as a whole?

> **2. Most systems are open; that is, they function within an external environment, or larger whole.** They affect that environment, and they are affected by the environment. The system and the environment affect one another through a variety of processes by which they exchange things like energy, resources, information, waste products, and materials, including the flow of people and managers.

The environment consists of all systems outside the organization that either directly or indirectly affect or are affected by the organization. The external environment continually provides opportunities and threats to the enterprise. The survival of any enterprise rests on its ability to capitalize on its opportunities and to minimize the impact of threats.

The terms "opportunity" and "threat" are relative terms; that is, few events in the environment are inherently opportunities or threats. Events become opportunities or threats in relation to the organization's ability to capitalize on them or its vulnerability to them.

Families, too, are affected by their environments. Consider the impacts of such things as neighborhood relationships, availability of church or other support groups, accessibility to retail shopping centers, and accessibility of medical and emergency services.

The proliferation of VCR "houses" provide an exponentially increased exposure to the world through video tapes that instruct. Positive influences are enjoyment, growth and development of a higher level of personal ethics. The negative influences are videos that debase and devalue people. The technology is wonderful. What choices do we make in helping it become an opportunity or a threat?

> **3. There is an organizing principle or basic "glue" that gives a system identity and purpose and holds it together.** In enterprises, this organizing principle is the ***mission*****,** which defines the identity and purpose of the organization.

For an organization, the mission usually focuses on the products or services provided, the recipients of those products or services (customers), and the value of those products or services to the customers. [We're focused on organizations here, keep in mind the same things directly apply to families and individuals.]

The mission is so important to organizations, that we give it a central emphasis in discussing how organizations work.

Then make my joy complete by being like-minded, having the same love, being one in spirit and purpose.
–Philippians 2:2

Mission and mind are synonymous, in this sense, like mind and means – open to, clear about, focused on, headed toward, collaborative. It doesn't mean being 100% in agreement, doing all things the same way, or blind obedience. We believe that all activities of an organization must ultimately be evaluated in light of their *compatibility with* and *contribution to* accomplishing the mission. In the kinds of systems that we are discussing here, namely human systems, the organizing principle is *psychological in nature.* That is, **what hold the system together are shared ideas, beliefs, and feelings of people who are part of the enterprise!**

By contrast, other systems are frequently held together by physical forces (e.g., the solar system is held together by the mutual gravitational force among the sun and the planets).

4. Each system is made up of smaller sub-systems and is itself a sub-system of one or more larger systems. For example, a family is a sub-system of the community or neighborhood in which it lives, and is made up of two or more individuals, each of whom is a sub-system of the family. For an organization, the departments or units are some of the sub-systems.

5. Each system engages in self-correcting activities based on feedback, which usually comes from the environment. A recent example of this is the Coca Cola Company changing the taste formula of its product based on feedback from customers — and then changing it back again based on more feedback from customers!

It is easy to see that some people systems do a better job than others of:

- gathering and interpreting information about themselves and their environment, and
- making use of that information to bring about self-correcting changes in the system.

Virtually all businesses that go out of business do so because they failed in some way to recognize signals that they needed to change something to remain viable.

Such factors as changes in consumer preferences, new strategies by competitors, changes in technology, or new legislation, if not heeded, can quickly bring the demise of an enterprise.

6. Systems have boundaries, which help determine what things are part of the system and which things are not part of the system. In most cases, these boundaries are not rigid and are subject to interpretation.

7. As systems grow, they are usually characterized by specialization of parts. Thus in families, people take on roles, such as mother, father, cousin, grandfather.

In small companies like ours, each person fulfills many roles. In the preparation of this manuscript, we act at the same time as managers, writers, typists, and computer operators. In a large company, those roles might be fulfilled by several employees with more specialized skills.

In small companies, the Personnel Manager does the whole job of personnel management, while large organizations frequently have specialists in human resource planning, wage and salary administration, training and development, labor and employee relations, employee benefits, and equal employment opportunity.

The Six Systems—A Tool For Describing, Diagnosing, and Managing Organizations

As an enterprise grows and becomes more complex, all of us have an increasing need for diagnosing the effectiveness of all functions in relation to each other . For this effort to be successful, we need a commonly understood, accepted, and supported concept of what systems constitute an effective organization.

There is a multitude of ways in which an enterprise can be divided into sub-systems. For some, a useful way is by function, such as finance, personnel, administration, engineering, manufacturing, production control, distribution, sales, marketing, and so on. While this breakdown is useful for many organizations, it does not apply to all organizations.

We have identified some basic systems that apply to all types of enterprises and that provide a useful way of describing, diagnosing, and managing an organization. We define six sub-systems that meet these criteria. They are:

ORGANIZATIONAL EFFECTIVENESS

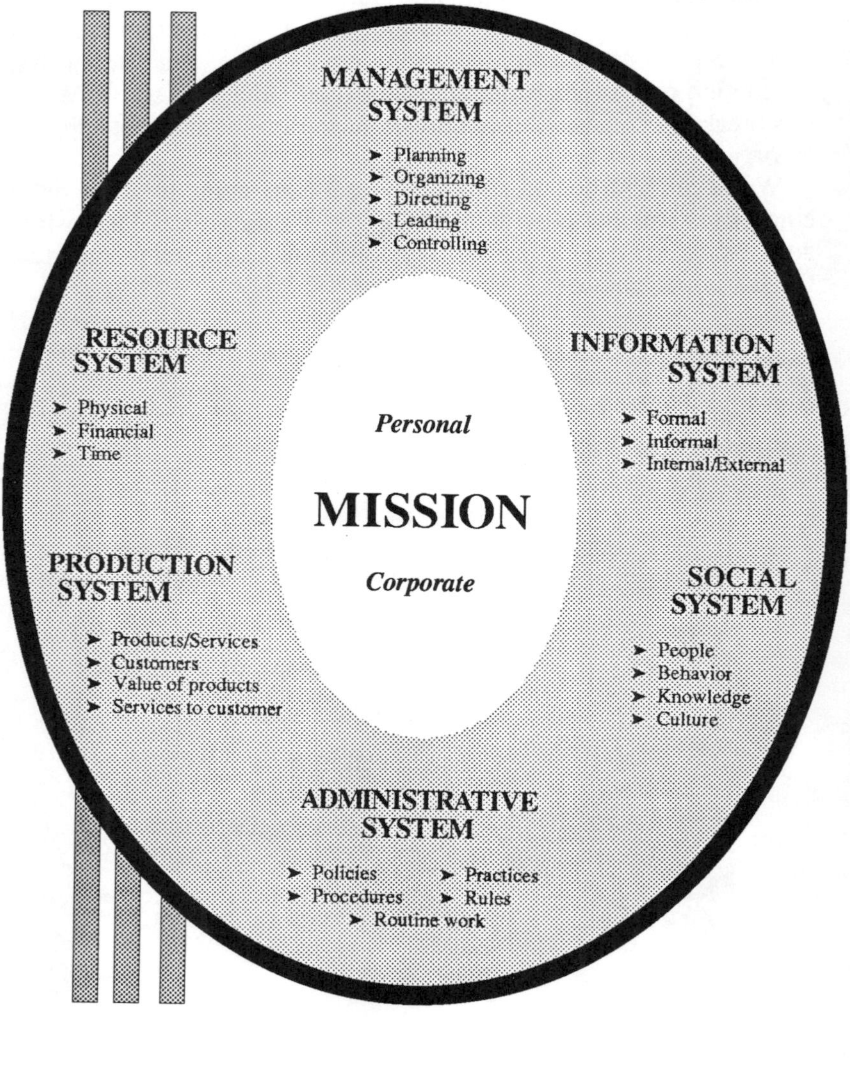

THE MISSION

The Mission is in the center, because it is the reason that the organization exists (its identity and purpose). It's the "glue" that holds it all together. In order for the system to function as a whole, the six systems surrounding the mission must relate to the mission and to one another.

The mission stretches us, individually and/or organizationally. It is not what we are doing now that increases current products and services!

It is our partly cloudy view of the future that provides us with hope, excitement and energy to keep pursuing those possible (not mystic) end results which our customers will value beyond our highest expectations.

The mission is always there, whether we have it written and posted for all to see or are just doing the work...no matter what the process, scope of authority, type of work or even *not* working.

What we **are** speaks openly about what choices we have made and tells the rest of the world **who** we are and what our mission is.

Even though we separate them conceptually, the six systems function interdependently; no system stands alone.

The Managing System

The managing system consists of all activities in the organization that give the enterprise identity, direction, and movement. How many times have you heard those words. Some know what they mean in today's environment, few know how to determine when they are being done, and how to help others do them! There aren't enough experienced managers teaching the rudiments of these functions, let alone successful managers who are open to sharing their expertise. These activities fall

MANAGING SYSTEM

- Planning
- Organizing
- Directing
- Leading
- Controlling

into five basic management functions - planning, organizing, directing, leading and controlling; and are applied in two managing arenas - strategic and operational. In Part 2, The Hard Side of Managing, we discuss these functions and arenas in detail and provide tools for effective action in the managing system.

The Resources System

This system consists of all activities in the enterprise that are dedicated to acquiring, developing, maintaining, preserving, protecting, and replacing its physical and financial resources. Physical resources include physical plant, machinery, equipment, raw materials, tools, fixtures, gages, test equipment, computers, and consumable supplies - the tangible aspects of the enterprise.

RESOURCES SYSTEM

- Physical
- Financial
- Time

Financial resources include not only cash, but also such things as receivables, inventory, credit, profitability, liquidity, equity, and other aspects of financial position.

Some of the activities that occur in the resources system are budgeting, capital improvement planning, financial forecasting, managing cash flow, banking, acquisition of capital, securities management, preventive and corrective maintenance, real estate management, and risk management. While these functions have been stated in "business" terms, their parallels in the family are apparent. Families can get into cash flow problems, or can get over extended in the loan commitment box. Preventive maintenance of a home is as important as preventive maintenance of the buildings in which a company operates.

Time is also a resource. Volumes have already be written on time management. For our purpose, time is a commodity and a scarce one. Some people spend it, others invest it, only God can create it. How do we use it? How do we cut from the "top" of our priorities? How do we say no? How do we "take time out?" How do we "provide, allow, encourage" time? How do we get quality time? How interested are you in answering this list of questions?

The answers to all the above questions relate to how competent each of us is at applying the ***Work/Life Systems*** approach to getting things done. Individuals profit, families profit, enterprise profits, we all profit when we "own" our own schedules.

The Information System

The information system is to an enterprise what the nervous system is to the human body. It consists of all formal and informal activities and processes for gathering, assimilating, interpreting, storing, retrieving, and disbursing information in order for the other systems to function. Included are all forms, media, and technology for communications and information flow about the organization itself and the environment in which it operates.

INFORMATION SYSTEM

- Formal
- Informal
- Internal/External

It would be difficult to overestimate the importance of the information system to the success of any enterprise. In fact, lack of success can often be attributed, at least in part, to problems in the information system. A most common difficulty is when people deliberately or unintentionally withhold useful information from other people or groups. Because this phenomenon is so prevalent, we have concluded that *the most prevalent form of theft in organizations is the withholding of useful information.*

Many people operate under the notion that "information is power." With this operating philosophy, they withhold, distort, or disseminate information as a means of manipulating, controlling, or achieving their own ends at the expense of others. Many are rewarded for individual success at doing this because there is no commitment to viewing performance as a team responsibility. Hence the individual's contribution may in fact be a minus to the organization. Personal gain, corporate loss. Such strategies, and there are numerous examples, deprive the enterprise of the vital information it requires to be successful. Furthermore, this kind of game-playing consumes a great deal of time, energy, and effort which could otherwise be used to the benefit of the enterprise.

Perhaps one of the best illustrations of this phenomenon is a real situation in one of our client organizations. The situation we encountered involved a Senior Vice President in a medium-sized, publicly held company. Over several years, this individual had become the subject of bathroom conversations and the office scuttlebutt. He had developed the reputation of being hard-nosed, uncaring, and brutally blunt, particularly with his peers and with other people outside the division he managed (interestingly, most of the people in his division really liked him). As a result of his reputation, many people avoided talking to him unless it was absolutely necessary, and then limited their conversations to bare essentials. Even the President had tiptoed around this fellow for six or more years, and did not deal with the serious productivity problems that resulted from the man's behavior.

It turned out that not only were several other people unhappy and affected by this situation, but the man himself was dissatisfied. When this all became clear, an effort was made to counsel the individual about his behavior, but the situation had gone too far for too long, and he ultimately left the company by mutual agreement with the President.

He subsequently found a position in another company that was well suited to his talents. Subsequently, he reported that he is happy and productive in his new work.

What caused this whole situation to deteriorate to the extent that it did was the withholding of information by many people for a long time. The president had been unwilling to counsel him about his performance; he withheld information from other people; other employees avoided contact with him. Because of his position and the vital nature of his work, the costs of this situation to the company were tremendous. Not only were the good ideas of a talented individual lost to the company, but many business opportunities were lost as well.

With the rapid accumulation of information and the advances in means for managing information, the possibility of information overload increases dramatically. Many of us can attest to the fact that it is possible to become overwhelmed quickly by the information that is available to us at the "push of a button." How do we sort out the information that is of value to us from that which is not? To help answer this, we have introduced the concept of **useful information.** Useful information is degined as relevant, valid, timely and reliable. These four criteria must be met for information to be useful:

1. Relevant — Fits the situation. Relevant information is pertinent to the work that we are doing or the situation in which we are involved. It has some value in helping us to understand the issue or situation or in helping us make or confirm a decision in respect to the situation. In purchasing a car, the price is relevant information for someone who has a limited budget, whereas for someone with unlimited funds, the price may not be relevant information.

2. Valid — Say what it means, mean what it says. In order to be valid, information must be accurate, meaningful, and presented in a form that is understandable and usable. It must accurately reflect what it is intended to convey to the user. For example, the Dow Jones Industrial Average was at one time a valid economic indicator. Now, as the economy shifts to a service/information economy, the validity of the Dow as a measure of economic activity must be questioned.

3. Timely — Not too soon. Not too late. Timely information is available when it is needed; neither too early nor too late. Sometimes when information is available before it is relevant, its potential value is not recognized, or it cannot be assimilated because of other information that is being handled at that time. Of course, we have all experienced the frustration of receiving a good piece of information one day after the report was due!

4. Reliable — Trust the source, human or other. This refers to the source of information. In order to be reliable, information must come from a source that can be trusted, whether that source is human, mechanical, or electronic.

CHARACTERISTICS OF USEFUL INFORMATION

Relevant →	*Pertinent to the situation*
Valid →	*Accurate* *Understandable* *Meaningful* *Useable*
Timely →	*Available when it is needed*
Reliable →	*Comes from a source that can be trusted* *(human, mechanical, natural, or electronic)*

If, for example, I have received some bad information from a particular individual in the past, I may be skeptical of information that person gives me in the future. Even if the person comes to me with valid, reliable, and timely information, I may not trust that person, so the information is less useful (remember the story of the boy who called "wolf!"?)

In order to be useful, information **must meet all four criteria: relevance, validity, timeliness, and reliability**. If it misses even one, it is not useful. In all enterprises, a primary goal must be to continue to increase and/or maintain an open flow of useful information. The result is better decisions, fewer conflicts, and fewer lost opportunities.

The Production System

Bear ye one another's burdens and so shall ye fulfill the law of Christ. For if a man think himself to be something, when he is nothing, he deceiveth himself. But let every man prove his own worth, and then shall he have rejoicing in himself alone, and not in another.
—Galatians, 6:2-4

PRODUCTION SYSTEM

- Products/Services
- Customers
- Value of Products
- Services to Customer

The production system includes all activities and resources involved in producing and providing the primary products and services of the organization to those who benefit from them. Marketing, sales, manufacturing, shipping, and service delivery are some of these activities.

This is where it all comes together, where the energy, efforts, and resources of the enterprise are directed toward fulfilling the identity and purpose. When each person, unit, and function has interdependentlyh performed the work for which it is responsible, the results will be success for the enterprise, satisfaction for the customer, profit for the shareholders, and fair compensation for the contributing workers.

This applies to families, churches, government agencies, and other nonprofit entities as well as to profit-making enterprises. They just measure success differently.

What is the production system for a family? It is the fulfillment of their goals, hopes, and aspirations through the individual and collective efforts of its members. It is the opportunity for each family member to fulfill his or her life's purpose by honoring and nurturing God-given talents and gifts.

The Administrative System

This system includes all activities and resources involved in maintaining routine, standard, normal activities, preserving the legal integrity of the organization, and managing exceptions. This is accomplished through various methods of regulation and standardization, including the following:

- policies, procedures, and practices
- budgeting systems and procedures
- personnel systems
- rules, laws, standards and regulations
- forms and directives
- procurement systems
- other ways of standardizing the conduct of business.

ADMINISTRATIVE SYSTEM

- Policies
- Procedures
- Routine Work
- Rules

Organizations invest a great deal of time, effort, and other resources in administrative activities both to fulfill their own needs for standardization and to meet many regulatory obligations.

Appropriately used, policies, standards and procedures can be tremendous contributors to the efficiency of an enterprise in that they prevent the necessity to "re-invent wheels" in new situations. Furthermore, they protect the organization from costly interventions by outside regulators.

The Social System

All of the people of an organization make up the social system. The focus of this system is on behavior, those forces in an organization that affect people's behavior, and the results of that behavior. Some of those forces include:

SOCIAL SYSTEM
- People
- Behavior
- Knowledge
- Skills
- Culture

- the organizational climate;
- individual and group beliefs and values;
- habits (defined as behaviors that were chosen at first, but, which through repetition and practice, have become more or less "automatic" responses to given situations.);
- knowledge, skills, abilities, experiences, competencies, hopes, fears, aspirations, needs, and desires of people;
- political and economic pressures;
- norms (mutually understood, informal standards for certain behaviors, such as production rates). Norms are usually unwritten and are frequently enforced by co-workers. For example, an employee who exceeds the "expected" production output may be labeled a "rate-buster" by co- workers, who may administer any of a number of "punishments."
- the formal and informal systems of consequences of behavior, which come in the form of rewards and punishments. The reward system can produce some ironic and unintended outcomes in an organization. For example, we did consulting work in one organization in which the executive managers were attempting, with limited success, to implement an interdependent teamwork approach to managing. One thing that prevented them from doing so effectively was their formal cash award system. While they expressed a philosophy of teamwork and interdependence, employees singled out for performance awards were those who had undertaken special individual effort to achieve some outcome. There were no criteria for recognizing and rewarding constructive efforts at teamwork.

The social system is generally the least understood and most poorly managed system in organizations. As one manager put it, "I can understand and get my hands on each of the other five systems that you talk about, but the social system seems gaseous to me!"

Well, it's hard to get one's hands on a big cloud of gas, so one of our goals in the **Work/Life Management System™** is to put handles on behavior and the more subjective aspects of an enterprise. More and more, people are coming to realize that the most valuable resources of an organization are its people. It is necessary to recognize that people are not just part of the machinery or equipment of an enterprise, but are a unique, living, dynamic system. Prudent management of the human side of the enterprise is a wise investment that always pays off.

We have seen many examples of executives whose bad behavior still gets the job done but at the expense of the stockholders and employees. Sometimes people can be exploited to achieve short-term gains, but over the longer run, the performance of the enterprise will deteriorate and good people will leave.

BEWARE OF THE MISAPPLIED FIX!

We have also seen many organizations that have carried policy formation so far as to unnecessarily constrict the activities of all or parts of the enterprise. Some managers, for example, will attempt to fix a problem in one department or division by establishing a policy that applies to all departments or divisions. This can create some ironic situations.

One company established a dress policy requiring all employees to wear "white-collar" business attire. This addressed the problem of people in reception, sales, and other public-contact positions having a poor appearance, but created some almost ridiculous situations for maintenance people and other behind-the-scenes personnel.

This is but one example of a common phenomenon in organizations that has come to be known as a "misapplied fix," and involves attempting to solve a problem in one part or system of the organization with a fix in another part or system.

In our experience, the most common misapplied fixes occur in the administrative system. Frequently, policy fixes are applied to problems in the managing, production, resource, and social systems. Some of these fixes might be helpful in the long run, but they rarely address the original cause of the problem.

One value of the systems approach to looking at organizations is that it provides a framework for diagnosing the location and causes of problems and directing the solutions to the right places.

SUMMARY

From Him the whole body, joined and held together by every supporting ligament, grows and builds itself up in love, as each part does its work
–Ephesians, 4:16

We have described how an enterprise can be understood in system terms. A general breakdown of organizations into six internal sub-systems illustrates its value in diagnosing and solving problems in organizations. The context or environment in which an enterprise functions must also be seen as a critical influence on the enterprise. It is important to recognize that although we separate the six sub-systems to describe and understand an organization, they do not function independently in practice. The six sub systems are all inextricably woven into the unique fabric that is the enterprise.

In the organization system, managers (social system) use and generate information (information system) in such forms as plans (managing system) and policies (administrative system) in order to manage physical and financial resources (resources system) and produce the products and services of the enterprise (production system).

Our desire is that all of us would develop a habit of considering the above systems as we deal with problems and future efforts. The Celestial Model has the spirit of intent flowing throughout as people weave in and out of each system seeking ways to assure interdependence and increase the excitement for working with each other. This spirit of intent refers to how others see us helping or getting in the way of being successful together.

Celestial Model for Managing

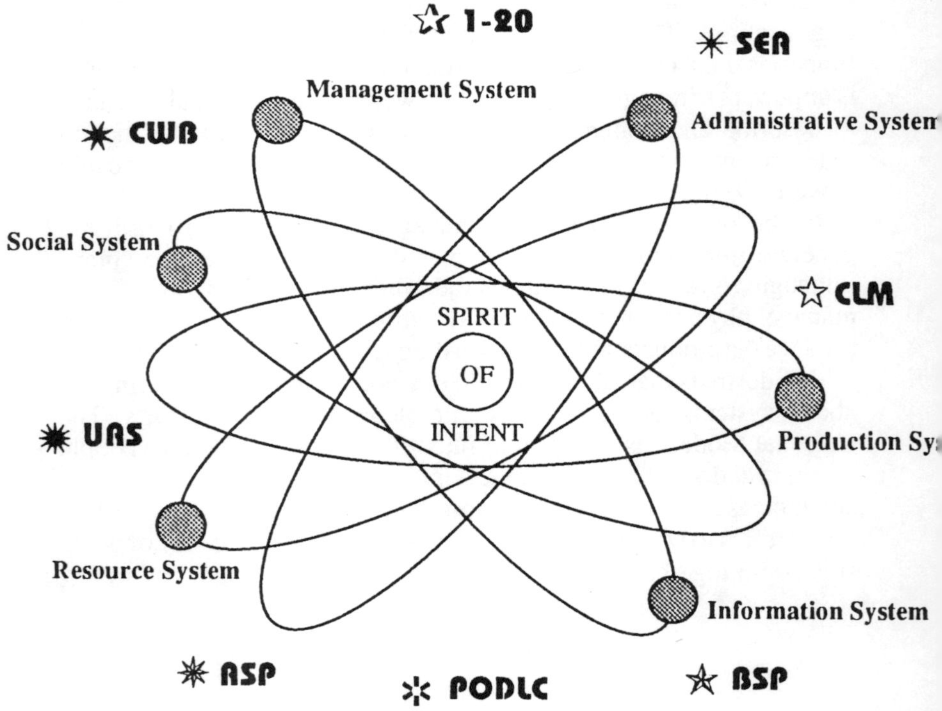

Part I

The SOFT SIDE Of Managing

Part I

The Soft Side of Managing

INDIVIDUAL AND TEAM EFFECTIVENESS

Rarely do we find anyone who would disagree with the statement **"PEOPLE ARE OUR MOST IMPORTANT ASSETS"**. Yet when reviewing corporate annual reports the only people named are the board of directors, the officers and some occasional other persons.

Many human resource directors report to other vice presidents, including the vice president of finance in moderate sized companies and the controller in others. Interesting enough, the training these people have generally is related to numbers, budgets, legal contracts, salary grids and "totems"–personnel rankings, a sequential listing of who is on top in value to the company.

Often the people promoted to human resource director positions tend to have limited operational experience. Their management experience, if they have any at all, comes from service organization activities like, personnel, administration, legal, security and safety.

There are exceptions to every rule. We are aware of some very experienced operational people in the human resource vice presidential level and they are at some very prestigious companies.

We mention this because a lot of the good people serving as top human resource officers who do not have operational experience will find **Part I "The Soft Side of Managing"** more familiar than **Part II "The Hard Side of Managing"** which deals heavily in the operational arena.

On the other hand, most of the other people in the organization will find this section of great significance because it gathers together important principles on motivation, behavior, communications, recognition, and culture.

This common sense approach to these subjects provides some challenges to our present ways of behaving in our personal and corporate lives.

We are going to take a look at :

Chapter 2 Work Behavior a Tool Toward Improving the Bottom Line

- the personality trap
- behavioral responsibility
- foundations for behavior (solid rock type not sinking sand)
- situations determine direction
- the development of whole persons
- a tool for seeing differences as opportunities

Chapter 3 Building Trust

- behaving at work, no longer an option to blow it
- devaluing vs valuing behaviors
- creative tension beats dysfunctional tension (easier on the heart)
- increasing the flow of useful information
- impact on productivity

Chapter 4 Working Guidelines

- working guidelines, communication tools that let you be you and me be me while we focus on getting the job done
- improving the quality of Work/Life.

Chapter 5 Giving and Receiving Valuing Feedback

- accepting and giving positive feedback
- criticism without blame (CWB)

Chapter 6 Uses of Humor

You will find some old friends and some new ones. Perhaps nowhere else is there such a fine gathering, under one cover, of information that helps us improve our relations with ourselves and others.

We find people in our working sessions quickly identifying with these tools, primarily from the point of view that "I hope so and so is *really* paying attention to this" — and those that *really* need this aren't here". When in most cases each person should be asking—"How well am I following these concepts? How willing am I to change? What can I do to help others?"

Chapter 2

Work Behavior:
A Tool Toward Improving the Bottom Line

Chapter 2

Work Behavior:
A Tool Toward Improving the Bottom Line

"And so since everything around us is going to melt away, what holy, godly lives we should be living."
II Peter, 3:11

How often have you made an appointment with a particular individual and set it 15 minutes early, because you just knew that person would be late? After all, it happened four times before.

What do you do when someone takes credit for your idea? How about when you are the object of put-down humor?

When you are asked to do a specific job with tough deadlines and are behind because others haven't completed their portion, which is necessary input into your work, how do you react?

How do you respond when someone else is coming unglued right in front of your face? Do you ever find yourself saying things like, "If Joe weren't so ______________, things would be just fine," or "If they would only get their act together, we could be more effective."? This and the following chapters are about dealing effectively with the complex issue of people and their behavior. The focus is the social system - people's behavior and things that affect their behavior. The subject of human behavior is complex. We focus on some key concepts and practical principles that help put handles on how to improve effectiveness by improving our behavior.

The bottom line is that both effectiveness and quality of work/life can be measurably improved when people accept accountability for their own actions and behave in ways that support and value themselves, others, and the enterprise.

Each human being is a whole person and brings that whole self into each situation. This chapter is about individual human beings and what they bring to enterprises of which they are a part.

OUR BEHAVIOR: WHO IS ACCOUNTABLE?

The idea that we are accountable for our own behavior can be both a blessing and a curse. On the curse side, if we accept accountability for our behavior and allow others the accountability for theirs, we can no longer:

- attribute a poor or ineffective job of communication with another person to that person's "lousy personality."
- blame others for our own mistakes or shortcomings;
- put ourselves or others in a rigid personality box and work against the possibility of change.

On the blessing side, this understanding enables us to:

- change, alter, or modify our behavior in order to be more effective in situations with other people;
- give and receive helpful feedback about our behavior or that of others;
- give ourselves and other people the opportunity to change when change is called for;
- take responsibility for the consequences of our behavior;
- be free of the burden of being responsible for the behavior of other people.

It is important at this point to distinguish between accountability and influence. Each of us allows ourself to be influenced by other people. This is both a normal and healthy situation; without it there would be chaos.

Parents exert influence on their children's behavior; supervisors and co-workers influence the behavior of their fellow workers; bank robbers influence the behavior of tellers. Nevertheless, each of us chooses how to behave.

FOUNDATIONS OF BEHAVIOR

I will behave myself wisely in a perfect way.
When wilt thou come unto me?
I will walk within my house with a perfect heart.
Psalms

What causes us to behave in the ways we do? The answer to this question is complicated, and as might be expected, the "experts" disagree.

The most general, and commonly agreed-upon notion is that what a person actually does in any situation is affected by:

1. Some things about the person or the self;

2. Some things about the situation;

3. Some unique ways that the particular self mixes with the specific situation:

THE SELF "MIX" SITUATION BEHAVIOR

The Self

It has been observed that by the age of six, most of a person's basic beliefs, values, attitudes, and behavior patterns have been formed. These foundations of the self are influenced by hereditary factors, such as gender, body chemistry, and other physical attributes, and by experiences with parents, siblings, and other people.

Lets think back to our own early childhood and recall the kinds of messages we got from other people:

Did we have certain "chores" for which we were responsible? What happened if we failed to do them (e.g., the bed wasn't made, the dog wasn't fed, our room wasn't cleaned, homework wasn't done)?

What ideas have we carried into adulthood based on these experiences (e.g., "We can't do anything right!" or "We are willing to do our share of the work.")

What kinds of behavior did we experience from our parents or other significant adults? Did they handle conflicts or problems in creative and effective ways, or did they handle them in dysfunctional ways? These experiences probably influenced the ways we handle conflict situations now.

Who got into trouble when sister clouted brother with a stick and brother blasted her in the mush with his fist? Was it brother, because "boys don't hit girls" (particularly when it happened out of earshot of the parents)? What other messages did we get about boys and girls? Are they still valid today?

Was our home environment relatively stable and predictable, or did we experience lots of upheaval, inconsistency, or mixed messages (e.g., being punished or praised for the same act at different times)?

These and many other experiences help the growing child to form ideas about what kinds of behavior are appropriate and effective versus inappropriate and ineffective. These ideas are carried into adulthood.

REWARDS AND PUNISHMENTS

People generally tend to continue to do things that get them rewarding or desirable outcomes. (Psychologists call this "positive reinforcement".

If, for example, we want to change a habit in ourselves or help another person change a habit or learn a new behavior, start by rewarding the new behavior frequently. Once the new behavior is learned, it can be best maintained by using a random rate of reward.

To understand this, think of the "one arm bandit" slot machines in Las Vegas. People put money in them over and over again, because maybe this time it will pay off.

Another example: a child really enjoys attention from her mother. She tries many ways to get Mom's attention without success and, as a last resort, emits a deafening scream. Mom turns to her with a disgusted look on her face and soundly (and in a raised voice) rebukes the child.

The result? If this happens frequently, which it does in many families, the screaming behavior becomes worse rather than better. This is because the positive value of Mom's attention, in spite of its form, outweighs the negative or punishing aspect of her rebuke.

The lesson in this example is to be really aware that what we think might be punishment in a given situation may actually be rewarding to the recipient. In work situations, getting chewed out by the boss can actually reward the undesirable behavior if the resultant attention from the boss or peers is rewarding for the individual.

HABITS

Based on accumulated experience of doing and learning, people acquire habits, which are behaviors that at first are done by choice, but which through repetition and reinforcement become "automatic" (that is, they occur with little forethought or intentionality). Many habits are difficult, although by no means impossible, to change.

Furthermore, many habits are very useful to have. Our work habit of maintaining a thorough and up-to-date calendar of appointments, along with a record of expenses, and client contact hours helps us to manage our work more effectively. Other habits, of which each of us can identify many, are dysfunctional, or at best, unnecessary, and deserve to be changed.

The Situation

Many aspects of the situation also affect our behavior. Some of these include:

- the reactions of other people to our behavior, which can be rewarding or punishing;

- the formal and informal "roles" in which we place or find ourselves, each of which carries with it prescriptions for how to behave (e.g., parent, supervisor, manager, teacher, trainer, consultant, union member, Christian, child, president, welder, minister, clerk/typist 3, and so on);
- the expectations of other people for our behavior;
- the "norms" of a particular situation (e.g., on an assembly line, the norm may be to produce 25 units of product per hour. Anybody whose performance is either significantly greater or lower than that norm is likely to be punished or even ostracized by the work group.)
- physical aspects of the situation, such as temperature, light, air quality, elevation, obstructions, condition of tools and equipment);

The "Mix"

The point at which *the self and the situation mix* to determine a person's specific behavior is where the business of understanding and predicting behavior becomes very complex. We'll limit this discussion to a few examples that illustrate the overall concept.

First example: Two employees with similar work assignments make similar mistakes on the job. The supervisor brings in each employee to provide feedback about their performance.

The first employee, who has generally low self esteem (i.e., does not see his or herself as being competent or worthy), based on early experiences of being criticized in the form of ridicule and put-downs, is embarrassed, handles the feedback poorly, and subsequent performance deteriorates. The second employee, whose self-esteem is high, uses the feedback as an opportunity to strengthen performance.

Second example: A young father-to-be, who is normally squeamish at the sight of blood behaves admirably and, in fact, is very helpful at coaching and supporting his wife during the birth of their child.

Third example: A person whom others have regarded as being shy and reserved courageously refuses to be influenced to engage in behaviors that violate his/her basic values.

Final example: Two members of a work group react very differently to an argument that arises. One, whose family history is one of arguments deteriorating into toxic, unpleasant brawls, either withdraws or does what she/he can to mask or minimize the differences of opinion.

The other, whose family experience included stimulating discussions, enjoys the discussion and uses it as an opportunity to sharpen his/her thinking and help the group come up with a creative solution.

BEHAVIOR AND PERSONALITY— WATCH OUT FOR THE TRAPS!

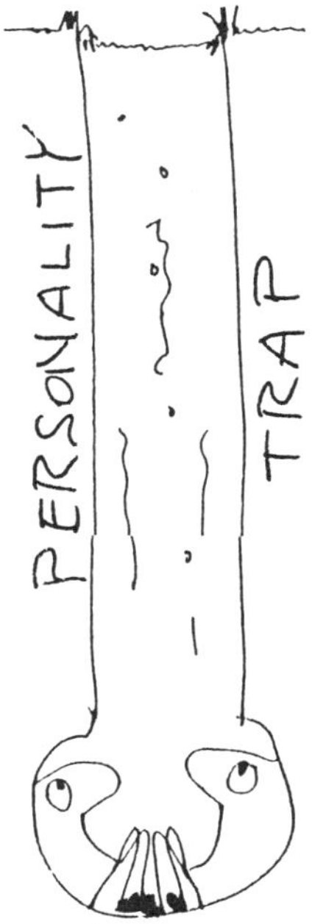

Don't let others spoil your faith and joy with their philosophies, their wrong and shallow answers built on men's thoughts and ideas, instead of on what Christ has said.
— Colossians, 2:8

For each of us, our first and most important point of contact with people is through our experience of one another's behavior. (While the subject of other, extrasensory ways of experiencing people, is fascinating, it is beyond the scope of this book.) We see, hear, and feel others as they do what they do, and it is from this experience that we form conclusions about them.

These conclusions are frequently

summarized as traits that make up the "personality" of the individual. The concept of "personality" is both useful and limiting.

Psychologists define personality as a collection of traits or characteristics that make up an individual - his or her typical way of responding to the world. This means that each person is in some ways predictable, that is, we come to expect certain reactions from others to specific situations and are surprised if they do otherwise. (Even people who are usually unpredictable are predictably so!)

From those predictable aspects of behavior, we attach certain personality traits for ourselves and others. What is important here is that we can observe only others behavior; others personality is only an inference or an interpretation of others behavior. A personal example may serve to illustrate these ideas:

Earlier in our marriage, my wife had primary responsibility for handling the family finances. We had established a budget, and she very competently saw to it that the bills were paid and that the money was at least as long as the month.

She had learned, through hard experience, that when unanticipated expenses or other unforeseen events caused a strain on our finances, I sometimes reacted in a negative way and asked for an accounting of how the money had been spent. She interpreted this as accusing her of poor handling of our money, and the conflict began.

From her point of view, she saw me as being sensitive about money matters and fearful about not having "enough." As a result of these traits (sensitive and fearful), she could predict my behavior in such situations.

I in turn saw her as being sensitive about things for which she had responsibility and unwilling to be objective in managing difficult money situations. What we had to ultimately recognize was that these inferences about one another were little more than our own judgments. We were setting ourselves and one another up in what we call "personality traps." The truth is that my judgments about my wife (or my boss or my work colleagues) mean something about me, not about the other person.

The personality trap comes in the form of rigid boxes that we build around ourselves and other people. The boxes are adorned with lists of trait labels that define the person and limit everybody's ability to change (much as a steel trap limits the ability of the trapped animal to move freely).

Had I remained in the personality trap with respect to my wife, I would have concluded that "that's the way she is, and therefore she'll always react the same way." Had she done the same to me, we would have become stuck with little possibility of getting past this difficult pattern of interaction".

Personality Conflicts - Real or Imagined?

In our consulting experience, we have seen numerous examples of people being stuck in the personality trap. This shows up in the form of "personality conflicts." Sound familiar? We find that we can go into any organization and ask the first person we encounter where the personality conflicts are, and the answers are immediate.

In most cases, the conclusion that two people have a personality conflict is a cop out – an excuse for not taking responsibility to see that effective communication occurs.

Furthermore, not only do the two parties involved in the conflict describe it as a personality conflict, but people around them reinforce and support the idea. The resulting pressures not to change and resolve the situation can be overwhelming.

Conceptualizing a conflict as a personality conflict brings with it other ideas that limit the possibility of resolution:

> "There's no hope of changing anything."
> "If that person would only change, everything would be OK."
> "I wish he would go away!"
> "I have to fight or give in."
> "There are people with whom I just cannot work."
> "I can only react to others."

Of all the conflicts among people that are interpreted as personality conflicts:

> 95%* (yes, that's 19 out of 20) are based on misunderstanding, and can be resolved by applying some simple and effective principles of behavior and communication;
> *and*
> only about 5%* are based on truly incompatible traits of the individuals involved.
> **(These percentages are based on our best judgement through our experiences over the past 20 years).*
> (Would you believe 80% and 20% – the point is that a high percentage is due to *misunderstanding*).

The costs to families, businesses, and other organizations of not dealing with conflicts are enormous. It is possible for people to learn how to effectively work with others. If we can maintain an awareness that change is possible for ourselves and for others, we can eliminate much unnecessary conflict and initiate and maintain more constructive working/playing relationships.

We see this as an obligation for people engaged in any form of enterprise.

WHOLE PERSON MODEL

Our behavior as projected to others

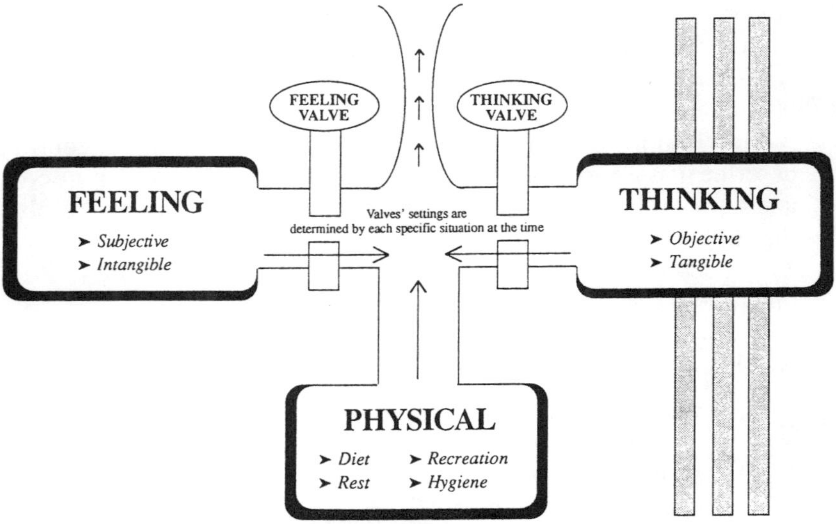

THE WHOLE PERSON

Early in this chapter, we referred to each human being as being a whole person. To illustrate what that means, we offer a simplified concept that dissects the whole person into three functioning components: the physical aspect, the thinking aspect, and the feeling aspect. By the way, we believe that our Christian spiritual selves underlie and transcend these three aspects.

The Physical Aspect

The physical self is the body and all of its functions. We experience one another primarily through the physical self and its senses. It is through the physical self that our behavior occurs. The condition of the physical self plays an important role in how well we function in the world. Some considerations in caring for the physical self are:

- Diet - which includes everything we put into our bodies through our mouths;
- Exercise - moving and using the body at or near its limits. We are not in the business of advocating particular exercise or conditioning programs. We simply offer the idea that people maintain an awareness of their own levels of exercise and make informed choices about it.
- Rest and Relaxation - Few people really experience the depth and quality of rest and relaxation that their beings require. We need to take an inventory of our own approaches to rest and relaxation. We need to see them as being important.
- Grooming and Hygiene - These affect how we present ourselves to the world and reflect how we think and feel about ourselves.

The Thinking Aspect

This aspect of the whole person is what many people refer to as "mental." These characteristics typify the thinking system:

- Logical
- Objective
- Rational
- Analytical
- Verbal (able to attach words to ideas)
- Linear (able to put objects, events, ideas, or words into proper sequences)
- Left brain.

In the world of business, the "thinking person" has been viewed as being the most well equipped to deal with the unfolding array of situations that must be met and decisions that must be made.

Furthermore, the logical, rational thinking self has been traditionally interpreted as a male characteristic. Females, on the other hand, have been understood to reflect the feeling self.

We categorically support the idea that both genders have the capacity to be a logical, rational thinking *and* feeling selves.

The Feeling Aspect

This aspect of the whole person is characterized in the following ways:

- aesthetic
- subjective
- emotional
- intuitive/creative
- holistic (seeing the world in whole patterns)
- non-verbal (generally unable to associate words with ideas)
- right brain

The feeling side of us is a tremendous source of energy, ideas, inspiration, and creativity. *By the way, most, if not all decisions are made in the feeling system.* All of the rational, systematic approaches to decision making simply lead us to the point at which we can select the alternative that feels best.

Reacting and deciding on the basis of feelings *alone* are irresponsible!

A key point that we want to make is that all of us come fully equipped with *physical, thinking, and feeling aspects*.

The importance of the feeling side has been greatly under-estimated, especially in the work place. Consider the following processes, all of which are in the feeling system: motivation, excitement, creativity, intuition.

Finally, we would emphasize that all of these aspects of the whole person affect one another. Our behavior reflects a combination of what we think and how we feel about a situation. Occasionally (or is it frequently?) our behavior reflects an imbalance between the thinking and feeling aspects. Sometimes when we become very emotional about something, we behave in ways that, had we balanced it with a bit of rational thought, we might have done differently. On the other side, we have known people who tend to shut down their feeling system output and behave in completely controlled, rational ways. Be assured that the feeling material is in there; those people are simply not letting it show. It also has been amply demonstrated that most, if not all, illness can be traced to an emotional base. Degenerative disease processes (heart disease, hypertension, ulcers, cancer) are known to have bases in how people deal with their emotional material.

Furthermore, there is good reason to believe that susceptibility to infectious disease is affected by our emotional state.

More and more organizations are recognizing the value of acknowledging and nourishing the whole person. We see previously "hard-nosed" managers being willing to be guided by their intuitions (and to acknowledge this).

People are becoming more aware of the importance of feelings and are more willing to allow feelings to play an important role in human interactions and decision-making.

Many companies are now providing opportunities, sometimes in the form of facilities on the premises, for people to engage in physical exercise. These investments in the whole person will surely continue to bring positive results.

PEOPLE DO DIFFER

Thus far, this chapter has focused on ways in which all people are similar. In this section, we recognize what your experience has probably told you: people do differ.

Seeing Differences as Opportunities Rather Than Threats

Live in harmony with one another. Do not be proud, but be willing to associate with people of low position. Do not be conceited. Do not repay anyone evil for evil. Be careful to do what is right in the eyes of everybody. If it is possible, as far as it depends on you, live at peace with everyone.
— Romans, 12:16-18

Most people in work, family, or other situations, encounter other people who are somehow different than themselves. Many times these differences are small and seemingly trivial, but all too frequently, differences are seen as obstacles to working together effectively.

In fact, differences are frequently seen as being very threatening. As a result, people are labeled, stereotypes form, and all sorts of barriers to communication and creative co-working are built.

One implication of this is that many of us would like others to be just like ourselves! Is that really what we want? We think not.

We believe that two essential things can make an enormous difference:

1. A shift in perspective from seeing differences as being threatening to seeing differences as being opportunities; and

2. Improving our skills at working effectively with people who are different from ourselves.

The first change is simply a conscious decision. If we are threatened by differences, it is because we have chosen to be so. We can simply change our perspective and recognize the tremendous potential, or opportunity, that is available through the effective blending of the skills, talents, and ideas of the people with whom we work.

Although this shift in perspective is simple, it isn't always easy. Something what does make it easier is to improve our skills at working with people who are different.

THINKING OUT LOUD

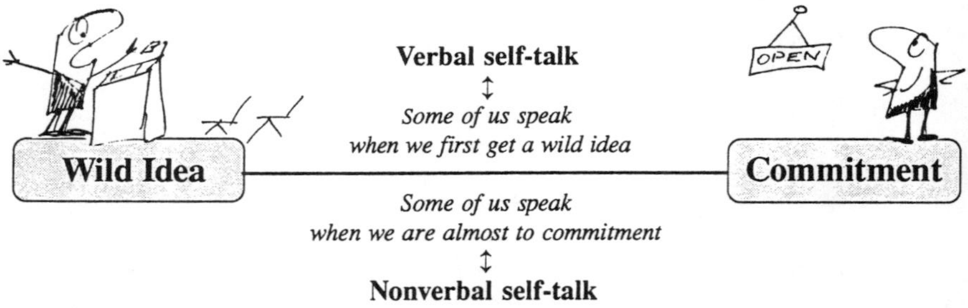

(1 TO 20)

At what level do you begin verbal self-talk?

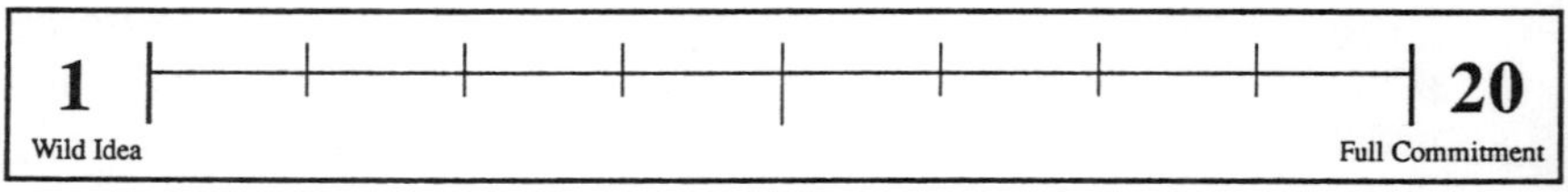

We developed the "1–20" concept as a result of a communication problem that confronted us. Since we began sharing it with client groups the past nine years, there have been numerous instances in which people have told us how this tool has made it possible for them to speak up with minimal risk and deal with tough situations, both at home and at work.

We'll describe this concept through a story of how this book was developed. When we began working together in our consulting business, we spent many hours sharing our conceptual understandings about how organizations operate. Periodically we would have some significant differences, and it quickly became apparent that we had some different ways of doing things.

While many of our differences were trivial in relation to a very strong developing working relationship, one difference became a minor annoyance to both of us and surfaced as a misunderstanding on several occasions.

The misunderstandings arose because of differences in how we process ideas. When I get a new idea, it is important to me to begin talking about it almost immediately. It is useful for me to "hear myself think" in order to process and evaluate ideas.

The tendency for some others, on the other hand, is to very thoroughly think through ideas before saying anything about them to anyone. For whatever reason, it was important to them to have fully evaluated and edited their thoughts before sharing them. Taken to their extremes, these approaches presented opportunities for conflict.

A typical conflict goes something like this: I would come up with a new idea. I would immediately begin describing the idea, usually very enthusiastically. Others reaction to my enthusiasm was that I was fully committed to the idea and ready to implement it, and others hadn't had time to think it through. I, on the other hand, interpret others silence as agreement, and proceeded to talk myself into the idea!

Finally one day we realized what was happening, had a good laugh, and worked out a concept to describe what was happening. We realized that some people need to "talk to think" (others have referred to this tendency as "auditory external" or "extrovert"), while for others it is important to "think to talk" (introvert).

The diagram below illustrates this idea. The horizontal line represents the evolution of an idea, from conception or first exposure at the left end, to full understanding and commitment at the right end.

Furthermore, we let everything above the horizontal line represent "talking about ideas" and everything below the line represent "thinking to oneself about ideas".

EVOLUTION OF AN IDEA

Thinking To Oneself About Ideas

Once others realized that I preferred to talk to think, they could relax; just because I was talking enthusiastically about an idea didn't necessarily mean that I was fully committed to it.

Furthermore, I realized that it is sometimes important to others to think things through before they begin talking about them.

In the diagram, the line represents the evolution of an idea from first exposure or conception to full understanding and/or commitment. Using that line, we have created a 1–20 Scale, with 1 representing the initial exposure to an idea and 20 representing full understanding and/or commitment. Intermediate numbers represent steps between these two extremes.

This 1–20 scale is an immediately useful tool for describing where a person is on a particular idea or decision.

For example, when I have a new idea, I will frequently say to others, "I have a wild idea", or "I'm at about a 5 on this idea, and I want to discuss it." The message to others is that I am not at commitment. I am also working on my behavior to allow others, who think differently than I do, to get some air time on issues.

Others find it important to work on being willing to enter the talking process earlier in their thinking. This gives people like me the benefit of knowing what they are thinking about and gives them the benefit of feedback and new information that is useful to them.

Couples have been able to use this tool as a means for checking out how far along the 1–20 scale each of them is, particularly on important subjects. Many times, conflicts of understanding can be avoided by simply checking out where the other person is on an idea.

This concept is also useful in the decision making process where more than one person is involved. The discussion leader or key manager can check out where each person is on the 1–20 scale in respect to his or her level of commitment to a particular decision. If everyone is at 15 or above, that is a good indication that a consensus has been reached, and little or no further discussion is necessary.

Frequently what happens is that one person may be at a 5 while all others are above 15. Checking out what is behind that person's position allows the individual to tell it as he/she sees it and frequently results in an even better decision in the end. This concept has also been helpful to executives who want to share some information on a particular issue or situation, or, who simply want to enter into a discussion of an issue without people over-reacting and taking their comments as a decision to act.

This builds creativity and teamwork when all people at the closest point of action are willing and able to interact earlier in the decision making process. It also relieves some of the unnecessary stress.

One final story about the "1–20" scale: When we described this concept in one working session, a woman jumped up and said, "Now I know what's been going on with my husband!" She went home that evening, and described it to her husband by drawing the diagram on a grocery bag.

The next morning she could hardly wait for our session to open up. Excitedly she exclaimed, "I've got to tell you what happened between my husband and me last night." Like good consultants always do, we said, "Say more about that." The summary of her response was that, as she described "above and below the line," her husband began to chuckle and said, "yes, I am below the line and have been trying to get above the line with you for 23 years...and this is the first time I've had a real chance." They talked together until 2:30 AM..

Other Approaches to Dealing With Differences

In the training, consulting, and human development fields today, there are many practitioners who offer methods of identifying and working with differences among individuals. Many of these programs include tests or other indicators of personality type, behavioral tendency, situational response, or other traits.

While we applaud and support these efforts to help people deal constructively with others who are different from themselves, we would also add a word of caution.

We have seen many instances in which the results of tests or trait profiles are used to people's disadvantage rather than to their advantage. In these cases, the labels, which are an inevitable result of the testing process, become stereotypes by which people place one another in "boxes" – the person "becomes" the label.

Labels become excuses for not being able to work together (e.g., "I'm a type X, and he's a type Y, therefore we cannot work well together.) Most responsible practitioners warn against this tendency, but it happens anyway. In chapter six, Putting the Basics Back in Managing, we spend more time on the impact of Labeling during the process of changing for the better.

SUMMARY

The first part of Chapter two laid some of the foundation material for the **Work/Life Management System**. Our intent was to clarify some ideas that we referred to as the self, the personality, the whole person, and behavior. Then, we offered some perspectives on how to work effectively with people who are different from ourselves.

These foundation ideas are important to the **Work/Life Management System**, which challenges us to:

- **Recognize and honor the integrity of the wholeness and individuality of each person.**
- **Use the idea of personality to help us choose appropriate behaviors that are effective and supportive in our relationships with other people and to avoid placing ourselves and others in personality traps.**
- **Avoid using the phrase "we have a personality conflict." The reason is we *are not* psychiatrists or trained psychologists – *we are* people who know what behavior helps or gets in the way of working together.**
- **Be willing to take accountability for our own behavior and give others responsibility for theirs.**
- **Give ourselves and others the permission and the opportunity to change when change is necessary.**
- **See differences as opportunities rather than as threats.**

We suggest that you take some time to put the "1–20" idea to work. Pick a situation in which you can use the 1–20 scale to let someone know where you are on an idea. *Have some fun with it!*

Chapter
3

Building Trust

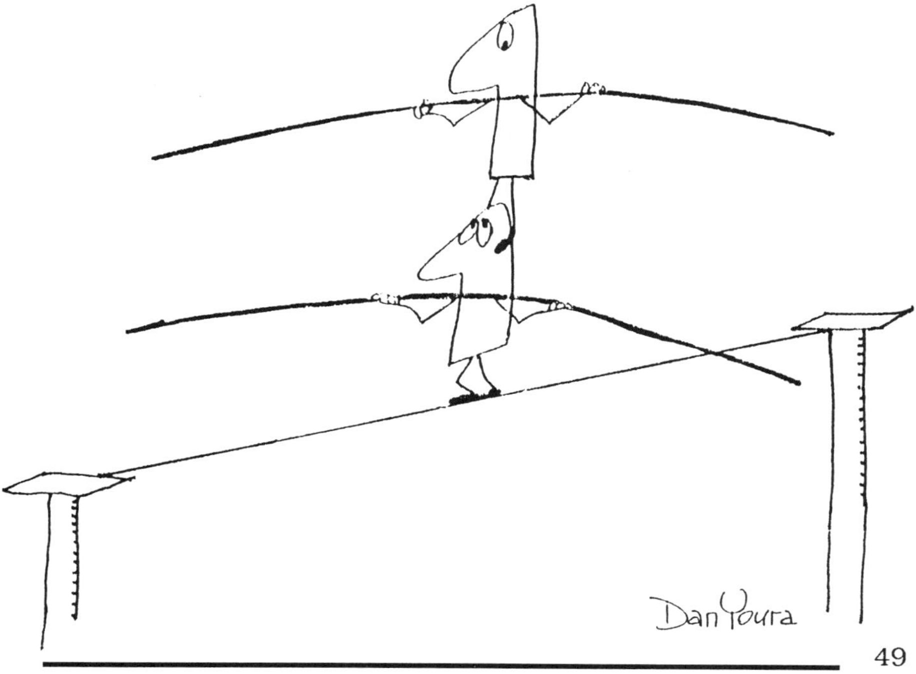

Chapter
3

Building Trust

BUILDING A PRODUCTIVE WORK/LIFE CULTURE

Over and over again, people are confronted with situations that challenge their abilities and highlight their inabilities to deal with one another in consistently effective ways. Even in the best of situations, conflicts arise, miscommunications occur, and people's feelings get hurt.

We are, after all, talking about human beings, who have their unique needs, quirks, foibles, attitudes, beliefs, and habitual ways of doing things. We do not, therefore, carry the naive hope of eliminating conflicts and misunderstanding, but rather to emphasize the following:

1. **Improving our effectiveness in working, playing, and being with other people.**
2. **Minimizing unnecessary conflicts and misunderstandings.**
3. **Learning how to deal with tough situations when they arise.**

WORK/LIFE CULTURE

For each of us it is true that "you are to me what my experiences with you have been." If we extend this idea to a family, a work group, a social group, or a whole organization, we approach the idea of the "work/life culture."

While we acknowledge the critical importance of the physical environment on people's effectiveness and well-being, we focus here on the social or behavioral environment.

For any person who is a member of an enterprise, the work/life culture is the summation of his or her experience of the behavior of other people in the system. Note the emphasis on the word "experience."

Frequently the intent behind one person's behavior is understood very differently by other people who experience that behavior. How many times have we said or heard others say, "I was just trying to help!"? Their intent may have been purely to be helpful, but they were seen by others as being an irritant.

Wherever we go, we find ourselves working together with other people, even on the highway, at home, taking in a movie, at a dance, and in church. Let's look at some ways of improving the ways we work together.

FOUR WAYS OF BEHAVING

In the course of our work, we have come to recognize four general ways of behaving, or strategies that individuals and groups of people adopt. None of these strategies is inherently effective or ineffective; it depends on the demands of the situation.

What often happens, though, is that people come to habitually rely on one strategy to the exclusion of others, regardless of the situation. The result is that their behavior is at best ineffective, and at worst, destructive.

We call the four behavior strategies dependence, independence, counterdependence, and interdependence. Here is a brief description of each of these strategies:

1. DEPENDENCE:
"If you win, I win."

When in a new work situation, it is important to depend on others to give appropriate orientation and training until the person is capable of performing the work. This is an appropriate dependent relationship with those people.

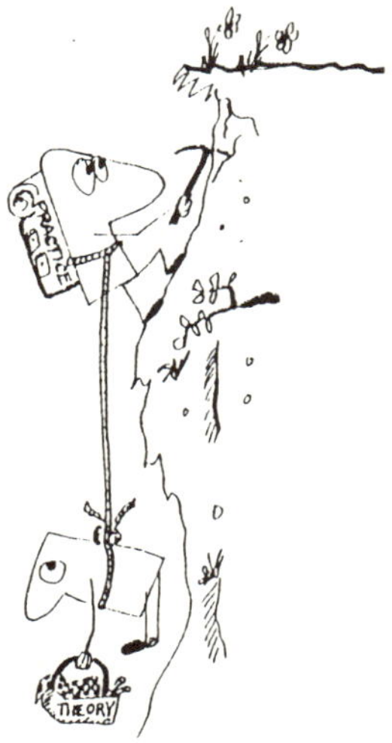

An infant is dependent on its parents for nurturing and protection. A growing child is dependent on his parents to provide a home, food, clothing, guidance, and appropriate discipline. Workers depend on others for information, materials, support, and other resources to get the job done. All of these are useful and appropriate dependent relationships.

We can also cite many examples of where dependent relationships are inappropriate:

- **An employee consistently waits to hear her boss's opinion before expressing her own**
- **A worker checks with his supervisor before taking even minor steps in his assigned work**
- **A middle manager, afraid to be accountable for her decisions, sends routine decision items up to her manager for approval, and the manager allows this "upward delegation"**

A classic marital dependency relationship showed up in a conversation recently with a couple. The husband is a prominent and prosperous physician in their community. The wife gives the impression as being totally subservient to her husband.

During the course of the conversation, she frequently down-played her own life and consistently deferred to her husband. At one point she said, "I have no talents." It appeared that she achieved her "successes" vicariously through her husband. Note that any dependency relationship involves two parties, the "depender" and the "dependee." Any ongoing dependency relationship is the responsibility of both parties. In fact, many such relationships are instigated by one person who seeks power over others.

Consider the individual who withholds critical information from others and then doles it out in pieces at a cost to the recipients.

People functioning in dependent relationships frequently come to resent it. For example, we know of one executive manager who insists that before any correspondence goes out of his department, he must have the opportunity to edit and approve that correspondence. The people who work for him have "gotten around the system" by doing more of their business by phone or not doing it at all, just to avoid the boss's red pencil.

2. INDEPENDENCE:
"I win or lose on my own."

The predominant theme in a strategy of independence is that "I have a job to do; just leave me alone and I'll get it done." Sometimes this is the only way that things will get done and is therefore an appropriate strategy. More and more, however, we are coming to recognize the costs associated with people trying to work independently. While independent action may be efficient in respect to time, many

opportunities are lost for the creativity and innovation that result from the synergistic effects of two or more people working together.

Our economy has moved from a predominant emphasis on production to a primary emphasis on service and information. In the production economy, work was simple, and people could work independently to fulfill their parts in the production machine. Now, the independent approach is not sufficient in an increasingly complex work environment.

Unfortunately, the educational system in the United States is not keeping pace with these changing needs. Students are given rote intellectual information and are rewarded for individual academic achievement (e.g., valedictorian, salutatorian, honor roll), while group processes such as teamwork, problem solving, communication, and creativity receive comparatively little emphasis. In fact, collaborating in schools is called "cheating!"

In the so called team sports, much attention is devoted to individual heroes or "stars." This failing in the public schools is just one factor in the rise of private, parochial, independent, and alternative schools.

3. COUNTERDEPENDENCE: "I win, you lose."

Counterdependence is probably the most destructive and widely used strategy. In a counterdependent mode, my aim is to win at your expense. It is based on the assumption that there must be winners and losers and that life is a "zero sum game" (i.e., a game like poker in which the winnings of one person come out of the losses of one or more other persons).

Our world is full of examples of counterdependent behaviors that drain energy and resources from creative enterprise:

- **The children competing for attention from mom and dad**
- **Politicians compromising their responsibilities to compete for votes**
- **Individuals, work groups, and companies engaging in various forms of sabotage to weaken their opponents and gain a competitive edge**

Again, we recognize the value of some types of "healthy" competition. The key here is how we go about winning and what the outcomes are for the winners and for the losers. To win at someone else's expense which negatively affects their life has little value.

4. INTERDEPENDENCE:
"Win-win" — The preferred way.

An interdependent strategy includes the best of the other strategies and a great deal more. It recognizes that each of us needs and can benefit from working cooperatively with others. It is based on the idea of synergism—that the whole is greater than the sum of its parts. It *celebrates* the diversities among people as strengths and opportunities rather than as threats, and places a high value on the contributions of each person involved.

An interdependent work/life culture is characterized by appropriate doses of dependence, independence, and counter-dependence, and, the following types of situations are evident:

- People accepting responsibility to initiate and maintain collaboration;
- People striving to maintain an open flow of useful information;
- High levels of mutual trust and respect among people;

- Heavy use of participative managing strategies;
- Minimal use of formal power and authority, high degrees of self-regulation, with leadership flowing to the person or persons with the most knowledge or skill for the particular issue, situation, or task;
- Differing viewpoints being aired openly and an emphasis on seeking outcomes that build on the contributions of all;
- People being willing to praise and affirm positives in others and give meaningful criticism without blame where it is appropriate;
- A preference for compromise over combat, and a willingness to give a little individually for the greater good of all.

The more experience we have, the more convinced we are that interdependence is the preferred work/life climate in work, home, and other situations.

The remainder of this chapter discusses some concepts and practical skills for building this type of culture.

An assumption that many people make is that the work/life culture that they experience is something that happens to them that is outside their control.

Our strong belief is that all people in any situation are co-creators of that situation, whether intentionally or by default. In the workplace, the people who make up the work force are responsible for the work climate that exists; they create it by their individual and collective actions. Furthermore, as we expressed in Chapter 1, each person is responsible for his or her own behavior. For the individual, the recognition that

> He is responsible for his own behavior, and he has power in creating and/or changing the situation if he does not like it, takes him out of the VICTIM role that many people assume.

The assumption of the victim is that the focus of control is outside himself; that other people control his destiny. Under this assumption, people abdicate their own power. It is our desire to help people *be aware of their own power and use it effectively.*

INTERPERSONAL COMMUNICATION

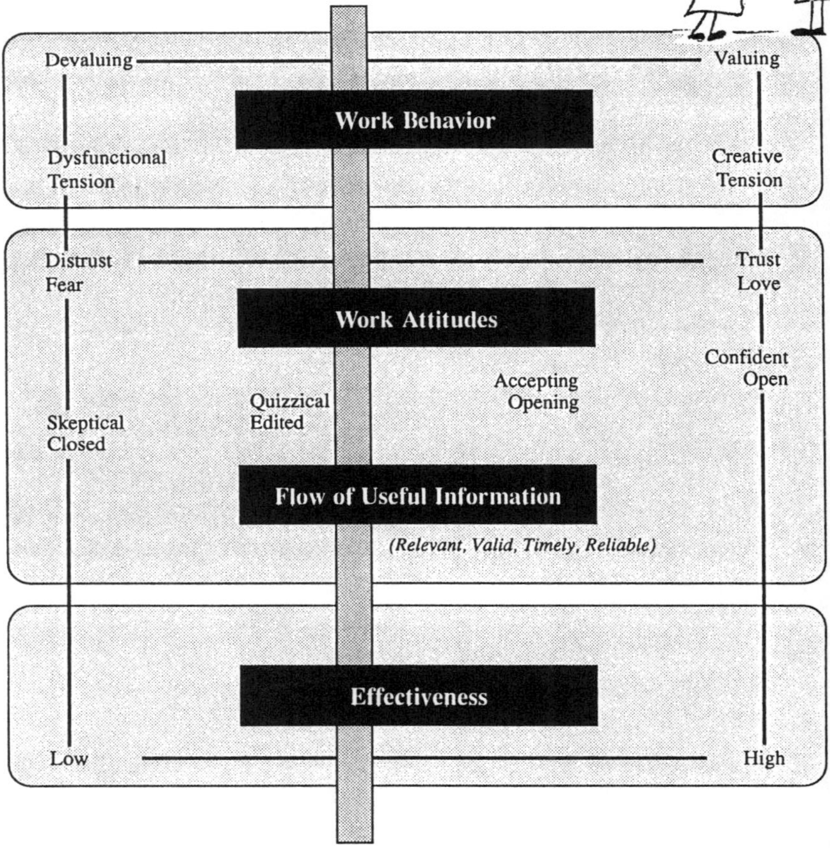

Most organizations spend only 17% to 33% of their time on valuing behavior!

We want to be on the right hand side.

BEHAVIOR AND EFFECTIVENESS

We are investing a great deal of space in this book to the subject of behavior. We do so, because in our experience, people have more difficulty dealing with the social system (people and their behavior) than with any of the other organizational systems.

We maintain that the social system has a profound effect on the enterprise; a well-functioning social system can make the difference between success or failure, or between getting by and achieving excellence.

In the discussion that follows, we illustrate the kinds of behaviors that contribute to more interdependence in the work place.

Work/Life Behaviors

To begin getting a handle on the complexity of behavior, we find it useful to describe behavior in enterprises along a continuum that is defined by two opposite poles: devaluing behavior and valuing behavior. The scale looks like this:

WORK/LIFE BEHAVIORS

Devaluing <——————————|——————————> Valuing

Devaluing behaviors are those that are negative toward other people, while valuing behaviors are positive and supportive of others. Many of the conditions of an interdependent work/life climate described earlier are based in valuing behaviors.

There are hundreds of ways that people can value and devalue others. As an exercise, think of as many kinds of valuing behaviors and devaluing behaviors that you can in a family situation; in the workplace; in other situations. It has been our observation that in many kinds of organizations most individuals and virtually all groups behave more on the devaluing side than on the valuing side, unless they have made specific, explicit commitments to do otherwise.

In our discussion of Working Guidelines, in chapter 4, we offer some specific ways to build a climate of valuing behavior.

Work/Life Attitudes

As is true for behavior, attitudes are complex and have been categorized and conceptualized in many ways. For our look at enterprises, a most useful way of categorizing the attitudes that people form about other people and situations is on the following scale:

WORK/LIFE ATTITUDES

Distrust <——————————|——————————>**Trust**

<——————(fear)<——————>(love)——————>

There is no more important attitude for developing a supportive work/life culture than mutual trust among the people involved. The basis of distrust is fear (e.g., fear of physical or psychological attack, fear of abandonment, fear of ridicule or reproach), while the basis of trust is love (not romantic love, but the care, concern for another's well being).

Unlike behavior, which we can see in other people, **we cannot see attitudes; we can infer them from our observations of behavior and we can ask people what their attitudes are.** Attitudes consist of our basic beliefs and feelings about someone or something and are related to the ways in which we behave.

The nature of this relationship has been the subject of debate for years—do attitudes affect behavior or does behavior affect attitudes? The answer seems to be "yes." We tend to behave in accordance with our attitudes, and we tend to form attitudes that are consistent with our behavior. A striking example of the latter is the way in which hostages form almost unbelievably sympathetic attitudes toward their terrorist captors.

To further help describe Work/Life Attitudes, let's look at a series of four "attitude stair steps" that move people from distrust to trust.

Being Skeptical. At the lowest end of the distrust scale is the attitude we call "skeptical." When we are confronted by a new, unfamiliar person, situation, or idea, our initial attitude may be skeptical, unless the person who introduces us to the new person or idea is someone we trust. In that case some of the trust transfers to he new person or idea.

Being skeptical of unfamiliar or threatening persons or situations certainly has survival value; it helps people avoid potentially dangerous situations. Other words that help describe a skeptical attitude are guarded, reserved, defensive, doubting, hidden, and fearful.

Being Quizzical. Based on our experience with a person of whom we were was initially skeptical, we may move to a new, less distrusting attitude of being what we call "quizzical." This movement is most likely to occur if we experience valuing behaviors from that person (e.g., a smile, a warm handshake, showing interest in me). At the quizzical level, we are less defensive, although we are still cautious and devote some energy to protecting ourselves just in case... The risks that we are willing to take to expose ourselves and our ideas are small ones at this level.

Being Accepting. Further valuing experience leads us to a new, more trusting step in our mutual attitudes that we refer to as "accepting." At the accepting level, we are finally able to work together effectively, because 1) we are devoting less energy to protecting ourselves, and 2) we are more willing to take knowledgeable risks, with less fear of being ridiculed, blind-sided, or otherwise ripped off.

Being Confident. At the confident level, we experience high levels of trust for one another and are willing to act on that trust. We let you be you, and you let us be us. We each respect and value the contributions that the other makes, and we are willing to be completely open with one another, including confronting one another when our behavior is inappropriate. There is little need to impress or deceive one another, and little energy is spent in protecting oneself from the other.

A pure, confident relationship is rare, and is a worthy target for co-workers, spouses, and others who live, work, play, or pray together.

In work/life situations, people's behavior and attitudes are related in the following way:

WORK/LIFE BEHAVIOR

Devaluing <——————————|——————————>**Valuing**

WORK/LIFE ATTITUDES

Fear<——————————|——————————>**Confidence**

In situations where people experience predominantly devaluing behavior, they are likely to develop attitudes of distrust toward one another, which in turn lead to more devaluing behaviors.

On the other side, when people experience valuing behaviors, they develop an attitude of trust, which stimulates more valuing behaviors. The most effective way to move from a situation that is characterized by distrust and devaluing behavior is for the people involved to change their behaviors. That is, if we want to build mutual trust, change our behaviors. The Working Guidelines, described in chapter 4, provide one means for doing so.

Flow of Useful Information

In Chapter 1 we described **useful information as information that is relevant, valid, timely, and reliable**. Information is the life blood of any enterprise, and anything that impairs the flow of useful information impairs the enterprise.

In our concept of useful information, we describe four levels of information flow, from closed, through edited and opening, to open.

Closed. At this level, very little useful information is flowing. Closed information flow is associated with situations of skeptical attitudes and devaluing behavior.

Edited. When we are operating at the edited level, we hold back a lot and give a little. The information that we are willing to share is at a level of relatively low risk. Some typical examples are:

- Choosing one's words carefully;
- Telling the boss what she/he wants to hear rather than what she/he needs to know;
- Making small talk and avoiding anything controversial.

The edited level of information sharing characterizes situations in which attitudes are at the quizzical level.

Opening. Here, we hold back a little and give a lot of information. We are operating at the accepting level, and are experiencing more valuing than devaluing behavior. We are therefore more willing to take higher risks with the information we provide to other people.

Open. At this level, we are willing to share any and all information and ideas that are relevant to the work we are doing or the situation we are in. Open information flow occurs when people are operating in valuing ways and have high trust for one another.

Adding the Flow of Useful Information line to our developing concept chart, we have the following:

WORK/LIFE BEHAVIOR

Devaluing <——————————|——————————>Valuing

WORK/LIFE ATTITUDES

Distrust <——————————|——————————>Trust

FLOW OF USEFUL INFORMATION

Closed <——————————|——————————>Open

Effectiveness

The bottom line for any enterprise is effectiveness - the degree to which it accomplishes that which it is intended to accomplish.

Effectiveness is based on the decisions that people make, and those decisions, in turn, are based on the quality and quantity of useful information available to the decision makers. With a closed flow of useful information, decisions will be poorer and effectiveness will be lower. Conversely, open information flow leads to higher effectiveness. This concept clearly illustrates one path by which the behavior of individuals in an enterprise impacts the overall effectiveness of the enterprise.

If people are concerned about their effectiveness, a most useful place to start to do something about it is with people's behavior. People are in charge of their own behavior and can change it if they are so inclined.

Chapter
4

Working Guidelines

Let us behave decently, as in daytime, not in orgies and drunkenness, not in sexual immorality and debauchery, not in dissension and jealousy.
Romans 13:13

We frequently hear people of all ages and walks of life say "Our real problem is a communication problem." When we pursue that comment further with them, we discover that a good deal of the **lack of communication is based on:**

- A lack of knowledge and skill at listening to what others have to say
- Not being sure that they have the message correct
- Not weighing response before sharing their side of the conversation

Working Guidelines are tools that we use to ensure that what is meant is what is communicated and understood. They are ways to carry out our responsibilities for being respectful, kind, clear, tough, effective, and authentic. They put meaningful, working handles on the concept of valuing behavior.

Each of us has his or her own experience. That experience may get in the way of being clear, candid, and caring. ***When we own our experience we can allow it to help us.***

Guidelines for working with others value each person's sense of history, while being personally authentic. By "authentic" we mean that a person's verbal and nonverbal behavior are congruent and consistent with what the person really feels and believes. Can you think of instances when your behavior or that of another person was not authentic?

As a part of their culture, all organizations and groups have "rules" for how to behave. Most commonly, those rules are unwritten, and generally they are not even discussed directly. People are just expected to know and abide by the rules of the game.

Unfortunately, many of those unwritten rules are devaluing and are deeply ingrained in the very fiber of the people working and/or living together. Some **examples of these unwritten, devaluing rules that we have encountered are:**

- Finding fault and pinning blame
- Giving put-downs and using put-down humor
- Withholding useful information to one's own advantage at the disadvantage of the enterprise and others
- Criticizing, condemning, and complaining.
- Speaking for others without their permission.
- Counseling in public, with little or no positive strokes.
- Running down oneself as well as others
- Talking in generalities and expecting detailed understanding
- Ignoring feelings and hiding behind verbal and written "bottom line" numbers, dollars, logic, terminology;
- Stubbornly "doing it my way" (don't confuse me with the facts)

In recent years, "human relations" training has been widely used in an attempt to overcome the negative consequences of these and other devaluing behaviors in the work place. Despite this emphasis, many people still have difficulty implementing the principles in day-to-day situations. What seems to be so effective in a workshop exercise on effective communication often seems irrelevant, inappropriate, embarrassing, or "corny" in real situations.

The appropriate "handles" just aren't there when the skills are most needed, and as a result, people have a lot of conceptual knowledge and very little working knowledge of principles of effective behavior.

One of the most effective tools that we have been able to offer to our clients is a set of Working Guidelines. Before we share our working guidelines, we want to emphasize a couple of points:

> **1. When members of a family, team, or group develop and build understanding, acceptance, and support for a set of working guidelines, they really have a lasting impact on the way people behave with each other.**
>
> **2. When we as individuals take the working guidelines seriously, regardless of the behavior of others, we are significantly more effective, feel better about how we are working, and are being more responsible for our actions.**

We define working guidelines as statements of behavior, which, when applied, improve the flow of useful information, help people communicate as equals, value the worth of others, and create a climate for increased effectiveness and enjoyment of work. A list of our working guidelines appears on the following page. We then discuss each guideline in turn.

WORKING GUIDELINES

I treat myself and others with trust and respect by:

- Behaving in a caring way
- Affirming everywhere and counseling in private
- Giving and receiving criticism without blame
- Using positive self-talk
- Encouraging and supporting valuing humor
- Working towards everyone's advantage
- Helping people be the best they can be

I communicate by:

- Focusing on issues, situations, and tasks
- Being specific
- Tailoring my communication to the situation

I work toward understanding, acceptance and support by:

- Listening, listening, listening
- Checking out facts and feelings
- Closing the loop on one idea before going on

I speak for myself and tell it the way I see it by:

- Expressing what I see, feel, know or believe
- Realizing how events affect me
- Explaining what I want from others
- Understanding what it means to me
- Defining conditions for success

I suspend disbelief and envision success for myself and others.

I have fun and encourage fun for others.

At first reading, the guidelines appear to be little more than common sense with which most of us can readily agree and perhaps conclude that they go without saying. However, in our experience with client groups, we find that, when we do a thorough job of building an understanding of the principles behind the guidelines and a working knowledge of how to apply these principles not only when the going is good, but when things are difficult, *measurable, dramatic improvements occur in the functioning of the group.* Common sense works!

We have applied these guidelines to families, church groups, management teams, project teams, political groups, work groups, and boy scout troops to name a few, and with equally dramatic results.

We invite you to give some serious thought to how you might apply these ideas in specific work, family, or other situations in which you find yourself. Think especially about how they might help you deal with difficult situations that involve conflict, strong differences of opinion, or other challenges.

We now offer a brief discussion of each of the guidelines:

I TREAT MYSELF AND OTHERS WITH TRUST AND RESPECT

Each of us has been given the precious gift of life. We are each unique and special. Knowing that, we have the privilege of believing the same about others.

For some of us it is easier to focus on trusting and respecting others, even at our own expense. We know of people who go out of their way to help others repair their home and leave their own in more disrepair. There are people in business that are patient and firm with their co-workers yet lose their cool at home. Of course the opposite of these situations is also true.

We need to trust and respect ourselves and others, know how that feels, and experience it in a routine way.

- **By behaving in a caring way.** First, caring does not mean avoiding tough situations. On the contrary, the most caring thing someone can do is to confront and get resolution to tough situations (e.g., poor performance by an employee; a friend, family member, or work colleague with a drinking problem).

Behaving in a caring way is easy when things are going well and can be very challenging when the going gets tough.

Lets think about our own work/life situations in which behaving in a caring way might be a more effective choice than we have made in the past.

Later in the next chapter, we offer a way of giving helpful criticism to others when it is appropriate. This process, which we call "Criticism Without Blame" offers guidance about how to give effective "negative" feedback in a caring way.

- **By affirming everywhere and counseling in private.** How devastating it is to be publicly criticized. Even when the criticism is appropriate, a human being deserves to be respected in public and in private (and hopefully following the principles of Criticism Without Blame!). When someone is to be criticized or "counseled," it is nobody else's business and should be done in private.

On the other side, when we have something good to say about another person, we will say it anywhere, including in the presence of others. This gives other people the opportunity to share in celebrating what is going well.

- **By giving and receiving criticism without blame.** Basically, it means that criticism is important when it is based in a valuing spirit of intent. We recognize the responsibility to be clear about what needs to be done differently and provide help to others as well as receive help ourselves to improve.

- **By using positive self talk.** Self talk recognizes that we as individuals have the capacity to influence ourselves by the conversation we carry on (with ourselves silently and out loud) about ideas, issues, situations, beliefs, visions, memories, labels, expectations, hopes etc. ***Positive self talk directly influences positive behavior.*** People have the capacity to talk themselves into feeling great even in tough times. Recently one of our clients stressed the importance of continuous reinforcement of a vision for success over the past few years. He acted according to that vision and now that vision is a reality.

There are personal growth programs that have a single focus on routinely setting positive "affirmations" as a means of more directly affecting the future. Painting positive images for our memory data bank is a worthwhile activity. Repeating these affirmations to oneself soon conditions our memory bank to believe with a sense of finality that what we have said is in fact true. Behavior change happens according to this updated memory bank. People will act according to their beliefs as committed to memory.

- **By encouraging and supporting valuing behavior.** The opposite is true when we use put-downs, including put-down humor. If there's one guideline that stimulates heated discussions in our client working sessions, it is this one where people want to hold on to devaluing behavior like put-downs. "Do I have to give up all my ethnic stories? Do I have to say kind things to my closest friends?"

When we share the idea of eliminating put-downs and put-down humor, we can almost always count on one or more people passionately working at justifying put-down humor.

Some say that with special friends, they have a good rapport and that they really enjoy sticking it to each other.

Some even say that without put-down humor, they wouldn't have much to talk about! How sad. By definition, we see put-down humor as humor that is at another person's expense. Much of the popular humor today is built on put- downs, including ethnic jokes, occupation jokes (e.g., lawyer stories), television situation comedies, and the acts of some of our well-known stand-up comedians.

What people like about giving put-down humor is the chance to be witty and clever. What people like about receiving it is the attention of someone focusing on them. But the cumulative effects of put-down humor take a toll. The giver fails to communicate real information, and the receiver's self esteem may be eroded.

By the way, put-down humor almost always reflects low self-esteem on the part of the giver. What is forgotten is that people, young and old alike, use this kind of humor as a means to avoid critical life questions, like dealing with minority or sex issues.

Put-down humor is also used as a cheap substitute for clear communication about difficult situations. In short, it creates and maintains unnecessary distance between people. It is usually hurtful to the victim, and it seldom adds value to a situation. Humor does not have to be at someone's expense to be funny.

We have to point out here that we are not suggesting that people eliminate humor from their lives. To the contrary, we see good humor as a vital ingredient of a healthy family or group. Life offers many opportunities to enjoy the natural humor that arises out of our human foibles.

Encouraging and supporting valuing behavior means not using put-downs or put-down humor, but rather respecting the individual, enterprise, race, creed, color, religion and gender by actively affirming positive behavior.

- **By working toward everyone's advantage.** This eliminates finding fault and pinning blame. We believe that nobody has ever been helped by being blamed. Finding fault and pinning blame are attacks on the person and result in diminishing the individual's sense of self worth by developing guilt and shame.

When we take time to ensure a meaningful gain for everyone involved we are completing the package for a good deal (which is defined as something good in it for all of us).

- **By helping people be the best they can be.** Each of us is responsible for who we are, what we are doing, and how we feel about ourselves and others. The way we are depends on our beliefs, visions, values, competency (which includes our combined intellect, knowledge, skills, and experience). When our spirit of intent is to help we will seek out positive ways to walk along side and consult with people as they work at capitalizing on their special gifts and expending the necessary effort.

I COMMUNICATE BY:

(In this section we are focusing on the more direct conversations, including everyday attempt to get at the bottom of problems, conflicts, differences, and tough decisions.)

- **Focusing on issues, situations, and tasks.** Many conversations, particularly when there is conflict or strong differences of style or opinion, deteriorate into personal attacks on the character of the other person.

This is not only a waste of time, but it also creates unnecessary polarizations between people and makes it more difficult to work together effectively. Use of this guideline helps people to keep the focus of conversation on the issue, situation, or task at hand.

Having the discipline to apply this guideline when difficult situations arise has an extraordinarily beneficial effect on the outcomes.

- **Being specific.** Specifics provide us with something we can work on; generalities (e.g., "things aren't going very well here") make it difficult or impossible to decide what to do.

Specifics may involve feelings, data, perceptions, interpretations, and evaluations of any given situation. There are times when specifics are withheld because of the lack of trust based on a very unfortunate past experience.

The free flow of specifics is a good indication of an enterprise where differences are valued and handled as critical to maintaining good communications.

- **Tailoring my communication to the situation.** Should I tell the whole story? What needs to be shared at this moment? How urgent is the requirement for my input? Do I come on strong or hold back a little? What sensitivities do I need to be aware of in relation to the other person? How willing are people to accept my input at this time?

U.A.S.

Understanding ↔ Acceptance ↔ Support

Understanding present situation:

- *Probe for clarity*
- *Check out facts and feelings*
- *Be up front about motives*

Acceptance:

- *Being heard is critical*
- *Check out positions on 1-20 scale!*
- *"Does not mean agree"*

Support:

- *How will this help? Why?*
- *Treat differences as opportunity vs threat*
- *Commit to the results*

I TAKE RESPONSIBILITY TO WORK TOWARD UNDERSTANDING, ACCEPTANCE, AND SUPPORT:

Work toward understanding, acceptance, and support (UAS) - A frequent cause of failure with employees, co-workers, children, spouses, and other colleagues in situations in which decisions are made, instructions are given, and/or commitments are made, is the failure to gain the understanding, acceptance, and support of those involved in or affected by the decision. We use these terms so frequently in our work, we have shortened them to "UAS." Here is what they mean:

- **Understanding**—comprehension of the decision or idea
- **Acceptance**—willingness to go along with the decision or idea (as opposed to agreement, which we cannot always expect). In addition it means each of us <u>must</u> be heard before we move on to support.
- **Support**—a commitment to act in accordance with the decision or assignment.

Lack of understanding can result in a lot of effort being expended in unwanted directions.

Lack of acceptance can result in conscious or unconscious sabotage of the work.

Finally, lack of support can result in half-hearted efforts or no efforts at all toward a goal (e.g., late or poorly done work).

Understanding, acceptance and support can be improved:

- **By listening, listening, listening.** A great deal of communication failure is on the part of the receiver. We often find ourselves barely attending to someone else's words as we prepare our next speech. We continue to work on listening for understanding when others are speaking. This eliminates a lot of misunderstandings. There are many books on how to listen. It is as simple as "doing it". What would happen if we had a national commitment to raise our listening effectiveness 50 percent by the year 2000? We suggest we'd have an excess of national money (no deficit).
- **By checking out facts and feelings.**— Check it out (facts and feelings) - For both the sender and the receiver of a

communication a useful rule of thumb is, "When in doubt, check it out, and the rest of the time still check it out." Checking it out is not a distrustful act. It is simply affirming what you hear and feel.

Again, meanings are in people, not in words. Failure to check it out is a major source of conflict of understanding. If we feel a conflict or misunderstanding coming on, take a moment to check out our own and the other person's understanding of what is going on.

When giving or receiving a work assignment, check it out to avoid a costly shot in the wrong direction. When someone's nonverbal actions appear to contradict what they are saying, check out their feelings. A small investment in checking it out up front can avoid tremendous costs incurred through misunderstandings.

- **By closing the loop on one idea before going on.**— This guideline helps to avoid what we call "popcorn" meetings, in which several ideas "pop up" and get briefly discussed, with no resolution on any of them.

I SPEAK FOR MYSELF AND TELL IT THE WAY I SEE IT:

The idea here is that as members of a work group, we have a responsibility to that group to offer our viewpoint or input, in a responsible way. If we withhold our legitimate input, we are essentially stealing from the group.

In fact, we believe that the most prevalent form of theft in organizations is the withholding of useful information.

This is particularly true when trust is low and devaluing behavior is rampant. People withhold information both deliberately and unintentionally.

We have found that when people are willing to offer their ideas, even when those ideas might not be popular, the group usually achieves a higher level of success.

- **What I see, feel, know, or believe.** I owe it to the group to share my knowledge and ideas in a responsible way as they fit the situation.
- **How what is happening affects me.** I do this with the intent of being helpful to the group and to keep the process moving.
- **What I want from others.** It's truly remarkable how many people are unwilling to simply and straightforwardly ask others for what they want or need in order to be effective, efficient, or happy. Instead we expect others to be totally sensitive and responsive to our wants and needs without our ever having to say a word. And then we get disappointed when they do not fulfill our wishes.

One of our colleagues, Dr. Dick Lazar, put it this way:

"When I know I need to get something done, I:

- Decide what specifically needs to be done
- Decide what I can do by myself
- Decide what help I want from others
- Get the help I want from others

OR "I get what I deserve!"

- **What it means to me.** One of the greatest barriers to effective communication is the failure to recognize that meanings are in people, not in words. When we clearly share what a particular subject or idea means to us, we reduce the possibility of misunderstanding.
- **Conditions for success.**— In communicating with others about tasks, projects, or programs of work, people often overlook the opportunity to convey those critical conditions which must be met in order to be successful.

For example, there may be critical information that we need in order to complete an engineering design or manufacturing process. By communicating this need up front, we increase our chances for success.

Perhaps there is some question about the availability of funds necessary for the start of a special project.

By being clear about the interdependence of work with others, we provide those we serve and those who provide service to us with a real opportunity for success. This minimizes the "oops!" and "we're sorry."

I SUSPEND DISBELIEF AND ENVISION SUCCESS FOR MYSELF AND OTHERS

Instead of focusing on other people's failings and false starts, we give them the benefit of the doubt and seek ways to help them succeed.

For example, many people work at losing weight. When they blow it, they need encouragement, not disbelief and ridicule.

One way that we limit other people's ability to make changes is to keep them in a "box." For example, if you are a friend or co-worker of ours, what are we likely to do is build a "box" with your name on it.

The box has rigid sides and a tight lid, and we write labels on the box that clearly describe our understanding of what type of person you are. Because it is important to us that you remain somewhat predictable, we keep you in the box.

If you should announce to us that you intend to make a particular change in your behavior, say, for example, to work on eliminating your use of put-down humor, we may look for the first opportunity to catch you at using put-down humor and shove you back in your box.

If, on the other hand, we suspend disbelief, we give you the benefit of the doubt and look for ways to help you achieve your goal.

When we use the power of affirmations to visualize people as being successful in very specific situations we will work at helping our visions come true. Part of this visualizing should include the principle of

LOOKING FOR THE THINGS
THAT PEOPLE ARE DOING RIGHT!

I HAVE FUN AND ENCOURAGE FUN FOR OTHERS

This is the last, but certainly not the least of our guidelines. We see it as being very important for people to enjoy the natural humor that arises in our day-to-day lives. Sometimes the greatest creativity and productivity are found during periods of fun. Having fun also involves the excitement of rising to a challenge and succeeding, or doing a good day's work.

IMPLEMENTING THE WORKING GUIDELINES

It is important to understand clearly that in order to effectively implement the Working Guidelines, it is necessary that people be willing to invest some time and energy in building mutual understanding, acceptance, and support for the principles behind the words.

It is not enough to simply hand out a copy of the guidelines, have people read them, and then resolve to do better at following the ideas. Our behavior arises out of the principles we have integrated at a deeper level of understanding, not those we carry as a surface veneer.

When we do follow up activities with clients, we find some lingering problems still eating peoples energy. We constantly re-emphasize using the working guidelines and at that moment most of those problems are handled. It seems so simple, however the discipline to keep applying these guidelines is critical.

It is worth taking the necessary time to discuss the guidelines and how they work. It is important that people have the opportunity to discuss how the guidelines might apply in their specific day-to-day working and living situations.

We give special emphasis to how to apply the guidelines in particularly difficult situations with other people. We also help people see the applicability of the guidelines in the family and other life situations.

Increasing our Batting Averages

A most important idea in developing commitment to the working guidelines is that of "batting averages." We believe that a frequent point of failure in human relations training is that people, having learned some hot new techniques, then make commitments to themselves to always behave accordingly. The result is like the fate of many New Year's resolutions: a brief demonstration of resolve, followed by a gradual (and sometimes precipitous) slide back to the old way of doing things. Human beings are human beings, and one aspect of being human is that we are fallible.

Setting up absolute commitments for one hundred percent success in the realm of behavior is an immediate set-up for failure. Under such commitments, as soon as a person "blows it," disappointment sets in and the experience is regarded as a failure.

The idea here is that instead of aiming for perfection, our goal in working on our own behavior is to improve our batting average, that is, to increase the percentage of "hits" in communicating and dealing with other people.

For example, now we can say that we do a better job of checking it out when we sense a disagreement or miscommunication with another person. Where in the past we would have been more likely to blame the other person for not paying attention to me, now we are am more likely to check it out.

By establishing personal goals to improve our batting average, we can celebrate our successes along the way and not be too hard on ourselves when we blow it.

Mutual Commitment

In working toward implementing the guidelines in any group of people, **it is essential to build a mutual, public commitment.** This means that people must indicate publicly to one another that they accept the principles behind the guidelines and that they intend to support the guidelines by practicing them in their own behavior.

One of the things that might get in the way of a particular group reaching acceptance and support for the ***Working Guidelines*** is that the wording might not feel right to them.

In order to reach acceptance and support, people must feel some ownership in the guidelines, that is, they must feel that they are somehow theirs. Obviously for the guidelines presented here, the wording is ours.

We encourage groups to develop an understanding of the principles behind our working guidelines, and then, if it is helpful to them, to change the wording to suit them, to delete any guidelines that they feel do not apply to them, and to add new ones that fit their situation. If necessary, they can scrap ours and build their own from scratch.

The critical experience in building mutually understood, accepted, and supported working guidelines is that groups of people take behavior and communication out of the realm of assumption and deal with them explicitly and say, "This is how we intend to behave toward one another."

Once people have made a commitment and developed a habit of applying the guidelines, the positive results are part of their experience base, and using them becomes more effortless.

Some Practical Tips

Groups and organizations that have been most successful in implementing Working Guidelines have typically done some specific things to maintain awareness and reinforce the use of the guidelines. Some of the successful ways of accomplishing this are as follows:

- **Post the guidelines.** Poster size copies of the ***Working Guidelines*** are posted on the walls or bulletin boards in offices and conference rooms (and even on some people's refrigerator doors at home!).

- **Pocket-sized guidelines.** People carry pocket-sized copies of the ***Working Guidelines*** in their pockets or wallets. When they attend a meeting, they pull out their copies of the guidelines to remind themselves and other of their commitment and to use for reference. We provide a printed, pocket-sized copy of the ***Working Guidelines*** to each participant in our working sessions.

- ***Working Guidelines* as the first agenda item for a meeting can be a very effective way of reminding participants of the guidelines and improving the effectiveness of meetings.**

This reminder need not take a significant amount of time in the meeting. Sometimes, just a simple reminder that the guidelines are in effect is sufficient. This tiny investment of time at the beginning of the meeting can reap a substantial return in effectiveness.

- **Revisit the guidelines when things get tough.** When a meeting seems stuck or is at an impasse, it is frequently useful to review the guidelines to see how they might help.

- **Follow-up review.** When a group makes a commitment to follow Working Guidelines, it is essential to set aside some time at a later date (we suggest 60-90 days) to revisit the guidelines, review how they have done, discuss how the guidelines may have helped in situations that did not go well, and reaffirm their commitment. In our experience, this is where the real payoff occurs.

Abuse

As a final note, it is important to recognize that just like any other tool, the ***Working Guidelines*** can be abused. People can use the guidelines to thwart effective communication by always waiting to catch someone violating a guideline.

Such abuses are a measure of how well the principles and the intent of the principles have been understood and integrated. If they are left at the level of a list of behavioral rules, the risk of abuse is much greater than if genuine understanding, acceptance, and support have been developed.

Chapter 5

Giving & Receiving Valuing Feedback

Chapter 5

Giving & Receiving Valuing Feedback

The ear that heareth the reproof of life abideth among the wise.
—Proverbs 15:31

Many of us have grown up with the notion that it is better to give than receive.

The positive side of this was to help us learn how to share our toys and candy, and as we grew older, our time, talents, and money. The negative side of this was that we were told what to do—not how to do it.

It is not unusual, in our consulting business, to find people at all levels who want to give feedback that helps others. In many cases their attempts are met with resistance from the people on the receiving end. The point here is that **very few of us ever received help with how to give and receive valuing feedback.**

He that refuseth instruction despiseth his own soul,
but he that heareth reproof getteth understanding.
—Proverbs 15:32

This chapter presents some practical approaches to giving and receiving positive feedback (validation) and "negative" feedback (criticism without blame). Both of these approaches are examples of valuing behavior, that is, behavior that is positive and supportive of other people.

Giving valuing feedback is a common desire among most people who want to have an ongoing and fruitful association with others. When valuing feedback is withheld, actual cost of doing business increases and the *QUALITY OF WORK/LIFE* suffers.

Recently we had lunch with a bright young person who left an executive job with a growing company for a similar company in the same field. The new company sought this person out and successfully recruited him because of two primary missing elements in his old work situation:

1. "I was totally unappreciated. There was no ongoing review of my work, no intangible rewards like being told I did a good job on this or that. Even money wasn't the issue."

2. "In addition, there were some changes being made over the past few months and nobody took the time to keep me up to date." So I was questioning—"where was I going to fit?"

Life presents us with many opportunities to give and receive feedback that is either positive or negative. It is our observation that most of these situations are handled poorly or not at all. Again, most people can talk about the benefits of an appropriate compliment or an effective criticism done well, but few really have the skill to do these things well.

Before describing validation and criticism without blame, here is a true story that happened in our family.

Robert and Jennifer are our twins who were ten when this story happened.. Since my wife and I both worked, it was important that they contribute to taking care of household chores. Through the previous five years (from the age of five) they learned to vacuum, wash floors, wash dishes, do laundry, clean bathrooms, clean their own rooms, mow lawn, pull weeds, and do light cooking. They did this work in varying degrees of completeness.

We have clearly defined responsibilities with routine inspection. However, there is one item that kept getting in the way of our mutual appreciation - they liked to eat my special chocolate covered, graham cracker cookies! (We had other kinds of cookies around the house that they liked.)

One day I discovered that most of the graham cracker cookies were gone, so I asked them the obvious question, "Who took my cookies?" The answer was, "I don't know!"

I made it clear that from then on, those cookies were out of bounds for them.

A couple of months later, sure enough, more cookies were missing. Once again I asked the question, and the answer was different, but just as predictable; each stated that the other had taken the cookies. I decided this had gone far enough, so in my great wisdom, I counted the remaining cookies and checked them for the next few days.

Later that same week, two cookies were missing. Now I had them! I proceeded to get them together and once again asked, "Who ate my two cookies!?" They knew the gig was up; both confessed, whereupon I administered a sharp rebuke and a whack to their backsides. The tears came, and I left for the other room.

As I pondered the situation, it became clear to me that I had blown it. Those two loving kids routinely do their chores well, perhaps better than most teenagers (and probably many adults). Why is it that I expected them to be perfect? Perhaps I was more the problem than they were. When had I taken time to tell them how much I appreciated the contributions that they make to our family? I cannot remember ever having felt so sorry for having been so harsh over such a trivial issue.

I called them into the family room and apologized to them. I took the time to tell them specifically how much Mom and I love and appreciate them and the help they give us.

As I reflected on that incident in light of our consulting business, it was clear that managers do the same thing with people who report to them. They are quick to point out small things that are not going well (usually in ineffective ways), and fail to routinely give credit for successes and accomplishments.

We refer to this phenomenon as the **"Two Cookie Syndrome of Management."**

We believe the inspection mentality of keeping track of things by finding what is going wrong should be replaced with the assurance mentality which is to catch people at doing things right.

We acknowledge the importance of handling things that aren't going right through the CRITICISM WITHOUT BLAME model discussed later in this chapter.

Catching people at doing things right comes from an old quality belief that quality is built into the product not inspected into the product. Inspection takes a lot of time and builds dependency on the inspector to find the problem. After all the inspector has to find something wrong, or there is no need for inspection. Many of us in our work and personal lives have a habit of looking for things that aren't going well. When we find them we say "Ah, ha I just knew there was a problem here".

There seems to be an undesirable characteristic of people to gloat at someone else's misfortune. That is why so much time is taken at coffee breaks for people to commiserate about their own troubles and those of others. Once again where have people learned to experience a more positive rewarding life with others?

Providing positive feedback at an early age hasn't always been the normal thing to do. When we were young we were told not to do this and not to do that. The burden for learning was carried by others. In some people this "not to " guidance was so strong that they felt anything was OK unless they were told "not to."

A young vice president for student affairs at a small Lutheran college was asked by a retired president emeritus " How is it going, Art?," to which Art replied," I don't know, nobody ever tells me." The retired president responded, "Vell, Ahrt, if you aver get a grunt of approval, construe it to mean high praise."

Because many people are relatively inexperienced and ineffective at giving compliments, we designed the validation process to help develop this skill.

GIVING POSITIVE FEEDBACK: THE PROCESS OF VALIDATION

Withhold not good from them to whom it is due,
when it is in the power of thine hand to do it!
—Proverbs 3:27

Positive feedback goes by many names: praise, reinforcement, acknowledgment, compliment, affirmation, "stroke," "warm fuzzy," to name a few. We use the term "validation" to describe a very specific and effective approach to giving other people positive feedback. The idea is to do so in such a way that the feedback is meaningful to and accepted by the other person.

We have run into many people who have a difficult time receiving compliments from others. Many of them have energetically denied that it is important to them to receive compliments; they claim that compliments are embarrassing, unnecessary, and usually insincere anyway.

Furthermore, many people have been raised to be humble, and therefore to accept a compliment is to violate their humility. Others feel that to give and receive compliments is "weak" or "soft" and therefore not in keeping with one's tough image. For these and many other reasons, people frequently fend off compliments that come their way.

It is our belief that regardless of what people may say, virtually all people, long to be recognized and validated by others. Furthermore, most people do not receive nearly as much validation as they want and deserve. We are certain about the positive and dramatic effects that validation has on the effectiveness and well-being of any enterprise, from families to major corporations.

One of the real joys of our work is that we have had the opportunity to share the concept of validation with thousands of people in a variety of work, church, school, and home situations. When given an opportunity to learn and practice the giving and receiving of validations, dramatic changes occur.

As we discuss the concept of validation, we invite you to consider the process from the point of view of both the giver and the receiver.

VALIDATIONS

Guidelines for practicing giving validations:

- *Be specific*
- *Talk directly to the person*
- *Make it genuine*
- *Be aware of feelings when giving validations*
- *Be aware of feelings when receiving validations*

Guidelines for practicing receiving validations:

- *Don't fend off validations — you deserve them*
- *Others deserve to have you receive their gifts*
- *Let others know what you would like to have noticed*

A validation is something good I see, feel, know, or believe about you and express to you.

The "and express to you" portion of this definition is very important. How many times have you thought something positive about another person and failed to express it to them. It may have been nice to have the thought, but it did the other person little or no good!

An effective validation meets the following conditions:

- **Be specific.** Avoid broad, general statements that are difficult to believe and easy to fend off (e.g., "You are a wonderful person!") Instead, make your validating statements specific:

"That report you just did really helped me to understand the issue." Specific statements are more believable, and the receiver is less likely to fend them off.

- **Talk directly to the person.** Notice how frequently people make speeches about an individual in the third person, when the person is right there. They go something like this: "I would like to thank Nancy for the fine job she did on this project."

A more effective way of validating Nancy would be to talk directly to her: "Nancy, thank you for the fine job you did on this project."

- **Make it genuine.** There are very few more distasteful experiences than to be presented with phony compliments. In fact, we believe that one reason many people are skeptical of compliments is their own history of receiving (or giving) phony ones.

There are many opportunities for genuine positive feedback to others. If we don't have a genuine validation for someone it is better not to say anything than to make up a phony one.

- **Be aware of feelings when giving and receiving validations.** We offer this challenge: Find someone and give them a validation that might not have ordinarily given. The person may be a family member, a friend, or a co-worker. When you doing it, be aware of personal feelings.

Are we self-conscious and awkward? Do we also feel warm and positive? What other feelings do we have? Also, check out how the other person feels. Did they try to fend off? What did their non-verbal behavior tell us about their reaction? By the way, what excuses are we making right now to prevent ourselves from doing this?

Here are some additional concepts to think about in respect to validation:

- **A validation is a gift from one person to another.** It is freely given. Furthermore:

- **The person receiving a validation deserves it.** And we mean "deserves" here in the most positive sense. Even if the person does not believe it at the moment, a sincere validation that meets the definition and specifications above is richly deserved. When we give a validation, we deserve to have you received . Have we ever tried to give someone a gift and have it refused? How did that feel? One of the things that prevents people from being willing to receive validations is the belief that it puts them in debt, that they then owe the other person a validation in return.

The important learning for us was that our being willing to receive validations from you is a gift to others in return; it is a fair exchange. One of the most important things we have ever done for ourselves is to acknowledge that we deserve other people's validation and are willing to receive it.

- **There are no strings attached to a validation.** Many times, "praise" has thinly veiled hooks in it which demand something of the receiver (for example, "John, you sure do a nice job of taking out the garbage!"). A validation does not contain these hooks. To summarize, a validation is something good we (I) see, feel, know, or believe about other and express to them.

Specifications for giving validation include:

- Be specific

- Talk directly to the person

- Make it genuine

- Be aware of feelings

Daily living presents many opportunities to give and receive validations; very few of these opportunities are taken. As noted in the story about the college student body officer it seems that in some work or family situations, a grunt of approval is to be construed a high praise.

We often hear the comment, "No news is good news." Almost

without exception, people in our client organizations express the feeling that there is not enough genuine recognition for well-done behavior.

Think for a moment about what might happen if in our country we achieved a mere five percent improvement in taking opportunities to validate others.

Because each of us is responsible for our own behavior, we offer the challenge of looking at our own experience as a giver and as a receiver of validations. If we see an opportunity for improvement, lets take it!

GIVING "NEGATIVE" FEEDBACK —CRITICISM WITHOUT BLAME

As water reflects a face so a man's heart reflects the man.
– Proverbs 27:19

One of the most effective applications of the ***Working Guidelines*** is in giving criticism to others when it is appropriate. By the way, some people in our line of work argue that criticism is never appropriate - that it diminishes the other person and is therefore never helpful and frequently harmful.

We acknowledge the point that most criticism as practiced does in fact diminish the receiver and cause more harm than good. However, we also recognize situations in which providing information that helps to fill in a blind spot for another person can be very helpful.

An important point here is that effective criticism involves providing the other person with information that they may not already have. And our intention in giving criticism is to call for the person's best, not to diminish the person through guilt and shame. Well done criticism without blame is a powerful form of valuing behavior; it supports the competence and worthiness of the other person.

In our discussion of the ***Working Guidelines*** in Chapter 4, we pointed out that nobody has ever been helped by being blamed. The purpose of blaming is to cause a person to feel guilty or shameful.

Many of us still cling to the myth that enough guilt or shame will cause a person to change his or her behavior. People may change their behavior, but rarely is it in a way that we would have hoped. The most typical change is to do whatever possible to avoid being the blamer. The challenge, as we see it, is to give criticism in the form of helpful information and to eliminate the blaming and fault-finding aspects of criticism. To accomplish this, we developed some guidelines for giving **Criticism Without Blame** (CWB). As you read them, please be aware that they are just guidelines, not a step-by- step cook book for giving criticism.

GIVING CRITICISM WITHOUT BLAME

We have found that giving CWB effectively usually requires some planning, particularly when the issue or situation is difficult or involves strong feelings. The subject of CWB can be an individual's work performance or behavior.

CWB can be used effectively in confronting people with drinking problems, drug problems, or other self-defeating or counterproductive patterns of behavior. Particularly for more serious issues, we recommend three phases in the CWB process:

1. Questioning the appropriateness of CWB

2. Planning the CWB session

3. Conducting the CWB session

Phase 1: Questioning the appropriateness of CWB.

Before going any further with CWB, check out whether CWB is really appropriate in this situation. We have found the following questions to be useful "filters" to sort out when and when not to use CWB:

1. What are my motives? Do I really want to help the twins, or am I upset and wanting to "get them" for disobeying me? As is also true for the remaining questions, this one must be answered honestly. If my intention really is to hurt or get revenge, then I should not do CWB.

2. **How clear and complete is my information?** Is it based on observable behavior and events, or is it based on rumor, hearsay, or innuendo? Is there other information that I should get before I reach faulty conclusions? For example, how possible is it that my wife took the two cookies for her lunch?

3. **How new is this information; when was the last time the person heard it?** It may be that they already have the information and to pursue it further may amount to nothing more than nagging. If they have heard it before, how did I present the information? Was it in the form of finding fault and pinning blame? Did I check out the twins understanding of what was being communicated?

4. **How likely is it that the person can do anything about it?** It's amazing how often we expect things of other people that they cannot possibly accomplish. Think of the zealous parent who wants his son or daughter to excel in a particular sporting event or profession, when the child has little aptitude or interest in that area.

It is important to consider whether or not the person has the capacity (skill, knowledge, information) and the support (tools, equipment, encouragement) to do what we expect of them.

5. **What condition is the person in (physically, intellectually, emotionally) to hear this now?** Even the most skillfully delivered feedback is likely to miss the mark when the receiver is "down" in one way or another. A little sensitivity to appropriate timing goes a long way. (However, don't get yourself into the trap of using this question as an excuse to never give CWB!)

6. **What condition am I in to give CWB now?** If I am in a highly emotional state, it is unlikely that I can do a competent job of giving CWB. It is important to wait until I feel more balanced.

7. **How committed am I to following through to resolution?** Without such commitment, my feedback may amount to little more than a parting shot.

8. **How likely is it that I, and not the other person, am the source of the problem?** Here again the challenge is to be really honest. It's very easy to take credit for successes and blame others for failures or problems. What am I doing that might make this a problem situation?

9. **How possible is it that what the person really needs is more validation instead of criticism?** The answer to this question is usually "yes."

I use these nine questions as "filters" to help me avoid giving inappropriate or ineffective criticism. They help me avoid "flying off the handle" and doing more harm than good. Having answered the questions honestly, if CWB still appears to be appropriate, I move to Phase 2.

Phase 2. Planning the CWB session.

In planning the CWB session, it is important to write down key points of discussion, particularly for difficult issues. Set aside enough time to do a complete job, and find a suitable, private meeting place, preferably on neutral ground.

Phase 3. Conducting the CWB session.

When giving CWB, get right to the point. Procrastinating or evading with idle conversation only builds tension and anxiety and makes it more difficult. In addition, consider the following pointers:

- **Follow the *Working Guidelines*** (Chapter 4). There are few situations in which it is more important to abide by these principles. It may be helpful to review the guidelines before the session and have them available at the session.

- **Check out the other person's understanding of what is being conveyed.** In difficult sessions, miscommunications can easily occur. We need to be patient, and work for a clear understanding.

- **Be open to new information.** Even though we may have thought we had all the relevant information, the recipient may be able to shed further light on why the situation occurred. Being prepared to drop or modify the criticism in light of this new information is very important.

CRITICISM WITHOUT BLAME

I ask myself:

- *What are my motives?*
- *What information do I have?*
- *What more information do I need?*
- *What condition is the person in to receive my CWB?*
- *What condition am I in to give CWB?*
- *What has the person heard already?*
- *What can the person do about it?*
- *What is my level of commitment to work it through?*
- *If the problem is behavior — who's is it ——mine? or others?*
- *How possible is it that what the person really needs is more validation?*

Write down the vital few points to work on in the form of end results:

- *What do the results look like as they are accomplished?*

Meeting with the person:

- *Find a private neutral place*
- *Avoid placing desks, tables between you*
- *Have— easel, blackboard, paper*
- *Follow: Working Guidelines; SEA; Data, Perception, Interpretation, Evaluation; Relevant, Valid, Timely, Reliable; U.A.S.*
- *Be open to new data*
- *Allow quality time*
- *Write key (SEA) points*
- *Write a mutual U.A.S. plan for both of us. Include: Followup; Rewards; Consequences; Timeframe*
- *Celebrate Accomplishment of Beatable/Achievable desired outcomes/validate*

- **Continually seek opportunities to collaborate** in generating alternative solutions to the problem being discussed. Keeping the tone of the conversation as a mutual effort at problem solving as opposed to a lecture or a "chewing out."

- **Check out feelings.** Sometimes strong feelings can get in the way of effective communication. It may be helpful to talk about feelings and then return to the issue. However, we avoid the mistake of focusing only on the feelings and losing the issue.

- **Clarify points of agreement, mutual commitments, and plans for resolving significant differences.** It is usually a good idea to write them down. Set and keep follow-up dates to check progress.

We recognize that this may seem like a great deal to do. However, our experience supports this method whenever serious problems crop up. Furthermore, recall that these are guidelines, not step-by-step instructions. It is important to adapt our approach to the specific situation. Sometimes the recipient of CWB reacts in defensive ways; some may react by dumping long-held frustrations. It is important to stay with the person without being drawn into a defend-attack-counterattack interaction. A couple of methods may help you deal with this situation:

1. **Being an active listener.** Paraphrase back what we've heard the person say for clarity. This doesn't mean we agree with them, but it does assure them that they have been heard.

2. **Checking out their understanding** by asking them to describe what they think we said and what it means to them.

One more thing—**there are no guarantees.** Just because we use these processes of validation and criticism without blame does not guarantee that we will be successful each time. Many things affect how a person will receive feedback. However, we are certain that when the principles behind these methods are followed, the likelihood of a successful interaction is measurably increased.

Chapter
6

Uses of Humor

BY
RICHARD ALLEN STULL

Chapter 6

Uses of Humor

(Richard Allen Stull is a nationally recognized educator and consultant in the field of managing. For years he worked with Louis Allan out of San Francisco where he contributed significantly to the Allan approach to organization planning. He has worked with many fortune 500 companies, and currently lives in Los Vegas pursing his many avocations including finishing his book on Humor.

I asked Dick to write this chapter because humor is so important to all our lives, and so much of it ranges from bad and distasteful to gloriously funny like Cosby, and Garrison Keillor of Prairie Home Companion and others mentioned by Dick in this chapter.

I also felt we needed some of the technical understanding of humor, Dick is eminently qualified to do. In providing this information Dick freely and professionally shows both sides of humor–both the put down and better humor.

Enjoy it, use it, it's worth more than what this book cost.)

Richard C. Gillespie

As a guest author in this book, I am pleased to contribute this chapter, and to acknowledge the part Dick Gillespie has played in my own life. It was he as much as anyone who encouraged me to complete a 35-year humor and comedy research project. Dick and I worked together in his firm, Work/Life Systems International in Everett, Washington. In addition, I came to know his fine family, a beautiful Christian family, dedicated to loyalty and righteous living. Dick has practiced the Work/Life Management System both in his personal life and in his nation-wide professional consulting assignments. And he loves to laugh! We both agree that a laugh on the job is an instant vacation.

Managing **is** Everybody's Business, but so, too, are fun and laughter. Work is not fulfilling unless we have fun doing it. It folds naturally into the soft side of management, the people part. Those of us who are successful, spend more time on our jobs than we do in any other life function, except sleep. We should, therefore, enjoy our work, it should have a tonic effect, it should be exciting, it should be fun. Said Benjamin Disraeli many years ago, "Life is too short to be little." It is too brief not to have some fun along the way: in that ride pool or commute, at the office, at the plant, on the road calling on a prospect, at church, in our home with the wife and kids, in the breakfast nook, in our living room with our relatives, or just in our own back yard sharing with a neighbor.

In addition, humor and laughter play an important part in many aspects of business, management, meetings, negotiating, and making presentation or speeches. The harried manager, supervisor or plant manager who does not tap this rich resource of humor is missing a vital and valuable link in communication skills. Those who truly desire to experience and enjoy the quality of work/life need to laugh.

Luckily, the good Lord has given us two great gifts as human beings:

1. **reason** to solve those problems in life and business that can be solved; and,
2. **humor** to handle those problems in life and business than can't be solved.

Do you, perhaps, recall the little boy in his crib during a terrible, hot, summer thunder and lightening storm? It was so violent that his parents were afraid that he might be frightened. They quietly opened his bedroom door to check on him. He was jumping up and down in his crib, yelling, "Bang it again, God, bang it again!"

It is this kind of fearlessness and free personality that give us our geniuses, persons capable of analogy, similes, metaphors, and paradoxes. Walt Whitman, great American poet, and champion of what he called "athletic democracy," who had to sleep for years with his retarded brother to keep him from crying, used to call grass, "God's handkerchief." And Thomas Wolfe, in his youth could see lightning as "God's flashbulb for taking pictures of planet earth." Humor begins in this kind of perception and insight.

What causes the smile, the laugh, or in special moments, the rollicking ripple of almost every muscle of the body? Philosophers, psychologists, comedians, and salesmen have been asking this question for many years.

We smile; sometimes we laugh. Ben Turpin said of himself that he was so cross-eyed that when he cried, the tears rolled down his back.

There was the glass blower with a carnival in Butte, Montana, who was struck with the hiccups and blew 200 percolator tops before he could stop.

Then, there was the senior Senator's answer to the freshman Congressman who remarked, on being introduced to him, "I had the honor of passing your house last night." "Thank you."

And, Fred Allen's inspired creation of the only armless sculptor in the world. He put the chisel in his mouth, and his wife hit him on the back of the head with a mallet.

Or, in the famous Fred Allen-Jack Benny radio feud of the 1930's, "Benny, until you were born, nobody knew what a cramp looked like."

What's different about an Italian dinner? In six days, you're hungry again.

Or, did you hear that the Communists have now started national million dollar lotteries for the people? Winners get a dollar a year for a million years.

As we shall see, most humor and comedy are based on some form of **ridicule** and **surprise**. These are, I find, the basic elements or common denominators of all humor and comedy.

George Bernard Shaw once quipped, "If the other planets are inhabited, the Lord must be using this one as his insane asylum." Mark Twain further pulled the latch string of insight with his now famous epigram, "Man is the only animal that blushed – or needs to."

IMPORTANCE OF HUMOR AND COMEDY

There are four basic antidotes for tension amid the crash and strain of modern day living:

1. taking drugs
2. exercising
3. religion, including prayer and meditation
4. laughing

Stress is most common in persons who:

1. live in the past; i.e., are neurotic, having had some wrenching, often early childhood experience, that cripples them emotionally
2. have developed, for a variety of reasons, a low self-esteem
3. have not found a way of getting themselves off their own hands by belief and faith in a higher life and spiritual model
4. cannot laugh at themselves.

Without getting too technical about it or going into detail, our research centers today are teeming with new findings which confirm that **laughter** releases in the body a mental alertness hormone, catecholamine which clears up the thinking process; acts as a kind of "mental jogging for promoting respiration, organ massage, and stimulating a hormonal balance and euphoria of the mind; releases the production of endorphins and encephalins in the brain, which are the body's natural morphine and pain killers; triggers the body's self-regulating immunological functions; relieves stress and depressive reactions; helps prevent burnout; elevates self-esteem; helps to put life into perspective in relation to its contradictions, pretensions, and deceits; and can, in general, brighten the corner where you are in the home, office, plant, or busy freeway.

Doctors today are actually prescribing humor for patients in hospitals. So, laughter is proving good medicine. Religion, too, has opened up the stained glass windows for laughter. As early as 1964, Elton Trueblood, wrote an entire book called, ***The Humor of Jesus.*** In it, this devoted Professor of Philosophy at Earlham College, recalled reading the Seventh Chapter of Matthew's Gospel to his eldest son, a four -year old. The scholar was feeling very serious when his little boy began to laugh. The child had laughed because he saw how ridiculous it would be for a man to be deeply concerned about a speck in another person's eye, while unconscious of the fact that he had a beam in his own eye. The boy had immediately perceived that the eye was not large enough to have a beam of lumber in it so that the very idea was funny. By analysis, we call this the humor of exaggeration, a very important kind of humor technique. Trueblood goes on, in his book, to elucidate 30 passages from Jesus's teachings which are humorous, including paradox, irony, parables, and selected dialogues.

Socrates stood up in the audience whenever he was caricatured by the early Greek dramatists. In this way, he said, the citizens could have even more fun as they saw him burlesqued from the stage. Some persons never get over their own sense of importance and conceit. They go through life self-centered and arrogant. Their minds are like a room full of mirrors, bounded on the North by themselves, on the East by themselves, on the South by themselves, and on the West by themselves. Every direction they turn, they see themselves. Humor and comedy can replace those mirrors with windows, let in the fresh air of laughter, so that they can reach out to others, and they to them.

I am sure you have noticed, as I have, that certain persons, when they get together, just seems to be happy, to laugh all the time. Almost any event, or even tiny circumstance, is somehow amusing, ridiculous, or funny to them. Sometimes, it is two sisters who simply laugh whenever they are together, about a crooked door, a bug on windshield, a limp dish rag, almost anything. It has been my own observation that whenever you have roughly 30 persons in close proximity for any length of time, say on a boat tour, a large family gathering, or working together in an office, in an Army barracks, there is usually one person, for example, a soldier in the Army barracks, who can imitate or make fun of the commanding officer, and get away with it. In an office one person, often an old hand, an old salt, with a sense of humor, can actually tell the boss off in front of others. These persons lubricate the social interface when there are frictions, can literally keep staff meetings from becoming a bore, or from becoming undemocratic.

In a department of some 36 employees in a corporation, where I worked for some ten years, we had a person who kept a Caesar Division manager in line. He could change the boss's mind in front of the group with a quip or anecdote to the benefit and silent applause of everyone in the department. If anyone else in the group, however, were to have challenged this Division manager in this way, he would have pulled out his authoritarian rapier, sliced out his protagonist's navel, and left the lint exposed!

My son, Dick Jr., and his marvelous mother-in-law, Gamile Sadak, spend hours laughing together. Can there by any better relationship than this between a son and a mother-in-law? They laugh so much, there is no need to cry.

A POINT OF DEPARTURE

Confucius once said that if he were given the power to govern the world, the first thing that he would do would be to concentrate on definitions, because action follows definition. In my new book, titled, ***Humor and Comedy in America: The Uses of Fun and Laughter,*** I have identified, classified, and defined:

25 basic types of humor and comedy
60 other varieties of comedic forms
20 formula jokes
20 techniques for developing and writing humor and comedy
20 techniques for delivering humor and comedy

as well as a special Appendix on the Comic's Vocabulary and another on the 100 best jokes of all time.

Here are just a few important definitions:

HUMOR: that which is amusing, comical, ridiculous or ludicrous, usually connoting playfulness or fun. Chaplin, in fact, defined comedy as playful pain

SENSE OF HUMOR: the ability to perceive and to express that which is amusing, comical, ridiculous or ludicrous

WIT: an astute, ingenious, intellectual perception; or, a judgmental ability to relate disparate ideas or things so as to amuse, ridicule, or illuminate

For example: "There is less there than meets the eye."
– William F. Buckley, Jr. Humor pictures; wit punctures.

COMEDY: a light, amusing or funny series of events, with a happy ending

For example: Shakespeare's brilliant play, "As You Like It," or popular sitcoms, such as "M*A*S*H" or "Cheers"

LAUGHTER: a physiological motor reflex produced by the co-ordinated contraction of 15 facia muscles, accompanied by altered breathing, and is usually evoked by that which is comical, ridiculous, or ludicrous

QUIP: witty, funny verbal observation, generally on the spur of the moment

For example; "He couldn't ad-lib a belch at a Hungarian dinner."
– Fred Allen

WISECRACK: a clever or sophisticated witticism, usually word-play about a particular person or thing.

For example: "His teeth had so many cavities,
he talked with an echo."
– Red Skeleton

EPIGRAM: a clever or sophisticated witticism, thoughtplay, or wordplay about a general group of persons or things

For example: "It is better to give than to receive,
and it costs the same."
– Sir Philip Gibbs

GAG: an intentional laugh – provoking remark set in dialogue or conversational form

For example: "Who was that woman I saw you with last night?"
"That was no woman, that was my son-in-law,
and I could cry every time I think about it."

ONE-LINER: a short gag delivered by one person, who both sets up the straight-line and springs the punchline

For example: "You can always tell an Arab.
When he gets up out of bed, he takes his sheet with him."
– Robert Orben

JOKE: a brief single-incident narrative, setting up a humorous situation, followed by a punchline, the suddenness of which surprises the listener by a twist, reversal, or unexpected outcome and the neatness of construction.

For example: An anonymous taxpayer sent a letter to the IRS, saying that he had cheated on his federal Income Tax eight years ago, and had not had a good night's sleep since then.

He enclosed $50, adding a note which read: "If I still can't sleep, I'll send the balance."

Another example: A friend of mine at Whirlpool Corporation, when I was doing an extended consulting assignment for them in Benton Harbor, Michigan, flew to Chicago with me for the weekend. He told me about his Department Manager there who had inherited all kinds of money, but was also highly placed in the executive ranks, yet was the cheapest man he had ever know. He and his boss were walking one evening down Michigan Avenue. Ahead of them was a poor, old beggar whose shoes were so bad that the soles were actually flapping loose. His boss stopped the beggar, reached into his pocked an d pulled out a roll of bills that would have choked a horse. He slipped off one of the large rubber bands, gave it to the guy, and said, "Here, put his around your shoe to stop the flapping."

STORY: an extended joke or anecdote, a long narrative account of some interesting, amusing, or ludicrous event

For example: Two successful Kansas farmers wanted to be sure that their sons got a college education something neither of them ever had. In their sons' senior year, these two farmers accepted an invitation on Parents' Day to visit a class at the University of Kansas.

They picked a class on Astronomy. The professor, in his lecture, related that the earth had a circumference at the equator of 25,000 miles and that the earth's estimated weight is 6.6 sextillion tons. For the mathematician, the professor explained, that is 6 x 10 to the 21st power, or followed by 21 zeros. But the earth is actually tiny in the universe, the professor pointed out, because it would take 1 million earth balls to fit into the space occupied by the sun. Some stars could hold a trillion earth balls; i.e.., million times a million earths, or 10 to the 12th power, or 12 zeroes.

As the farmers left the lecture hall, Zeke turned Zep, the other father, slapped himself on the left leg and said, "You know, Zep, I guess it don't make so much difference whether the Republicans git in this year or not!"

PUN: a humorous use of words in such a way as to suggest different meanings and applications; or, words having the same of nearly the same sound but different meaning

For example: A Wisconsin farmer with poor relatives in East Germany herd that a food package he had sent them had never arrived. Putting a braved face on the matter, he cabled them: "CHEER UP! THE WURST IS YET TO COME."

In my opinion, the pun is not, as is so often mentioned, the lowest form of humor: the practical joke is. Pun requires intellect to compose it, can be charming, and can be funny.

In my research, as mentioned, I have identified another dozen or so types of humor and comedy and an additional 60 varieties of comedic forms.

My own favorite type of humor is SUDDEN REALITY. This is usually a story, an accurate description of reality, of things as they are, reminding us of what we already know, feel, or refuse to admit; and, at times, illuminating those urges, emotions, and denials in an altogether different and entertaining way.

For example: The two current masters of this art form are Jerry Clower, country humorist, and Garrison Keillor of Prairie Home Companion radio fame.

From my own experience, here are two examples:

At Strong, Carlisle, and Hammond Company in Cleveland, Ohio, where I had my first job, our boss called six of us subordinates into his office and said, "All right, men, if there is anything I hate, it's a "Yes Man. Do you men understand that?"

And we all bobbed our heads up and down and burped in chorus, "Yes we do!"

Or, another of my favorites occurred on one of my major consulting assignments for Monsanto Chemical Company. A true story. Nearing retirement, the top Vice President was an old Dutchman from the Hague, authoritarian and tough. He called in his General manager, was boiling mad about something and as they argued, fired him on the spot. The General manager said, "You can't fire me: I QUIT." He turned to leave and inadvertently. Walked into the Vice President's office closet and banged the door closed.

When he came out of the closet, they both began to laugh. They recognized how foolishly they had behaved, apologized to one another, shook hands, and this incident saved one of the great Vice Presidents of monsanto Chemical company. Within a year, this General Manager was promoted to replace his boss as Vice president upon his retirement.

The morale of this story is, of course: the next time you are fired, walk into your boss's closet.

Another example from home life, a true story is about my own father, who, at the time was Industrial Sales manager for the State of Ohio in the White Star Division of Standard Oil Company of New York. My parents raised four children. After one hectic Sunday, when all four of us had been notoriously noisy and naughty, my father went to his office Monday morning, buzzed for his secretary, and immediately dictated a memorandum to his children, titled COOPERATION IN THE HOME. That evening, when he came home, he placed a copy of it on each of our dinner plates:

TO: Bob, Dick, Marian and Bill Stull
FROM: Dad
RE: Cooperation in the home

1. Come to the table when called and wait for the others to be seated. After grace, offer to pass something, then begin to eat.

2. Enter into interesting and intelligent conversation. An occasional joke is generally sufficient. Don't gang up and try to be funny all through the meal. Avoid all loud and irrelevant arguments. Don't cut in when someone else is talking. Don't reach for it: ask for it. Follow the rules of table etiquette. Then, it will appear natural away from home. When you leave the table, ask to be excused.

3. After taking a shower or bath, put the soap in its proper place so that it will not soak up water. Hang up your bath towel so it dries out. Rinse and clean out the tub for the next person. Put your dry, dirty clothes in the clothes hamper, not on the floor.

Don't waste toothpaste and powder: you can't clean your teeth with the excess splashed around in the sink. Clean out the washbowls and stand when you have finished.

Ask to use the bathroom when someone else is in it, and abide by their decision. Bathrooms are at least semi-private, even in large families. Then, turn out the bathroom lights, and close the door quietly when you leave.

4. If a wastebasket is overflowing, don't try to force more refuse into it. If you notice that something has missed the basket, pick it up and make the deposit yourself.

Don't leave empty drinking glasses sitting around anywhere – living room to kitchen. Old apple cores, gum, and candy wrappers should never be permitted to remain on the living room stands, dining room table, or in ash trays. And don't toss them into the fireplace.

After reading, put your books and magazines away. When you have finished reading a newspaper, fold it in regular order so the next reader doesn't have to straighten out what you have mussed up.

Everyone should wash and wipe his or his own dishes after a midnight snack.

When someone is on the telephone, turn down the TV or radio.

5. Offer to help your mother, and mean it. Instead of arguing with her take her part.

If you will observe and do these simple things, our home will be much happier — you'll enjoy it, too.

WHAT IS FUNNY AND WHY?

We have seen that much in the entire work/life situation is funny. There is a lot of fun at work and at home. Our children can be all sort of fun. Their playfulness creates an atmosphere of fun. It simply makes sense to enjoy them at all ages and stages in their development. Try to help them create a sense of humor to see the funny, the bright side. Plan quality time with your family, with focus on your spouse and children. So far as the children are concerned you'll be surprised how fast those days pass, and once gone that cannot be repeated.

The two basic elements of most humor and comedy are:
1. RIDICULE (SUPERIORITY)
2. SURPRISE (SUDDENNESS)

These elements are as ancient as the harsh humor of the Old Testament, where there are twenty-nine references to laughter, out of which thirteen are related to ridicule, and interestingly enough, only two linked to joy. The New Testament takes a more positive look at life. Today the building block of most humor is still the joke. What makes a person laugh is largely a matter of individual and social conditioning. ***Psychology Today*** did a reader survey of some 14,5000 subscribers' response to 30 jokes. No specific pattern was found, though each joke printed could easily be analyzed in terms of ridicule and surprise. There is nothing wrong with ridicule, if it makes us share in the foibles of humanity and pegs us, like Job, in the scheme of things. But we do not need to be cruel. There is such a thing as good taste. If it can offend, it will offend.

What is funny is a compound of attitudes, perceptions, thought, feelings, values, and interests. To explode this chemistry depends upon at least three factors, if , for example, you are exploding a joke:

1. There must be sufficient intellectual, linguistic, and cognitive experience with the joke subject matter to elicit ridicule and to stimulate surprise.

2. There must be a mood of fun or playfulness; otherwise, the joke will be rejected.

3. The joke itself must not threaten the value system of the listener.

Consider the following joke: A burglar broke into the home of a modern artist. The artist, however, caught a glimpse of the thief and made a sketch for the police. Within a few hours, thanks to the sketch, the police had arrested two vultures, a rusty tractor, a gorilla, three large baskets of fruit, and a Russian wolfhound.

Now, if you did not know intellectually that much of modern art is non-representative and concerned with color, design, and substitution, if you did not know that museums live in fear of hanging new school paintings upside down, if you did not know that often a modern artist paints an orange by painting the juice, if one of your parents had just been shot by a burglar the night before hearing the joke, or if your religion forbid disfiguring or distorting the human body in anyway, you probably would not laugh at this joke.

Most of the raw material of humor or comedy is tragedy. That is the reason ridicule and surprise are the key elements. Often, we are too embarrassed to cry. Laughter is often our first line of defense against life's frustration. We laugh because we prefer not to fight or flee or make ourselves sick by suppressing the tension.

OTHER USES OF HUMOR AND COMEDY

Sales persons, being social, often use humor. Public speaking is another area, or to break stiffness at a meeting, negotiating. Public speaking stands out because more and more executives are having to stand up and speak to defend their companies and our society in areas in which they believe.

In public speaking the main uses of humor and particularly the joke, since it is the building block of humor, are:

1. an ice-breaker opening, to put your audience at ease
2. getting and sustaining attention
3. advancing speech themes or topics
4. change of pace, relaxing the audience during a speech
5. making a point or clinching ideas in speech content
6. final summary or positive close.

The retirement party used to be an important area for the use of humor. Often the employee was given a gold watch or the office manager the clock off the wall that he had been watching for 52 years! Today, more common is the business roast, which is just what it sounds like, a chance to toast over the hot ashes of someone who is retiring or we want to honor. It is a tongue-in-cheek affair, like the Dean Martin Roasts on TV that got them started. Originally, they were developed by the Friar's Clubs in New York and Beverly Hills for show business celebrities. Some companies actually give courses on how to plan, write, and conduct a business roast. Some social groups, even the PTA, have tried them, and they have proved themselves as fund raisers for many organizations. The honored guest is roasted in fun, his or her foibles and eccentricities exposed, but also their accomplishments and contributions to their organizations, usually with jokes, anecdotes, and a good-natured ribbing and fun.

CONCLUSION

As you work your way through this book and make the concepts your own by applying them in your daily activities, you will find that people in the soft side of management are serious, but also flawed and funny. There is really no need to pretend that we are more than we are; but, we can all become more than we are. We cannot always have it our way, but we can live by the fifteen word philosophy of Teddy Roosevelt "by doing the best we can, with what we have, where we are, right now." And everything can be funny from the alphabet to the zealot; from the philosopher to the saloon singer. Some wit put it this way:

To be is to do. – Neitzsche
To do is to be. – Heidegger
Do be do be do. – Sinatra

Henry Ward Beecher put it this way: "A man without mirth is like a wagon without springs. He is jolted by every pebble in the road.' James Thurber found humor to be a very serious thing: emotional chaos remembered in tranquility. Christopher Fry saw that comedy filters tragedy because "comedy is an escape, not from truth but from despair: a narrow escape into faith. It believes in a universal cause for delight, even though knowledge of the cause is often twitched away from under us, which leaves us to rest on our own buoyancy in faith. In tragedy every moment is eternity; in comedy eternity is a moment. In tragedy we suffer pain; in comedy pain is a fool, suffered gladly."

The story has been told for years about the guru, the wise old teacher who was dying. His followers line up next to his bed, from the most brilliant at the head of the line to the oaf at the end of the line. The brilliant follower leans down and asks, "Oh, wise one, what are your departing words?"

"My final words," murmurs the dying leader are: "Life is a river." The brilliant one repeats these words to the person next to him in line, and the message travels like wildfire down the line, "Our leader says, "Life is a river." When the message reaches the oaf at the end of the line, however, he asks, "What does our leader mean, life is a river?"

Now, that message travels back up the line: "What does the wise one mean, life is a river?" What does the wise one mean, life is a river?" The brilliant follower leans over the leader again, as the guru is breathing his last breath, "What do you mean, life is a river?" He pleads. And the teacher shrugs his frail shoulders as he answers his final words, "So, it's not a river."

As we have seen in this final chapter, persons who laugh tend to have less stress and live longer. Humor can make bad days more bearable, tension more tolerable, disasters less devastating, teachers better teachers, bosses better bosses, and subordinates better subordinates. We know, too, that laughter increases wellness, productivity, and creativity. It decreases stress, depression, and burnout.

One psychiatrist put it this way: "If faced with a choice between the loss of a leg and his own sense of humor, he said he would lose a leg – because we have two legs and only one sense of humor." Humor helps up put life into perspective, tells us the truth about ourselves, and we begin to wonder why nobody has ever mentioned that Gorbachov carries a map of the Philippines around on his forehead.

In closing this chapter, let me leave you with

A RECIPE FOR HAPPINESS

Take:

1 heart full of love
2 portions of understanding
2 handfuls of generosity
1 dash of faith
1 heaping tablespoon of forgiveness
1 cup of laughter

Combine these ingredients and stir frequently with tenderness. Sprinkle freely with kindness — and serve daily.

Part II

The HARD SIDE Of Managing

Part II

The Hard Side of Managing

Wherever two or more people are gathered together to accomplish some specific work the processes of managing happen. Managing is both a formal and informal happening and depends on the **shared knowledge, skills and experience of the people working together.**

Each particular situation helps to dictate how people will work together. Many organizations are clear about what needs to be done (what physical, financial, and human resources are needed to get it done), *yet are not at all clear about how they are going to work together to get it done!*

In most organizations, the basics of managing are still reserved for those people who have people reporting to them. They still have the caste system for different levels of supervision. The caste system philosophy suggests that there is a level of information about managing that is only for supervisors, middle management and executives.

We maintain that although the scope of work broadens at the top of the organization and narrows at the bottom, the basic philosophies and tools for managing are necessary for all people. **Managing the organization is EVERYONE'S BUSINESS** in direct relation to their scope of work.

The information in Part II sets the stage for providing a solid foundation for managing an organization. These same philosophies and tools are necessary for individuals as they go about managing their personal and work lives.

Our concept of the managing arena is presented in the **Managing System Overview** page 114 which displays the functions that are performed in the work of managing (planning, organizing, directing, leading, and controlling), and the arenas in which those functions are performed (strategic and operational.)

As we note in the matrix above, planning, organizing, directing, leading and controlling are basic functions. These functions have stood the test of time. Each has a vital role in defining the work of managing for success. We will discuss each function in more detail in the following chapters.

The STRATEGIC arena, houses the managing work that focuses on future direction, movement, change, continued growth and prosperity. Managing in the strategic arena focuses on establishing INTENT on the part of the enterprise to accomplish something. There is no implied or stated commitment of organizational resources, nor is there commitment to specific objectives in the strategic arena. There is at some point a commitment to a strategy, before continued work is done to "prove" the value of having that strategy become a part of the operational business plan.

The OPERATIONAL arena, focuses on making specific commitment of organizational effort and resources, and on execution of planned activities in order to accomplish the organization's strategy.

This generally includes current year budgets, projects, products, services and initial stages of new products and services being developed. Here is where the actual commitment and action take place as a result of having performed the functions of planning, organizing, directing, leading and controlling.

Part II Hard Side of Managing describes the managing system and provides tools and concepts for effective managing.

The chapters are organized as follows:

Chapter 7: Putting the Basics Back into Managing Discusses strategic managing in its simplest form as a discipline for integrating future efforts into the reality of today's decisions.

Chapter 8: Strategic Managing Discusses operational managing, where the actions of today are designed for acquiring wealth so that additional capital is available for enduring growth and prosperity. This chapter will summarize the completed ***Managing System Matrix.*** We provide some additional ideas on how to use the Matrix as a quick reference tool for improving communications among people doing work in both present and future arenas.

MANAGING SYSTEM OVERVIEW

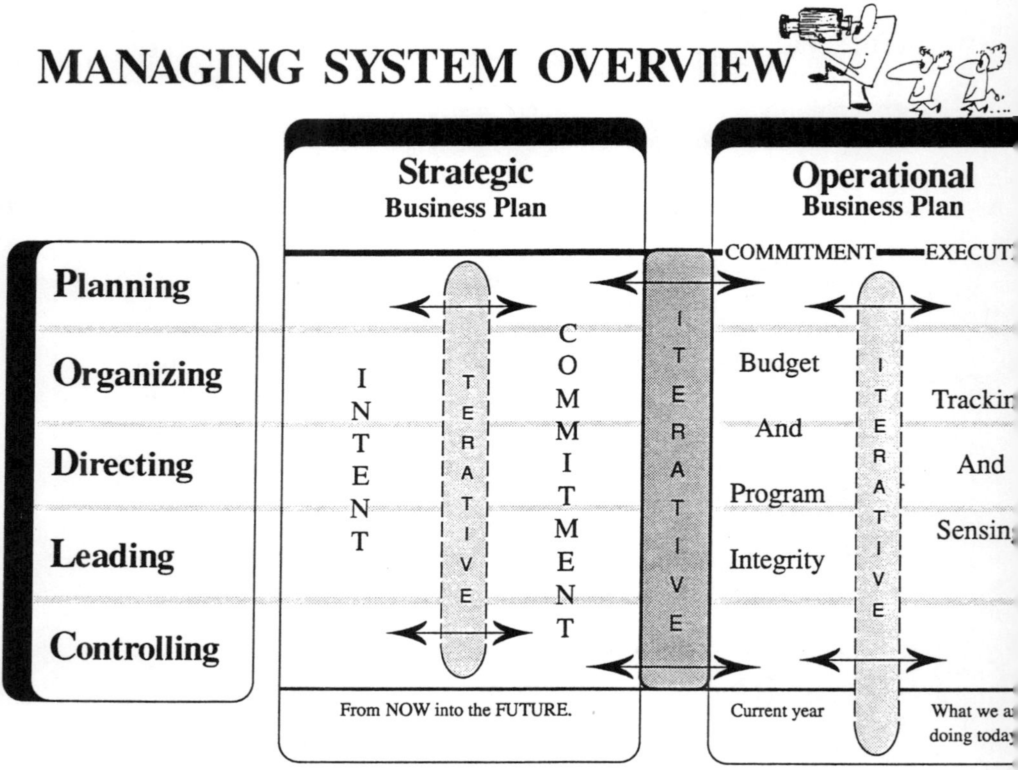

Chapter 9: Operational Managing and the Business Plan Executing the plans for current year activities. Here where the action begins to get results.

Chapter 10: Operational Managing: The Task of Doing the Work is a written document for tracking and sensing the vital work and performance evaluation. The Working Agreement fulfills a basic need for communicating clearly about vital work in ways that help implementing the principles of the managing system and their integration with the Production, Resource, Information, Administration, and Social Systems presented in Chapter 1.

Chapter 11: The Working Agreement: A Managing Framework for Assuring Success Provides a very useful tool for getting mutual agreement on getting the job done.

Chapter 12: Making the Working Agreement Be a Vital Part of today's Reality provides specific ways to develop, implement and maintain ***Working Agreements*** to aid in growing and staying profitable.

Chapter 7

Putting the Basics Back into Managing

Chapter 7

Putting the Basics Back into Managing

What do we still remember about PLANNING, ORGANIZING, DIRECTING, LEADING, AND CONTROLLING (PODLC)?

Maybe the real question is "why should we?". After all, don't several years in managing exempt us from all this education stuff? The answers to these questions are "it depends." We know of people with a lot of experience in both staff and line roles who have increased their effectiveness significantly by reviewing and applying some basic principles of managing.

New and old companies have failed because not enough attention was paid to PODLC. For example:

Some start-up companies have failed because they were underfunded. Others have failed even though they had a lot of venture capital (other people's money). They failed to control their expenditures, lost a sense of urgency, and a sense of financial integrity. The well dried up and another good idea didn't make it because of inexperienced managing.

A fifteen year old multi-million dollar company over-committed on a new product for the market, under-performed on product design and delivery. The result—Chapter 11 bankruptcy.

This chapter offers a quick review of five basic functions of managing—planning, organizing, directing, leading, and controlling. This review sets the stage for the development of managing system tools in subsequent chapters.

PLANNING

Planning is the process of establishing mission, goals, objectives, and tasks that set direction for the enterprise and guide its use of resources.

Put more simply,

Planning is thinking ahead and preparing to act in the present.

This idea of acting in the present is an important one. Many people and organizations engage in planning as if the purpose of doing so were to create plans. This frame of reference severely limits the effectiveness of planning, because it fails to tie planning to the day to day work that is done in the enterprise. As we see it, the ultimate purpose of planning is to help us decide what to do today, with the emphasis on results, both personal and corporate.

Planning is the process that results in plans. An organization without specific plans is like a ship without a rudder. What would happen to a ship if it left port without updating critical weather information during hurricane season?

Some organizations fail to update their business plans during their volatile business cycles and many fail to have written business plans. Sometimes plans take on a life of their own.

A lot of effort is spent involving people in "futuring" both near in and far out. The plans are written, placed on the shelf and never see the light of day. Successful plans have coffee stains, cross outs, and iteration after iteration based on current useful information.

Plans and planning are interdependent. Plans represent a point in time where there is a common sense of understanding, acceptance and support.

In the definition of planning, we mentioned several elements, including mission, goals, objectives, and tasks. Taken together, and in the context of vision, beliefs, and values, these elements form the mosaic of the planning process. We will look at each of these elements separately and their effect on the planning process.

Mission

In a logical, ideally designed effort, planning proceeds from a broad, longer-term focus to a narrow, immediate focus, with each step following gracefully and logically from the preceding one. Thus, an enterprise begins with a broad sense of its identity and purpose, or, its mission. Recall in Chapter 1 our discussion of mission as the central, unifying theme for an enterprise. For businesses, the mission boils down to deciding, "What business are we in?"

Answering the following three questions thoroughly goes a long way toward defining the mission of an organization.

1. What are our products and services?

2. Who are our customers?

3. What is the value of our products and services to our customers?

On the face of it, these questions are deceptively simple. In practice, they can be positively menacing.

Some may want to try answering these questions individually at first and then compare answers. Were they easy to answer? How similar or different were the answers for the different people?

How important is it that we have mutual understanding, acceptance, and support for the mission of our enterprise? How long did it take us to come to a mutual understanding of our mission?

We know of one case in which the senior management team of a major corporation extended their management retreat by three days just to work through the confusion and lack of clarity they had about their mission!

Clear identity and purpose for people within an organization provides a solid foundation for motivation and effectiveness. Usually identity and purpose are described in position descriptions.

The ***Working Agreement*** (see Chapters 11 and 12) provides an effective tool for describing and communicating each person's role in the enterprise. When it is clear that each person has a meaningful and a recognized part of the whole, then the organization's mission takes on real life. Another idea is to spend an evening with the family to discuss the "mission" as a family. We might ask ourselves, "Who are we? For what purpose(s) do we exist as a family?" Keep it light, and be prepared for some interesting discussions.

Mission is the primary focus for all individual and organization resources. When the mission is unclear, the organization is out of focus, energy is wasted, people become depressed, tired, cantankerous, and withhold useful information. This affects all people in the organization just like it affects all people in a family when their real purpose is out of focus.

Values and Beliefs. If the mission is one of the building blocks of the foundation of an enterprise, its values and beliefs form another building block. Values and beliefs represent the basic philosophy that guides the actions of the enterprise through its people.

T. J. Watson Sr. built IBM Corporation on three foundation beliefs:

1. Respect for the integrity of the individual

2. Striving for excellence in the quality of products

3. Providing the best possible customer service

As Mr. Watson saw it and practiced it, other things about the company could change, but the basic three beliefs remained firm. In our own consulting business, we have articulated some "shared beliefs," or beliefs to which all of us who are part of the business can subscribe. Here are some of them, along with a brief discussion about how each helps to guide us in our work:

•*We see enterprises as systems.* This belief or orientation about enterprises enables us to recognize that any changes or interventions that affect one part of the enterprise are likely to affect other parts as well. Sensitivity to this helps us to avoid creating unwanted negative effects of the work we do with clients.

•***We see the social system as a largely unrecognized key facet of the working process of any enterprise, and therefore deserving of time and resources of the enterprise.*** This belief, coupled with our systems orientation, causes us to focus attention on the human side of the enterprise and to help our clients understand how to work within the social system to enable people to work together more effectively.

•***We believe in "in-process" design of our consulting work.*** The most "simple" of human enterprises are complex systems that are constantly undergoing change. In our consulting work, we are constantly gathering new information and adjusting our design accordingly. Of course this has to be done in a responsible way and not haphazardly. Many of our clients have praised our willingness to change the design in ways that were most helpful to them.

•***We are willing to raise and address the "hard" questions.*** A while ago, I had separate phone conversations with two men who are co-owners of a medium-sized company. Over the years of their business association, they have developed some habitual ways of working together that are self-defeating. One of these is that when difficult questions arise (e.g., what is our pricing strategy in today's market?), they deteriorate into an attack/counter-attack mode and end up polarized. Dealing with hard questions must be done skillfully. By using such principles as are expressed in the ***Working Guidelines,*** polarizations and conflicts can be minimized, and fruitful, synergistic conversations can occur around tough issues.

•***We practice what we teach.*** It's difficult to imagine not doing this, yet we have seen consultants who, in our opinion, teach teamwork and cooperation to their clients, and practice independence and divisiveness with their own colleagues. Our integrity is at stake if we are unwilling or unable to do the things that we share with our clients. Fortunately for us, we know that what we share with others also works for us. (We are constantly working on our batting average in both practicing what we teach and our faith).

•***The spiritual part of our lives is important to each/all of us.*** The Bible is our source. Being a Christian is the basic practice of our Work/Life approach. We do not preach a religious line to our clients, but it is important to us to live, work and abide by our spiritual values and let others know that part of us.

We offer you the idea of sitting down with your family and/or your work colleagues and discovering what your shared beliefs and values are. It is also instructive to discuss what beliefs and values are not shared among family members or work colleagues. Where there are differences, how can we deal with them effectively?

Vision. A "vision" is a statement of how we prefer the future either as an individual or enterprise. ***Visions are rooted in beliefs and values and are sources of hope, energy, inspiration, and excitement.*** They are further enhanced by our knowledge, skills, and experience.

The art of visioning takes practice. As a sculptor, musician, and painter practice, practice, practice, so must we as we go about our business of visioning the way we see ourselves managing and the end results of that managing.

Frequently we ask people to list their visions for their organization. They painfully struggle to come up with something that makes sense. Finally a number of the people have said "I've followed so long that I don't have a vision". This comment comes from people at the top levels as well as those throughout the rest of the organization.

Marriages grow stale because couples fail to visualize a joyous future, even in tough times. Mom's and dads fail to show their children how to look beyond todays tough times.

Note that visions are an important step in orienting an enterprise and/or an individual in a particular direction. Visions are not fantasies, or hallucinations. Nor do they represent commitment; they are expressions of hopes in various stages of clarity and usefulness.

Goals

Goals may be defined as broad statements of desired outcomes; something to be accomplished. In some ways this is a very limiting view of a goal. It only answers the "I wish, I want, I will" expectations and outputs. For example:

A company has decided that next year the gross revenue will be $8.7 million. This is based on the combined hard work, wisdom, and good judgement of all the functions of the company. Their visions are all geared toward getting to the goal. When this is satisfied they breathe a sigh of relief and begin the cycle over again. Generally this "next year" cycle starts well before the end of the $8.7m cycle ends. *When the focus is on coming to the end of a previously made commitment there is little openness to new ideas*. The focus should be on celebrating completion of the results we are looking for and visualizing beyond this end result!

Mid-way through the third quarter there is a significant increase in revenue from an unexpected source. We are home free; the goal of $8.7m WILL be met easily. Hence a profit limiting sigh of relief occurs, and a great opportunity to keep the pace up and really have a banner year is significantly reduced.

Effective goal setting is a dynamic process from the very beginning– starting with visualizing the future less clearly to finally doing our homework and visualizing it clear enough to plan and take specific action to accomplish successful end results.

Since goals are spawned in our VISIONS ***there is inspired hope, excitement, and energy.*** These are feeling elements of the decision making processes. When the $8.7m was originally understood, accepted and supported, there was a lot of legitimate "feeling" with the "can do" attitude that is not written on paper. People visualized getting to the goal, not what it feels like having met the goal — Which they should have done! Visualizing the end results as already complete. Visualizing helps us get ready to enjoy the future!

Let's restate the goal in dynamic terms:

- **Our revenue for FY__ is at $8.7 million**
- **The profit picture is on target**
- **Return on investment is at our stockholders level of expectation**

  We are rewarding our people for continued improvement in their productivity beyond this revenue bench mark. (With this type of visualization people will know there is more in it for them as they continue beyond the $8.7m and instead of a sigh, there is excitement and hope.)

Intangible goal setting such as visualizing customer satisfaction, behavior change in the way people interact in tough times, and general conditions for success on tough issues has an equally powerful impact on the success of a company.

Objectives

We want to warn you, the following can be seen as dry, technical reading, it can also be seen as a much needed tool to clean up the difference between goals and objectives. This distinction is critical when the working agreement tool is used later on.

Objectives are statements which tie quality, quantity, time, and resources to accomplishing goals. They are specific and may be intangible as well as tangible. An objective covers who is doing what, by when, using what resources, to accomplish outputs that satisfy goals at the maximum cost benefit to both the customer and the company.

One objective for meeting the $8.7m revenue goal might be : Having the marketing and sales team experienced in using the ***WORK/ LIFE MANAGEMENT SYSTEM*** tools to:

- Increase the flow of useful information in a manner that customers are willing to confide their concerns as well as hopes for the products and services they are looking to buy.
- Resolve field issues in valuing ways that customer criticisms are seen as opportunities and customers causing problems are given criticism without blame.
- Increase the closing rate on sales by 20% within six months.
- Have customers feel they really are being served.

A related objective might be:

- The W/LMS training is completed by _____ at a cost of $_____ and is conducted by the training department using both live and video tape presentations.

To summarize, the following offers another way to describe goals and objectives.

Goals–state end results, desired outcomes and referred future.

Objectives–state the *how to* for accomplishing goals.

Tasks

A task is the actual work that is done or the effort that is expended to accomplish one or more objectives.

We specify a task in written form using these elements:

- **Objectives stated to satisfy previous goals.**
- **Activities necessary to accomplish objectives.**
- **The value of those activities in terms of outputs to meet goals.**
- **Conditions for success which spell out help (behavior/ resources) we need from others.**
- **Measurement criteria for evaluating outcomes of the activities in light of the task objectives.**

In 1972 we started helping people see that the task is the central focus for getting all work done. It is the organizing principle for tracking and sensing vital work. We can do visualizing, set goals, establish objectives and fail, if we don't articulate the task clearly.

The task is another of the vital ingredients in the ***Working Agreement.*** We will cover this in later chapters.

Vision

↕

Goal

↕

Objective

↕

Task

- Activities
- Value
- Conditions for success
- Measurement
- Effectiveness

By the way, we write goals, objectives, and task statements only for the important things to be done. This system is to help us, not to make slaves of us. If we waste energy and time writing trivial goals and objectives, we may not have time to enjoy doing the work!

Our discussion of planning has been a lengthy one. Planning represents a complex set of interrelated activities. The orderly process from broad to narrow focus outlined above is rarely followed precisely in practice. It is more commonly done in an iterative fashion; that is, people move back and forth among visions, goals, objectives and tasks.

For instance, developing a specific task may bring to mind other objectives and goals that need to be articulated. Or in the process of doing work, new information comes to light that requires a change in one or more key goals or objectives.

Planning must be a flexible, ongoing process that guides the enterprise and is guided by current information about the enterprise and its environment. **Once again, planning is thinking ahead so we can act responsibly today!**

ORGANIZING

It has been said that the world's first management consultant was Jethro, father-in-law to Moses. Jethro's contribution was to make the seemingly unmanageable task of leading the Israelites out of Egypt more manageable by creating a division of labor. Instead of having Moses be responsible for everything, he helped organize the work by assigning certain key responsibilities to certain individuals and groups. Jethro's effort represented the managing function of organizing—**designing and developing an organization and establishing the arrangement and relation of work to be performed by individuals and groups in order to carry out the plans of the enterprise in an efficient and effective manner.**

Formal vs. Informal Organization.

The formal organization is what is typically represented in an organization chart; it is the formal allocation of functional responsibilities and authority levels in an enterprise.

At home we rarely have organizational charts, yet successful families have a clear sense of who's in charge ona specific job, what's to be done, and at what acceptable quality level.

Successful formal organizations are set up to make sure that the form of the organization, as reflected in organization charts, follows the necessary functions to accomplish the work. Form follows function is a very important guideline when considering reorganizing.

Informal organizations represent what actually happens in the day to day functioning of the enterprise.

For example, groups of people within an enterprise develop their own practices, values, norms, and social relationships as they work together. These *informal organizations can be either supportive of the larger enterprise, or they can conflict with the direction of the enterprise.* Counterproductive informal groups frequently form when the formal organization fails to meet the desires or needs of some or all of the people. (Unions form in new companies when this isn't done. Frankly, in some organizations, unions are the primary way for people to be heard because supervisors fail to do it, and some don't even see it as part of their job).

From our systems perspective, as discussed in the beginning of this book– e.g. production systems, information systems, resource systems, social systems, administrative systems, managing systems, we see the formal organization as being designed and implemented through the managing system. The informal organization is a manifestation of the social system. In subsequent chapters, we will discuss the organizing function as it is carried out in the strategic and operational arenas of the managing system. Here is another thought for this section on organizing: see if you can guess when the following quote was written:

"We trained hard, but it seemed that every time we were beginning to form up into teams, we would be re-organized. I was to learn in later life that we tend to meet any new situation by re-organizing; and a wonderful method it can be for creating the illusion of progress while producing confusion, inefficiency, and demoralization."

Sounds like a relatively recent statement, doesn't it? In fact, this statement is attributed to Petronius Arbiter and was written in 210 B.C..! Apparently one of the most common misapplied fixes for problems in organizations for at least two millennia has been to re-organize.

Have you ever experienced a re-organization that was intended to organize around a problem? *Organizational structure is frequently the first element to be addressed whenever a problem arises.* The results of re-organizing to solve specific problems (e.g., to avoid firing an unproductive relative of the boss) can be quite humorous (and costly to the enterprise).

The organization is a framework, not a straight jacket. People have differing needs for structure and format. The ambiguities of no formal structure and shifting informal organizations are too much for many of us to handle. Structure provides for discipline, confidence, and a realization that there is someone someplace who can give reassurance. For others, much more is accomplished with less structure, particularly where the situation involves fewer people in the critical information chain.

We find this true as our teenage twins are growing up. They need a lot of structure at 13, some yet at 18, and hopefully just a haven for security and rest as they reach their twenties.

DIRECTING

Assignment and clarification involves giving work direction to individuals, teams, projects, and units based on plans and assigned functions. Giving work direction implies that one person influences one or more others to do something. It also means being very aware of how we give direction. Is it done in a valuing way, where people are involved with the opportunity to contribute from their competency? This can be a tricky business, especially when the particular one or more others are not interested in being influenced!

The most appropriate and effective approach to giving and receiving work direction depends on the situation. Four aspects of the situation that make a difference are:

1. The task itself. Different styles are appropriate when the task is structured vs. unstructured; simple vs. complex; routine vs. unique. For the more simple, routine, structured tasks, more directive approaches are appropriate, while for unstructured or complex tasks, more collegial or participative styles are usually more effective.

2. Personal relationships among the people involved. Where relationships are based on cooperation and valuing behavior, there is usually less need for direction that is based on formal authority.

3. Formal and informal authority relationships. If the enterprise emphasizes formal authority hierarchies, then more formal, directive styles are usually practiced to achieve work direction, in many cases this directive approach gets in the way of involving people at their highest level of competency.

4. The knowledge, skills, experience, attitudes, and temperaments of the people involved influence the way direction is given to accomplish a particular task. A very experienced and knowledgeable executive we know has such confidence that he manages very successfully by patiently asking questions, sharing his visions, and routinely sensing and tracking results against his strategic and operational plans. Usually, for less experienced people, more formal, thorough work direction is required.

Many people are more secure and responsive when work direction is given clearly and thoroughly from a higher authority. Others are stifled or constrained by work direction that is too rigid. They are self-starters who require only a clear sense of the objective and are then turned loose to creatively accomplish the desired outcome. The PREFERRED way!!

A person's SPIRIT OF INTENT has a lot to do with how people receive and give direction. The SPIRIT OF INTENT is that sense and feel we have as a basis for doing the things we do. If our spirit of intent is to value people, our actions have a better chance of being received in a positive manner. If our spirit of intent is to devalue people, chances are our actions will be received in a negative manner.

If the SPIRIT OF INTENT of the person who is giving and receiving direction is to help and value, then cooperation is more readily assured. Behavior other than this eats up the energy and good will of both parties and gets in the way of the flow of useful information.

There are times to be tough, times to be permissive, times to be autocratic, times to be production/profit oriented, times to be benevolent, and times to be participative. However, none of these need to be at the expense of respecting the integrity of each individual or the organization.

How do a manager and subordinate deal with each other when their respective backgrounds and experience come up with different approaches on how to handle a situation? Hopefully when this or similar situations arise, there is modification on the part of one or the other or both; they work at working with each other. If this is not possible after a period of time, one of the parties will probably be transferred, quit, or take some other action.

When directing people it is important to recognize that to some people the job and organization is the primary purpose in life and to others the paycheck is all that matters.

There is pressure in our society to make jobs more challenging, to enlarge jobs, to encourage people to be more participative, and to take more initiative. The assumption is that this will result in a more productive and satisfied worker. Managing includes making sure that we are in the type of work that fits our competency.

A satisfied worker is not necessarily productive, nor is a dissatisfied worker unproductive. We know of people at all points of action of organizations that fit both these categories. The satisfied worker may be liked by most people, easy to get along with, and at the same time gives less than is required.

At the same time the productive dissatisfied worker is eating up the energy of others through a negative spirit of intent. Either way, the directing effort suffers.

Directing is an ongoing function that fosters the discipline to get the job done and the freedom to decide how it gets done, with whom, in a particular situation that uses all resources most effectively.

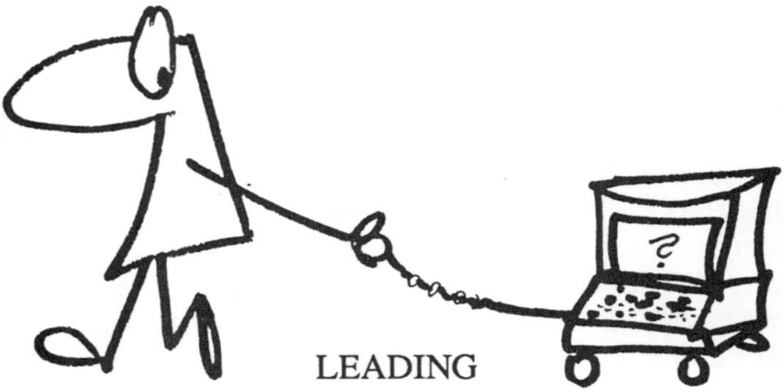

LEADING

The leading function has a direct link to the SOCIAL SYSTEM mentioned in chapter one. The social system includes people's values, attitudes, habits, beliefs, knowledge, skills, experience, competencies and behavior. Leading calls on all these elements through the art of visualizing the preferred future in a manner that fosters some sense of hope, excitement and energy for the present as well as the future. E.g.– a youngster having trouble at school with a teacher may see the future as bleak, and with no hope. By helping the youngster visualize what it looks like when both the teacher and youngster are in "Tune" with each other–and work to get there–then some hope returns.

LEADING INCLUDES ESTABLISHING AND MAINTAINING A DESIRED ORGANIZATIONAL CULTURE THAT ENABLES INDIVIDUALS, TEAMS AND THE ORGANIZATION TO SUCCEED IN A QUALITY WORK ENVIRONMENT. The Organizational culture is based on mutually held and accepted values, beliefs, and norms that guide and direct people's behavior in the enterprise. What happens when family values, beliefs and norms are locked into and locked onto valuing people and being productive in ways that serve GOD and mankind?–We know and experience more of the opposite!

The present culture exists because it was spawned from our past experiences of working together. There are some places where the culture is such that people enjoy coming to work, and others where the culture is so poor many people are leaving, and those staying are there out of fear of not being able to find a different job.

Leading provides the energy for constantly determining whether the way we are going about getting the work done is still the BEST way for us to work today.

- ***What habits do we want to keep?*** What habits do we want to add in place of some that are getting in the way of our visions for the future?
- ***What memories do we want to keep*** that continue to help us stay on course?
- ***What new memories do we want to create*** that will help us visualize the future in terms of hope, excitement, and energy?
- ***What beliefs do we want to strengthen*** to keep us doing those things that value people, maximize our resources, and continue making us profitable?
- ***How clear are our corporate beliefs?*** How well known are they by our employees? What evidence is there that confirms our efforts to practice what we believe? How congruent are our personal beliefs about working with others and our stated corporate beliefs?

Leading consists of those activities which create a climate where people feel confident, motivated, and inspired to pursue their work, and see that work as being consistent with

1. a mutually understood, accepted, and supported direction, and

2. who they are and what they value as individuals.

Leading also includes giving opportunities for people to use their talents and abilities sometimes in new, unorthodox, and creative ways.

Notice that we give more emphasis to "leading" than to "leader." Everyone in an enterprise, regardless of formal position, can engage in leading activities. The emphasis given by many management writers to leaders misses this critical point. ***Leading is a set of activities that can and should be carried out by all people.***–Managing is everybodys business at all points of action.

When a particular individual's knowledge, skills, or abilities fit a particular situation, he or she should have the opportunity to contribute meaningfully and influence decisions that are made. We refer to this as SAPIENTIAL AUTHORITY—or authority based on wisdom or knowledge.

The following reflect some basic support ideas for developing a solid practice of LEADING in an enterprise:

- ***Be concerned about the quality of work/life*** and act on those things that either get in the way of or contribute to a quality work/life experience. Concern for the well being of the human side of the enterprise is like building up credit in the bank. In tough times, the people will be there, willing to help beyond normal expectations. Moms and dads will be there for the children and children will be there for mom and dad.
- ***People must have meaningful work in line with their talents, abilities, and experience. (And the opportunity to learn and get new ones.)*** If this cannot be fulfilled at the present time for certain individuals, at least let them know that and give them opportunities to be creative about the work they have. Work at helping people grow within their talents and aptitudes, even if it means helping them find more challenging work with another enterprise. Everyone wins in this situation.
- ***Trust our own instincts in working with others; analyze the situation carefully before going against our instincts.*** Instincts tie directly into the SPIRIT OF INTENT. Again where the SPIRIT OF INTENT is to value people the actions will meet with much less resistance.
- ***Be willing to "spin the vision" and encourage others to do so.*** Visions create hope, energy, excitement, and inspiration. In our own consulting business, we have been able to pull ourselves up from difficult financial situations by taking time to clarify our visions in terms of todays reality and hope for tomorrow.
- ***Remember that leading is a legitimate role for all people in an enterprise, managers and non-managers, parents and children.*** Everyone can inspire growth or creativity in a given situation.

In keeping with this idea, it is important to be open to new ways of looking at things. IBM founder T. J. Watson articulated this principle in October, 1935, during the height of the depression:

"The ability to see a problem from every angle and to reverse, when need be, all pre-established convictions provides the light of inspiration and constructive thought."

Leading is the activity of linking competencies with tasks, opening doors, affirming risks, letting it happen, being accessible, encouraging participation, giving and receiving feedback, depending on others, asking for help, admitting mistakes, providing support, making resources available, and legitimizing failures. Key to achieving this is working together to create a culture that is characterized by openness, love and trust.

CONTROLLING

We define controlling as gathering information about the organization and its environment and using that information to the advantage of the organization.

The controlling function involves:

- Establishing standards of performance
- Assuring that continuing activities meet standards
- Measuring performance
- Taking action to correct significant departures from standards
- Seeking new opportunities
- Ensuring that the mission, goals, and objectives of the enterprise are appropriate and are being accomplished.

Controlling has a twofold emphasis:

1. Staying aware of external happenings that have potential to impact the overall internal functioning of the enterprise. Additionally, it means that present directions, resource utilization issues, staffing changes, changes of any sort must first fit into the overall scheme of things before action occurs.

2. Seeking to evaluate the appropriateness of existing plans in light of new information. Increasing the flow of useful information is critical to the success of controlling. Being open to new information requires finely honed skills at listening, inquiring, paying attention to detail, and being confident about how to check out the original intent when being pushed for a decision to change part of existing planning.

Information is gathered for control purposes, and conducted through the activities of TRACKING and SENSING.

TRACKING is the formal control processes of establishing standards and parameters, gathering information pertinent to those standards and parameters, and taking action to correct significant departures.

As a basic formal control process, ***TRACKING*** involves the following:

- ***Establishing standards.*** Standards are criteria of performance. Normally they are selected points in a program, project, or work effort where measures of performance are taken in order to evaluate progress in relation to plans. (At home these standards could be how clean we keep our rooms, the way we treat each other and the types of entertainment we permit.)

- ***Measuring performance.*** Measurement of performance usually involves observing what is actually happening, comparing it with what was planned, and noting deviations. Three distinctions can be made in measuring performance:

  •• ***Especially*** important that there be understanding acceptance and support about how progress will be measured.

  •• Subjective and intangible measurement should reflect evidence of some change in behavior, feelings, excitement, hope and or energy as viewed by those affected by the effort previously committed to change. For example: If we commit to being more open to others ideas, then we measure this by talking to those people with whom we have committed to improve our openness.

  •• Measuring intangible/subjective planned end results is merely a straight forward common sense approach of stating upfront what its going to take for us to know when we've met our commitment. Not doing this creates continuous stress on work process where generally some one ends up losing and some one winning in place of successfully accomplishing the job together.

- ***Interim vs. final outcomes.*** **Interim assessments of progress are useful for detecting deviations early enough to avoid more costly problems later. If the interim control steps are taken properly, the final outcome is usually pretty well assured.**

- ***Effort vs. results.*** **For some endeavors, it is appropriate to measure effort as well as results. For example, a research and development effort usually involves risks and uncertain outcomes. A control process that emphasizes effort along the way enables the R&D team to be sure that they are approaching the problem in the most appropriate way. Then** regardless of the outcome, they can know that they gave it the best possible opportunity to succeed.

CAUTION: Results are still the primary measure in the market place. We want a car that runs well, not one that tries to run well. Stockholders want to make a profit that rewards them for their investment. Coming close just doesn't cut it.

Budgets as Control Devices. **Many people perceive a budget as a license to spend the budgeted amount. This notion results in such ludicrous practices as end of fiscal year spending sprees under the threat of "use it, or lose it." Budgets are the price of the plan–not a license to spend. It represents what the enterprise is willing to pay in order to accomplish the plan.**

Budgets permit managers to see what monies are being planned to be spent by whom, for what purposes, against what programs. Effective budgeting allows authority to be more freely delegated to the people who have responsibility to carry out the work. This discipline of allocating resources actually frees people up to act.

Ongoing variables affecting cash flow, such as labor costs, material costs, or aging of receivables, may necessitate in process changes in actual spending. Routine monitoring of actual spending in relation to the budget allows for informed judgments along the way about whether to change spending practices or to change the budget in order to make it more realistic.

Some common pitfalls in budgeting are:

- ***Making budgets so rigid and detailed that they become cumbersome.*** We have seen situations in which the budgeting process is so detailed and time-consuming that it has virtually taken on a life of its own. The costs to the enterprise of such detailed budget work far exceed its value. Furthermore, people come to resent the effort and the distraction from their "real" work, and it becomes a de-motivating process.

- ***Being budget-driven rather than plan-driven.*** In these cases program decisions are made based on previously determined budget allocations. This is backwards! We recognize that enterprises are frequently limited in what they can do by limits in their financial resources, but it is then necessary to create realistic plans within the overall financial limitations and then allocate the budget accordingly.

- ***Using budgets as an umbrella for inefficient management.*** Sometimes the excuse, "We could have done better, but we didn't have enough dollars" is just that—an excuse. People have a responsibility to manage resources in an efficient manner. This applies to families as well as to business, government, and other organizations.

- ***Creating rigid, inflexible budgets.*** This is also a pitfall in planning. The real world is in a constant state of flux. Any planning or budgeting process should allow for appropriate changes to be made as new information becomes available. The consequences of not doing so are lost opportunities, and, in some cases, the steady demise of the enterprise due to the dread disease "*hardening of the categories*!" Where traditional, we've done it in the past, mentality prevails to keep stability for stability sake!

3. ***Correcting Significant Deviations.*** A thorough problem/possibility analysis effort is required to determine which deviations are significant and which to pursue with appropriate action. It is important to have a commonly understood, accepted, and supported system for determining what the SITUATION is, what are the EXPECTATIONS for resolving the situation, and what ACTIONS are necessary to accomplish the expectations. The following SEA problem analysis and decision making model represents a quick tool for staying on track during the resolution of a situation.

FORMAL TRACKING requires a sense of discipline and integrity on the part of the people doing the tracking. Personal needs and personal greeds often get in the way of patience, persistency, and

SEA

S ituation:

- *What is going on (WIGO)?*
- *What should be going on (WSBGO)?*
- *What could be going on (WCBGO)?*

E xpectations - Targets:

- *What desired outcomes are necessary to handle the vital few problems/possibilities described in the situation?*

A ctions:

PRESENT	↔	FUTURE
➤ *Adaptive (live with it)*		➤ *Preventive*
➤ *Interim (Meanwhile ...)*	↔	➤ *Contingent (If)*
➤ *Corrective (Shut off the valve)*		
	↔	

accuracy in the information gathering process. Successful people do what less successful people fail to do and that is to work at tracking the vital few with an occasional eye on the trivial many and trivial mandatory.

SENSING is the informal processes of getting a "feel" for what is going on in the organization and its environment. This feel has all of our values, attitudes, habits, beliefs, knowledge, skills, experience, competencies and visions at its beck and call. It is important to acknowledge the critical nature of feelings in the decision making process.

Of the five managing functions, controlling seems to have acquired a bad name among people in the workplace.

We have asked several client groups what kinds of connotations they have experienced for the concept of control, and a good many of them are negative.

People have come to understand control as surveillance, snooping, checking up, persecuting, finding fault, pinning blame, punishing, and otherwise making life difficult.

Unfortunately, there are some good reasons why the negative reactions to controlling occur.

One of our client organizations had developed the practice of periodically conducting management reviews of their line operating units.

So far, so good.

However, people in the operating units feared, despised, and disparaged the reviews and the review process; it was a de-motivating experience.

To conduct the review, the top executive manager and three or four of his staff would show up at the unit, interrogate people, and rate the performance of the unit on a scale that had zero points as the highest possible score!

The unit started at zero, and points were subtracted for each problem or infraction that was uncovered.

As parents, many of us do similar things with our children. Sometimes we find ourselves in an "inspection" mode, seeking to find what the kids have done wrong and all along missing all the wonderful things they are doing and being. ***Perhaps we would do better to pray, praise and give thanks for what they do, mistakes and all, as long as they are working at valuing others.*** Perhaps, we should even consider adults the same way. As we look for how things are going we should pray about it, look for something good, and give criticism without blame as appropriate. Reviews, when done with the SPIRIT OF INTENT to help are worth their effort.

If an enterprise is to succeed and flourish, it is imperative that useful, motivating and appropriate control processes are in place. Usually a good blend of formal and informal control activities is appropriate.

Every individual in an enterprise has an opportunity and an obligation to continuously sense how things are going and to anticipate potential problems and opportunities. Again, enterprises that are characterized by openness, love, and trust tend to encourage this kind of constructive sensing. People do it because they want to.

QUALITY ASSURANCE AND QUALITY CONTROL.

A final subject under this general discussion of controlling is that of Quality Assurance and Quality Control.

Quality Assurance (QA) means establishing the quality philosophy and strategy of the enterprise up front, and preferably in writing. It also involves describing the efforts that will be undertaken to assure that the quality philosophy is reflected in the products, services, and activities of the enterprise. For a manufacturing company, QA plans might be made in the areas of research and development, marketing, sales, personnel, manufacturing, distribution, customer service, and engineering.

In contrast, Quality Control (QC) is the effort that is undertaken to constantly monitor the progress of work, through intermediate steps to the final outcome. Control is most effective when it is as close to the source of a potential problem as possible and when standards and methods of measurement have been clearly defined. An old concept being given new life is called statistical process control (SPC) as a vital tool for achieving total quality.

Quality control costs are subject to constant review. The "gotcha" philosophy of inspection is expensive. The finding something right approach adds value to inspection. A good blend of QA and QC activities usually provides the most effective controlling strategy in an enterprise.

The following chart illustrates some of the distinctions between QA and QC:

PLANNING——————>EFFORT——————>RESULTS

QUALITY ASSURANCE	↔	QUALITY CONTROL
looks forward in time	↔	**looks backward in time**
involves planning and "do it right" orientation	↔	involves inspection-action-reaction "fix it" orientation

Even this brief exposition reveals that planning, organizing, directing, leading, and controlling are complex managing functions. Appropriate fulfilling of these functions helps to guide an enterprise through the good times and through difficult times. We will provide more discussions of these five functions in subsequent chapters as we explore how they are applied in the STRATEGIC, and OPERATIONAL management arenas.

OPERATIONAL ARENA

The operational arena is more focused on managing activities that move the organization from STRATEGIC INTENT to COMMITMENT (of objectives and resources) and EXECUTION TO ACCOMPLISH / RESULTS / OUTPUTS. The operational arena is really where the current business plan *lives* and guides all efforts to get the job done–which is committed for completion now, this month, this quarter, and this year. In other words it spans all the work necessary to insure that the products and services of the organization are taken care of and at the level which results in growth and prosperity.

We divide the operational arena into two parts, Commitment and Execution.

Commitment is establishing and making commitments to specific outputs and to resources (physical, financial, human, time) required to achieve those outputs. The written product of these commitments is usually in the form of operating plans and associated budgets.

The key to managing in the tactical commitment level is gaining understanding, acceptance, and then SUPPORT (UAS) prior to formal commitment.

Understanding means taking the time to make sure that all the players are of one mind about the situation. All the available useful information is on top of the table and there is clear evidence that the players are confident of their role and how to play it.

Acceptance means having the undivided attention of the other players while sharing information with the final net outcome being no less than " at least we've been heard" even though we don't agree. As we have gathered, acceptance doesn't mean agreement!

Support means that we've reached a point of confidence where I am able to take action as though it were mine. I own the decision. Publicly I behave as though my complete commitment is behind the decision.

Gaining UAS requires skills that value people, help others work in creative tension, and are experienced in managing for synergy. The tools for acquiring these skills are found in the sections which cover ***"Individuals and Work Teams"*** and ***"Managing Change."***

Experienced managers are well aware of the importance to reduce to writing the vital few commitments of direction, outputs, and resources. Written commitments are valuable because they ensure a reasonable base for tracking the implementation at the EXECUTION LEVEL of Operational Managing Arena. Written material gives us all a chance to "check out our facts and feelings" about what we committed to others. Remember

MEANINGS ARE IN PEOPLE NOT IN WORDS

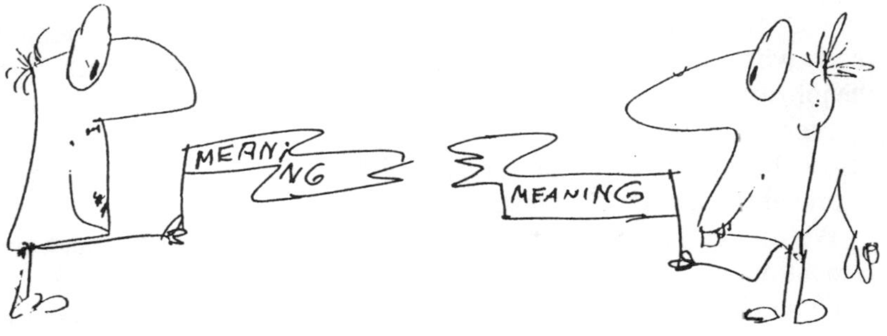

so if there is any doubt about what is written, now is the time for clarification before action is taken in the EXECUTION LEVEL.

EXECUTION level of the Operational Arena is the specific day to day action and utilization of committed resources by individuals and groups in order to carry out operating plans.

Up to this point all work is in preparation for THE DOING. **Sometimes we get so busy preparing to do the work that there is little energy left to produce our products and services.** For many of us who have worked up through the ranks the fun is in the doing. Our experience with others is that "the hunt is better than the kill" (that is they prefer to keep developing plans). Both the doing and planning are necessary for being successful.

Successful people ensure success by paying attention to detail at their level of execution with review, monitor, and approval interspersed as appropriate.

Execution forces the best laid plans into the reality of foreseen and unforeseen difficulties. Here is where the creative juices flow and frustrations accumulate. Where the spontaneous occurs faster than the orderly positioning of things can cope. Where decisions to deviate from planned work are seconded guessed by all people more than one foot away from the heat of schedules, sales, cash flow, and payables.

Execution provides for ongoing activities of formal tracking and informal sensing with the end result being feedback on performance. This becomes celebration time. When action begins to move away from planned targets tracking and sensing quickly validates the change or makes a mid course correction to get things back on track.

Project and individual performance assessment and review is rewarding when the Managing Systems are working smoothly. The

Managing System is most commonly known about and the least commonly understood. Perhaps it is because we skip over common sense knowledge with the idea "we know that – we've seen that before" yet don't have these ideas as part of our bones! These basic elements are bench marks for managing. When we see ourself heading for trouble, we should stop—look for deviations from these basics, and listen to the many ways open to get back on track.

Execution is in constant tension with the Commitment because what we started out to do is our best position at the moment. None of us walk on water, nor do we have all the information to make perfect decisions. It is an ITERATIVE process. This means that we are always genuinely open to new information and will test that information against our targets, and change where the change helps us **to acquire wealth and gain additional capital to grow and prosper**. That is why we are all in business. The other peripheral benefits are great, but are of little value if we don't grow and prosper.

The OPERATIONAL ARENA is everybody's business. Staff support people look with pride at their contribution for getting things in place for line people to produce the products and services in high demand by customers. Line people celebrate accomplishing the targets and give due regard to the support of staff people. It is truly fun to be interdependently successful worth every bit of effort.

In the following chapters we will present how to do STRATEGIC and OPERATIONAL managing.

Chapter 8

Strategic Managing

Chapter 8 Strategic Managing

Where there is no vision the people perish
—Proverbs 29:18

This chapter discusses the **Strategic Managing Arena** (see the Managing System Matrix in the introduction to Part II). We emphasize strategic managing as including, but being much more comprehensive than strategic planning. Strategic planning is only a part of strategic managing.

STRATEGIC ARENA

Strategic managing is broad management that gives the organization identity and purpose, relates the organization to its environment, and establishes INTENT TO ACCOMPLISH STATED DIRECTIONS OR OUTCOMES IN LIGHT OF ITS MISSION.

The key focus or orientation in the strategic arena is INTENT, the scope of strategic managing is generally broad, and the time orientation is generally longer term. Managing in the strategic arena establishes the intent of the enterprise to fulfill a particular identity and purpose, to accomplish certain broad outcomes, and to reflect certain philosophies or values. Originally we described the strategic arena with the word intent only. However early '90 while meeting with Jack Creighton the president of Weyerhaeuser and describing this part of a presidents job, he remarked that it should include commitment to a strategy as well. This made sense, and after further discussion with others we modified our Managing System tool to include Jacks suggestion. This true story is shared to show that all of us must be open to the ideas of others.

When people thoroughly involve themselves in the strategic arena there is clear evidence of openness, excitement, hope, and trust. The ideas, issues, problems, possibilities and resulting planning are of tremendous value to the organization.

Typically, executive managers have as their prime responsibility strategic managing; therefore, they could be expected to spend most of their time operating in that arena. Mid-managers and First-line managers have less strategic responsibility and more operational responsibility.

People at all levels have some responsibility in each of the management arenas. For example, many times, non-managers are the people who have primary contact with the customers of the enterprise. The information they can get about customer behavior and reactions to the organization's products and services can be of great value in strategic managing.

In our experience with numerous client organizations, we have seen a great deal of confusion about who is working in what arena. Here are a few classic examples of this confusion:

- An organization invests in a strategic planning process. Once the plans are completed, people who are affected by those plans interpret the strategy as *commitment* rather than as *intent*, and are offended when the plan is not carried out to the letter.

- At a management team meeting, one member spins a vision that is so exciting to the other members that they immediately initiate action to fulfill the vision. By short-cutting the strategic planning process and completely omitting the completed staff work required to responsibly develop operating plans and commitments, they undertake a half-baked effort and interfere with other ongoing activities.

The business of FUTURING is very important. Lets look at FUTURING and Strategic Managing in a little more depth.

FUTURING AND STRATEGIC MANAGING

The strategic arena holds all futuring activity and relates this activity to the planning, organizing, directing, leading and controlling functions. Some of this futuring activity might include. The organization's current self image and that of the future, mid and long term. For this to occur the individuals at all levels of the organization must contribute their part of the future mosaic:

- **People with a more narrow scope of responsibility should be encouraged to "step ahead in time" and visualize what it looks like to have their contribution significantly increased and how it feels to be successful at doing this value added work.**

- **People with more broad responsibilities should encourage others to share their visions and build on each others ideas. Then add their own to the process and the cumulative efforts of all will exponentially increase the value of the futuring work.**

- **Everyone should be keeping up to date on current events, trends, developments, and choices with summary implications for the future.**

- **As a result of the work above, the organization may come up with a cumulative understood, accepted, and supported preferred future. But it should keep in mind that the preferred future is in the INTENT ARENA ONLY!**

- **Open communication is central to strategy of all futuring activites.**

Futuring is a critical part of every manager's job because it increases the flow of useful information that is critical to real significant change for the organization.

Futuring in the strategic arena provides the opportunity for people to be open instantly to new opportunities. There is confidence that, before the new is committed to, a lot of COMPLETED STAFF WORK is done. (Completed staff work means that before decisions are made there are clearly stated outputs, resources to accomplish the outputs, and agreements on how to work together to get the job done.) When the completed staff work from the OPERATIONAL ARENA is finished the decision can be made to do or not to do.

The set of activities that has come to be known as "futuring" is part of the broader role of strategic management. Futuring cuts across all of the functions of strategic managing. It is a set of activities that enables the organization to establish appropriate strategic plans based on an informed view of the near- and long- term future. Futuring involves four basic steps: observing, forecasting, spinning the vision, and building strategies.

OBSERVING

Observing involves gathering and interpreting information about the organization and about its environment. This is the strategic controlling function. Internally, the effort is aimed at identifying existing and potential strengths and weaknesses.

- What is it about the organization that contributes to its success?

- What are we good at?

- What resources do we have that we can count on to keep us productive and competitive?

- What are our weak spots?

- Where are we vulnerable?

- What trends do we see developing or continuing that signal changes in the way we operate?

1. Forecasting

Where observing is more analytical and "objective," ***forecasting is more of a creative art.*** Very sophisticated models exist for forecasting certain phenomena (e.g., the weather, stock prices, the economy, earthquakes); even so, there is a degree of uncertainty involved. For organizations, the forecasting task involves deciding which of many observed events and trends are relevant to the organization and predicting how those events and trends may affect the organization.

The sorting task is not always easy. From an unmanageably large number of observed events and trends it is necessary to distill a manageable vital few on which to focus. Some possible criteria to help this sorting process are:

- Those representing significant opportunities or threats, as opposed to those representing inconsequential opportunities or threats;

- Those over which the organization has a high degree of control or influence vs. those over which the organization has little control or influence;

- Those that are urgent vs. those that are not.

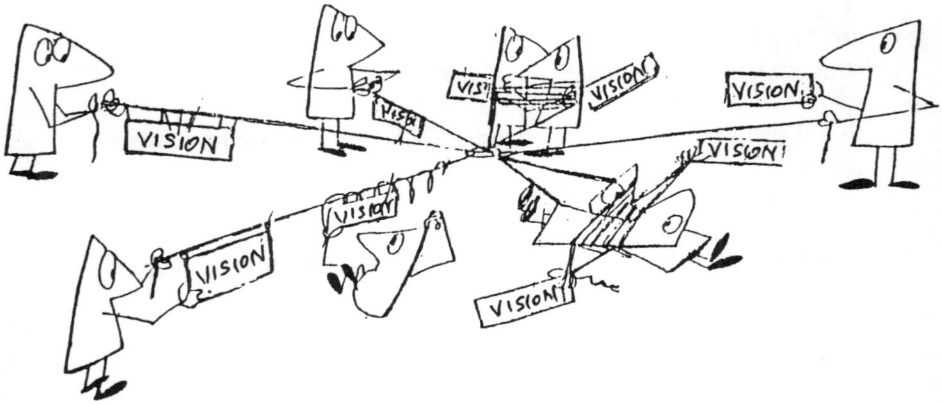

2. Spinning the Vision

Recall that visions are statements of preferred future for the organization that are rooted in beliefs and values, that are developed in light of the observations and forecasts about the organization and its environment, and that build energy, excitement, hope, and inspiration for the enterprise and its people. Spinning and articulating the visions for the enterprise is a strategic leading function.

3. Building Strategies

Based on the information assembled in steps 1, 2, and 3, it is important to establish strategy, that is, to identify key result areas, establish goals, and develop broad policy (strategic planning).

Some situations or trends that come out of the futuring work may not be appropriate to incorporate into the strategic plans of the enterprise at this time. For these areas it may be necessary to establish intent to continue to monitor and evaluate the situation. A future date may be set at which time a more informed decision will be made about whether to develop strategy in that area.

MANAGING FUNCTIONS IN THE STRATEGIC ARENA

We now discuss each of the five managing functions (planning, organizing, directing, leading, and controlling) as they are applied in the strategic arena.

Strategic Leading

A great deal of the energy for ***Strategic Managing*** comes from the work in the leading function. Strategic leading is an inspirational role for the enterprise. It affects the "culture" of the organization - the beliefs, values, and attitudes of the people who make up the organization.

Effective strategic leading builds hope, energy, excitement, and commitment to the enterprise. (Gen. Schwarzkoph displayed this skill as he set the stage for Desert Storm activities in the Gulf War.) This is accomplished by "carrying the flag" for the enterprise—sharing, talking about, and taking pride in the mission and assuring that everyone is aware of the mission.

Another facet of the strategic leading function is the role that ensures the continued well-being and availability of resources for the enterprise. Probably the most notable example of this is the work that Lee Iacocca led at Chrysler Corporation to procure "bail out" financing from the Federal Government. Regardless of one's opinion about the propriety of federal intervention in the survivability of private enterprise, it has to be acknowledged that Iacocca's work almost certainly saved the company and inspired its people to move ahead creatively.

Leading includes the "art of visualizing" what tomorrow looks like today. The "Art" portion of visioning ties directly to peoples *feelings* about the future in a manner that describes the misty, foggy and partly clear portions of the future. Visualizing the future has a lot to do with people's past and present memories, habits, beliefs, and visions. Present situations that include positive growth, and prosperity trigger a multitude of new ideas and opportunities.

Negative situations that are handled as threat vs opportunity eat up the energy of people engaged in exploring the future direction and movement of the organization. The "art of visualizing" includes skill at turning negatives into positives while spinning a vision for the future.

Strategic Leading means setting aside the cares and accomplishments of today and establishing a climate for people experimentation where people will "go with the flow" toward new and unthought of dimensions in their work. This is done by design, not luck. If luck is important to you, use the definition of luck which says " Luck is where preparation meets opportunity." Lao-Tzu, a 17th century Chinese philosopher, observed that:

"A leader is best when he is neither seen nor heard;
Not so good when he is adored and glorified; Worst when he is hated and despised. Fail to honor people; they will fail to honor you. But of a good leader, when his work is done, his aim fulfilled, the people will say, "We did this ourselves."

It is still important to restate that we spend little time focusing on the noun *leader* and most of the time on the verb *leading*. The reason for this is that leader has the reputation of being a person in the hierarchy and consequently leading is for the special few. Our experience confirms the strong belief that **LEADING IS EVERYONE'S BUSINESS.**

How often have we heard one of our good ideas come back to us from someone else? That is one of the premier complements. Strategic Leading involves Risk. **A good idea doesn't care who has it, as long as it gets used.** Many good ideas get lost because of poor presentation. The INTENT mode usually has many ideas in some state of being incomplete which at the same time raises a lot of hope and excitement. ***The RISK is that someone will move the idea into the OPERATIONAL ARENA before its tim***e. Like good wine, let it develop to its full maturity and then success.

Leading happens more quickly when enabling questions and statements are used to solicit information. This is particularly true when seeking "soft information" such as how people feel about their work, about the decisions that were just made, about their contribution and expectations for the future. We might consider using the following:

- When someone is describing a particular situation and we feel there is more than has been revealed, we should ask them to " say more about that." This indicates a willingness to hear the whole tale. It is very important to hear the whole tale.

- There are times when people need to " think out loud" in order to express where they are at in a particular situation without being committed to a particular position. Once this is done their contribution increases exponentially. Encourage them by simply stating "THINK OUT LOUD AND SHARE WITH ME WHAT YOU HAVE IN MIND. Perhaps I can help or at least build on your idea."

- Feelings are critical in all phases of work. The question "how do you feel?"—when tied into the possibilities of the future—generates many opportunities to test out the level of energy, hope and excitement for that particular idea, option, alternative etc.

- There are times when we need to come to closure on a particular issue. It is at this point where the question " What do you recommend?" forces the discussion into the next stage closer to commitment

LEADING BY LISTENING AND ASKING IS SIMPLY TOO IMPORTANT TO *ASSUME* THAT PEOPLE MAKE A CONSCIOUS EFFORT TO WORK THIS WAY IN THE STRATEGIC MANAGING MODE. Many people go through life just hoping that maybe, someday, someone, will take time to LISTEN to them, and ask for their opinion, with the spirit of intent to value that opinion. This simple effort opens up the real opportunities for ***Strategic Leading.*** The following chart provides examples of some strategic leading activities:

- Making the mission available to all employees

- Involving employees in developing the mission

- Spinning a vision for the future of the enterprise

- Involving people in spinning the vision for the future

- Representing the enterprise in the broader community

- Lobbying for legislation favorable to the enterprise

- Seeking support for the enterprise from others

We could make the point, how does this all fit into the family by recalling the comments of young children when either mom or dad was headed for the Gulf War and they needed to be included in when will mom/dad be back, whats going to happen to mommy, to me? They wanted to know what this war (mission) was all about. They wanted to be listened to!

STRATEGIC DIRECTING

Strategic Directing consists of those activities that establish an overall organizational "climate" that supports the accomplishment of strategic plans. It answers the broad questions:

- How do we do things around here?
- What methods, procedures, philosophies do we endorse and follow as we work together?
- How do we intend to gain the understanding, acceptance, and support of the people operating under these stated conditions in the future?

There are times when new forms of giving work directions have a key role in determining the effectiveness of bridging the gap between strategic managing and operational managing. Strategic directing presents an opportunity for exploring these new directions with the involvement of those who may be affected by the new and different ways of giving direction.

Frequently, management teams have difficulty carving out enough time to effectively carry out their strategic directing roles. Our directing effort has well established habits, memories, and beliefs that often get in the way of our ability to break through into the ongoing world of strategic managing.

After all, the real world is made up of solving problems and making decisions, not this "what if" esoteric business. This habit of taking direct action gets into the blood and seems to be satisfied only when the LUST FOR TAKING ACTION IS SATURATED and people look for ways to get away from it all. Why? Because the same problems keep occurring.

Memories of past wasted effort in long sessions away from the office in retreat settings, piles of paper, and no tie in to operational managing contribute to this lack of commitment to strategic managing.

Beliefs such as "If it ain't broke don't fix it" and "Our business is too dynamic to take the time away from the office, (after all who would run it while we are gone)" suggest that these people are "fear-sighted." When fear controls present day activities its next to impossible to visualize the future. Strategic directing sees the present SITUATION for what it is—as an opportunity, not a threat. What we do end up with is put in a 3 ring binder, put on a shelf and conveniently lost to our memory (CLM). This convenient loss of Memory (CLM) is a malady that lingers on and on whenever there is a chance to back out of something, or deny it ever existed. Some of the best symptoms of this malady are when people say

–"I don't remember saying that
–you must be mistaken,
why I'd never–".

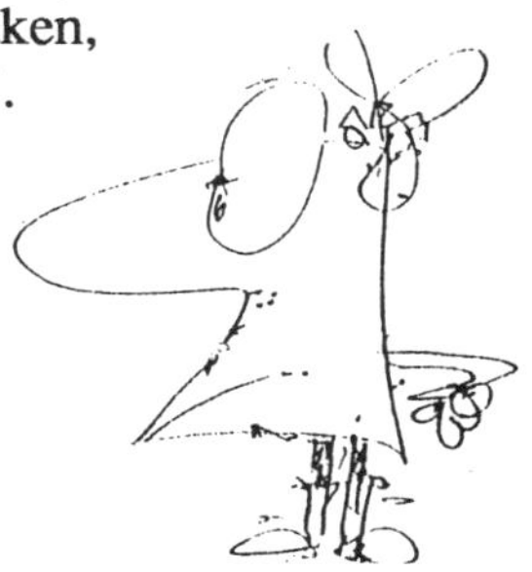

None of us is guaranteed tomorrow. What would it be like to work with others as if there is no tomorrow? What if we were never given the capacity to "think ahead into the future," so that we can more clearly act in the present? What if there was no way to anticipate success? Our customers reaction to our products and services? That's what happens when we fail to do strategic managing, and strategic managing must have the directing function as a vital part of its effort.

The following are some examples of ***Strategic Directing*** activities:

- Articulating the beliefs and values of the enterprise
- Involving people in building shared beliefs and values
- Establishing broad policies and procedures
- Having clear responsibilities for operationalizing company strategies

Strategic Planning

"Paul Bunyon and Babe the Blue Ox" were fictitious logging characters who accomplished outlandish feats like digging the GreatLakes, and building mountains. One of these stories took place in the dead of winter where it was so cold that words froze and filled up the space until the spring thaw.

Sometimes people have trouble visualizing how all this talking (i.e., strategic planning) is going to make sense when they get back on the job and continue the business of making a profit. Their memory of "that planning session" becomes a bunch of words all being thawed out at the same time. Sure they were written down, but have you ever tried to wade through that stuff six months later?

Strategic Leading and Strategic Directing provide the opportunity for Strategic Planning to mean something. **The visions, hope, excitement, and energy of Strategic Leading and the gathering of the right people at the right time, behaving in valuing ways, with clear identity and purpose in mind from Strategic Directing help Strategic Planning become a critical force in Strategic Managing.**

The documented work coming out of ***Strategic Planning*** is clearly laid out to capture the vital few elements affecting the future of MISSION, GOALS, and BROAD OBJECTIVES.

Vital few refers to the 20% of our effort that gets 80% of the results. So if we are spending 80% of our effort on work that nets out only 20% of our expected results, we need to cut that out and focus on more productive work. These elements include both the "hard" portions of an organization like money, facilities, products, services, formal information, structure, and the "soft" portions like behavior, hope, excitement, visions, beliefs, concerns, customer satisfaction, image, and culture.

Visualize documented Strategic Planning as an edited video tape. Feel the emotion as significant views of the future are shared in openness and candor with trust and confidence in the integrity of all participating. Recapture the significant information that helps focus scarce resources in directions that ensure prosperity, growth, and development and the feelings of people as they unite around this hope for the future. Think of how good it feels as a person who fed ideas into that Strategic Planning effort to see some of them being considered as part of the future direction and movement of the organization.

Keep in mind that Strategic Planning reflects the intent of the enterprise to apply resources to accomplish certain outcomes.

Effective strategic planning requires useful information about the environment in which the organization operates and about its own internal strengths and weaknesses. These are strategic controlling activities and will be discussed further.

Time horizon is a very important consideration in strategic planning. For some enterprises, the strategic time horizon is many years or even decades in the future. The U.S. Forest Service, for example, must plan for managing the entire life cycle of trees in the National Forests. Other enterprises have relatively short strategic time lines. For software houses, medical technology manufacturers, and other high-tech endeavors, the entire cycle from identified need to first delivery of products may be as short as six months.

Strategic planning for farmers can vary from six months for getting into the hog business to years for fruit orchards. Farmers are affected by as many external variables as any other business we can imagine. More and more, farming is becoming big business, and skillful application of basic managing functions is critical for survival.

The centerpiece of strategic planning comprises the strategic goals (again, broad statements of desired outcome). Goals can be developed in many areas including product and services, marketing, financial resource, sales, corporate image, public relations, human resource, and quality.

A common error in planning is to over-plan, that is, to try to plan for everything. As a result, many enterprises suffocate under the weight of their own planning efforts.

In order to avoid over-planning, we recommend that the first step in strategic planning be to identify key outputs where the planning effort will be focused. Key outputs are those areas of the enterprise for which one or more of the following is occurring:

- ***New threats or opportunities are presented by the environment.*** Examples include a new competitor coming onto the scene and threatening to erode the client base, technological changes, changes in customer behavior or preferences, new regulations that affect the business, opportunities to develop new products or services.

- ***Recent performance has leveled off or deteriorated.*** Example: Customer complaints about a particular product line have increased significantly in the past six months.

- ***Resource limitations threaten the ability of the organization to conduct business as usual.*** Example: Budget constraints are now making it less possible for many Federal Government agencies to fulfill their public service ideals of being all things to all people.

Establishing key output areas is an important early step in setting priorities for the work of the enterprise and for orienting the efforts of the enterprise in a particular direction. Goals are then developed in each of the key output areas.

It is important that these goals be consistent with the mission of the enterprise. If, for example, a goal is established to develop a product line or market that falls outside the stated mission, then one of two things needs to happen. Either the mission needs to be reconsidered and changed to accommodate the new product or market, or the goal should be changed or dropped.

The list below presents some specific activities that fall into the strategic planning cell of our managing system matrix.

- Writing long-term goals
- Deciding to enter a new market
- Developing a statement of the mission of the enterprise
- Spinning a vision for the future
- Conducting "futuring" activities
- Planning to send the kids to college
- Planning how to live after the kids go to college
- Planning for retirement income

One of the additional challenges in ***Strategic Planning*** is to be able to live with the notion that this is a never ending job. The dynamic nature of our culture and scientific findings force attention to detail that hasn't become a reality in the market place today and may never become a reality as it is today.

No one knows the time and place of an innovation that will make it real for today. ***Strategic Planning*** keeps our heads up constantly searching for those opportunities, while Operational Managing keeps our feet on the ground by tying operational planning into the commitments of today's scarce resources, mission, goals , and objectives. The twins graduate high school in June, how does that change the way we as a couple use: our discretionary time? Our vacation? Our home? What do we do with all this left over room?

The **STRATEGIC PLAN** is the documented effort by those involved in formalizing the strategic managing effort. This plan is used as ongoing input to the major commitment and execution decisions made in the Operational Arena.

The strategic plan requires ***ongoing*** activity to keep it useful. The strategic plan is in the INTENT mode, which means that there is room for new information in an ITERATIVE process for updating, and gaining understanding, acceptance, and support from all the Executive Team.

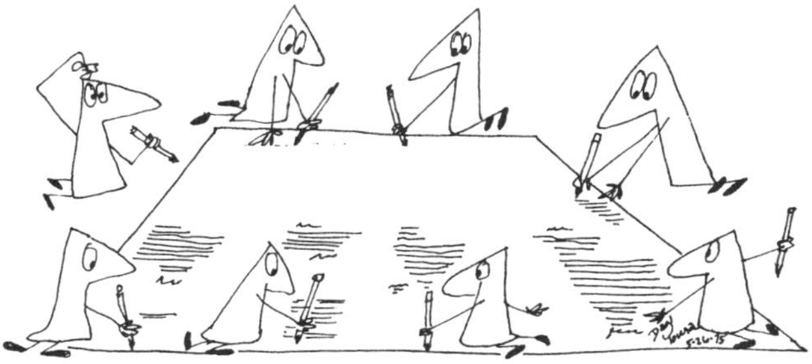

Strategic Organizing

Strategic Organizing sometimes gets ahead of the strategic plan. A long held belief by numerous people is "let's get the right organization in place; then we can go about doing all these great and wonderful things" (without the benefit of a strategic plan). Well, what is strategic organizing?

Strategic organizing is the process of designing an organization at the macro level to best carry out the strategic plans. This is where the total work of the enterprise is divided into manageable parts in a way that is most compatible with the strategic plan.

The people involved in matching the structure to the strategic plan should comprise a mixture of talents including these three functions:

1. CONCEPTUALIZING—Should have a strong conceptual understanding of organizational theory, the things that have worked and the problems with concepts that didn't

2. COMMUNICATING— Should be competent in the multimedia arena along with personal "process" skills that enable people to gain UAS of the structural changes in a win / win mode.

3. IMPLEMENTING—Should have LINE and STAFF experience throughout the organization with formal and informal influence based on actual performance and commitment toward getting the job done.

Organizational structure refers to the formal architecture of the enterprise - the broad division of labor. Two main considerations apply in developing an organizational structure: departmentalization, and levels of authority.

A key process in strategic organizing is departmentalization. Decisions have to be made about how to best organize to accomplish the strategic plan. Some of the possibilities for departmentalization include:

- By function—This is a familiar way of organizing. A typical functional organization consists of departments or divisions that are formed around specific functional areas. Examples include engineering, production, marketing, sales, and administration.

- By product or service line—General Motors, for example, has separate divisions for Cadillac, Chevrolet, Pontiac, and Buick.

- By geography—Some larger enterprises establish divisions in separate geographic locations. Many franchising operations, for example, have regional headquarters.

Most medium to large organizations are combinations of the above types. For a geographically organized enterprise, each regional office may be organized functionally. Other organizations may have product line divisions that are responsible for manufacturing and sales, while other functions, such as marketing, R & D, finance, purchasing, and personnel are centralized in the company headquarters. There are plenty of exceptions to this too.

Of course, other forms are also possible. Some enterprises, particularly those whose work involves project or program work, choose to organize in a "matrix" or "project" structure. Unless carefully managed, these forms can and do create problems with scheduling and multiple reporting relationships. (The Work/Life approach helps to guard against these exposures and enable matrix or project structure work very effectively.)

Decisions also have to be made about the number of levels of authority in the organizational hierarchy. Some organizations are very "tall"—that is, they have a relatively large number of levels in the hierarchy. We have worked for some client organizations for which the entry level worker is 8 - 10 levels below the chief executive. Other organizations are more "flat"—that is, they have very few reporting levels.

The chart below contrasts some of the features of tall and flat organizational structures.

Tall Organizations:		**Flat Organizations:**
larger organizations	↔	smaller organizations
less flexible to change	↔	more "nimble in a pinch"
more costly (because of more managers who receive higher pay)	↔	less costly
slower information flow	↔	faster information flow
narrower span of control (number of people reporting to a supervisor)	↔	wider span of control
more opportunities for promotion	↔	fewer opportunities for promotion
appropriate for more creative unstructured work	↔	appropriate for more routine, structured work

With today's shift from an industrial economy to an information and service economy, many organizations are recognizing the limiting effects of large size and tall chain of command.

We see a clear trend in the years ahead for larger, mechanistic, bureaucratic forms to give way to smaller, flatter, more organic forms of organization. As this occurs, it becomes especially important for people to be aware of the managing arena in which they are working.

The distinctions between executive, middle, and first line management will be less clear, so everyone will have greater responsibility in both managing arenas. Even with the less structured forms, the distinctions between intent (strategic arena) and tactical commitment and execution (operational arena) will be even more important.

The following list illustrates some activities that fall into the category of strategic organizing:

- Designing a broad organization
- Deciding where to locate plants or stores
- Developing organization charts for the whole enterprise
- Determining what functions will be centralized
- Creating or abolishing organizational divisions
- Deciding to go from a line/staff structure to a matrix
- Working through project team from a cross section of the business with focus on the task

Strategic Controlling

Strategic controlling deals with the broad issue of analyzing and understanding the internal and external environment of the enterprise. It involves gathering useful information to

1. analyze the internal environment of the organization (strengths and weaknesses)
2. maintain current knowledge of the external environment (opportunities and threats to the enterprise)
3. evaluate the effectiveness, appropriateness, and relevance of the organization's strategy in light of its strengths and weaknesses and external opportunities and threats.

EVALUATING THE EXTERNAL ENVIRONMENT—ENVIRONMENTAL ANALYSIS

- What happens when decisions are made without understanding the market?
- What happens when a key competitor does an end around and captures a significant portion of our market share with a new product, advertising, or price strategy?
- How well do we keep up with technological developments that could either strengthen or erode our business?

(When the in-laws call on Friday night and announce that they will be there early Saturday morning to stay the weekend, this could be seen as a threat to the much anticipated peaceful weekend. On the opportunity side, it forces us to clean the house, which we needed to do anyway, and it provides an opportunity for some good time with extended family members.)

These kinds of questions emphasize the opportunities and threats that affect an organization. The external environment is a complex system that can be both supportive and hostile to the enterprise.

It is vital to the survival of the enterprise that useful (relevant, valid, timely, and reliable) information be available about the threats and opportunities that may be presented by various parts of the environment. This information, which is obtained as part of the strategic controlling function, enables the enterprise to evaluate, verify, and modify where necessary its strategic plans.

Assessing the environment of an organization can range from a fairly simple, straightforward matter to a costly and complex program of research and evaluation. At a minimum, an enterprise needs information about its:

- ***Customers*—Who are they?** Is our advertising reaching them? What are their wants, needs, desires? Are their needs changing? Where are they? How much are they willing to pay?

- ***Competitors***—Who are they? In what ways could they (do they) take business away from us? What new products/ services are they developing or offering?

- ***Suppliers***—Can we count on a steady supply that meets our standards, and at prices that we can accept?

- ***Regulators***—What effects will new legislation or regulation have on us? How will business tax changes affect us?

How does this information affect the family? Each of us is a customer to the other.

- We compete for air time, T.V. selection, who gets the "lazy boy" chair.
- How do we get the dough we need?–new clothes, education
- Who needs to know what time to be home, go to church, school, work?

It is also useful to be aware of how indirect action components of the environment affect the organization. For example, technological advances can bring opportunities and threats. Economic conditions strongly affect the buying behavior of existing and potential customers. Changing social, political, or cultural attitudes cause changes in the way our customers, competitors, suppliers, and regulators behave. Which ones are significant and how will they affect us?

In the practice of ***STRATEGIC MANAGEMENT,*** enterprises define their environments as they see them at the current time, based on the best available information. In our experience, good information about the environment is already known by many people in the enterprise. It simply needs to be collated and assimilated into a compound picture of the whole.

Where good information is not available, the value of obtaining that information must be weighed in light of the cost of doing so. In addition, information should be obtained from a number of perspectives, and should be checked for its validity.

Evaluating the Internal Situation (Situation Analysis)

Information about internal strengths and weaknesses of the company is also essential for building effective strategy. In order to be complete, internal information should be available about each of the six sub-systems of the enterprise (Managing, Information, Resources, Production, Administrative, and Social Systems; see Chapter 1). Given valid information about the current situation (strengths and weaknesses), the question becomes:

"What are the possible alternative strategies that we could choose that capitalize on our strengths and either minimize or rectify our weaknesses?"

This process will frequently drive the enterprise back to a reconsideration of strategic goals, objectives, and in some cases, mission.

Situation analysis also takes many forms. The most complete form is a thorough SITUATION AUDIT with formal data gathering in each of the six sub-systems. The most informal approach involves armchair speculation about how things are within the enterprise. Most enterprises choose a combination of formal and informal approaches. They conduct formal audits in areas of high risk or in which minimal data exists, with less formal data gathering in some areas, and speculation and educated guesses in others.

Quality Assurance Planning–A Vital part of Total Quality

An important part of strategic controlling is developing and articulating the quality philosophy of the enterprise and then establishing a quality assurance strategy. This strategy represents the intent of the enterprise to plan quality assurance. It is necessary to analyze the needs for special quality assurance standards or procedures, and to evaluate the impact of these standards or procedures on the feasibility of producing and delivering the products or services.

The list below displays some illustrative activities that fall in the strategic controlling category:

- Establishing quality assurance standards and goals
- Conducting formal analyses of the internal situation
- Performing employee surveys
- Doing situation audits
- Being aware of human resources data bases
- Assuring resource inventories
- Making industry comparisons
- Conducting informal analysis of the internal situation
- Having informal conversations with employees in the work place
- Sensing meetings with groups of employees
- Using suggestion boxes
- Minimizing speculation and educated guesses
- Conducting formal analyses of the external environment
- Doing market research
- Analyzing of competitors threat
- Monitoring legislative action
- Establishing industry comparisons
- Performing research through electronic data bases
- Accomplishing library research
- Conducting informal analyses of the external environment
- Reading trade/business publications
- Attending conferences, conventions, meetings
- Reading newspapers

SUMMARY

We have discussed the strategic managing arena as a unique managing effort, where the work done is in the INTENT mode and relies heavily on hope for the future backed up by ongoing useful information.

This hope comes from the visions of people who are willing to surrender to a purpose that fulfills their need to get things done. By surrendering to a purpose people more clearly discipline themselves to focus their energies on that purpose with excitement and energy. The strategic arena provides the platform for developing the details for accomplishing that purpose before commitment of resources. By taking time to do completed staff work (including $, time, quality, quantity, etc.), the purpose has a better chance of happening when formally entered into the live arena of today's activities.

The work performed in each of the managing functions affects each of the other functions interdependently. The planning function holds the responsibility for articulating the clear purpose. The ***LEADING FUNCTION*** captures the SPIRIT OF INTENT in the form of visions for the future and becomes a source for PURPOSES that are further developed in each of the other functions.

Strategic managing is a vital arena that provides for the future direction of the enterprise. It is a challenging process that requires discipline, particularly for people who are accustomed to taking a "nose down" perspective to deal with day to day work.

Strategic thinking takes a "nose up" orientation and a willingness to look creatively into the unknown future.

Those who believe that sitting with one's feet on the desk, gazing off into space, and daydreaming amount to a waste of time may be right in some cases, but frequently that is precisely what is needed to create the new ideas and bring a fresh perspective to the enterprise.

In order to think strategically, one has to be willing and able to grasp the complexities of an organizational system that is operating within and engaging in constant exchange with larger systems. Furthermore, one must be able to think simultaneously about the long-term and the short-term future, tolerate ambiguity, and be willing to risk being incorrect at least occasionally.

The OPERATIONAL ARENA is in constant creative tension with the STRATEGIC ARENA. Their relationship is one of thrust and parry, thrust and parry. We describe this process as the ITERATIVE approach toward seeking a common UNDERSTANDING, ACCEPTANCE AND SUPPORT for tactical commitment and execution. The next chapter describes the OPERATIONAL ARENA in more detail.

MANAGING SYSTEM MATRIX

	ARENAS		
	STRATEGIC Business Plan (INTENT → COMMITMENT)	**OPERATIONAL** Business Plan — COMMITMENT	**OPERATIONAL** Business Plan — EXECUTION
PLANNING	Strategy ➤ *Stating mission* ➤ *Defining long-range goals*	Business operation plan ➤ *Immediate goals* ➤ *Specific objectives* ➤ *Budgets*	Actions ➤ *Project development* ➤ *Functional tasks* ➤ *Individual activities*
ORGANIZING	Broad Strategy ➤ *Divisional* ➤ *Functional* ➤ *Geographic*	Labor Divisions ➤ *Departments* ➤ *Work groups* ➤ *Authorized positions*	Staffing ➤ *Project Teams* ➤ *Individuals*
DIRECTING	Broad Work Direction ➤ *Whole Organization* ➤ *Divisions*	Work direction for ➤ *Divisions* ➤ *Operating units*	Task Direction ➤ *Project Teams* ➤ *Individuals*
LEADING	Inspirational Focus on ➤ *Company mission* ➤ *Vision* ➤ *Beliefs*	Unit / Department / Team ➤ *Mission* ➤ *Vision* ➤ *Beliefs* ➤ *Building* ➤ *Maintenance*	Focus on Support and Enabling Activities for Individuals and Work Teams Motivation
CONTROLLING	Environmental analysis ➤ *Internal* ➤ *External* Marketing strategies Quality assurance plan Performance definition	Budget analysis Attainment reporting Management information system Management reviews Functional reviews Quality assurance system	Work Sensing & Tracking ➤ *Performance Appraisal* ➤ *Ongoing Sensing* Quality Control

Chapter 9

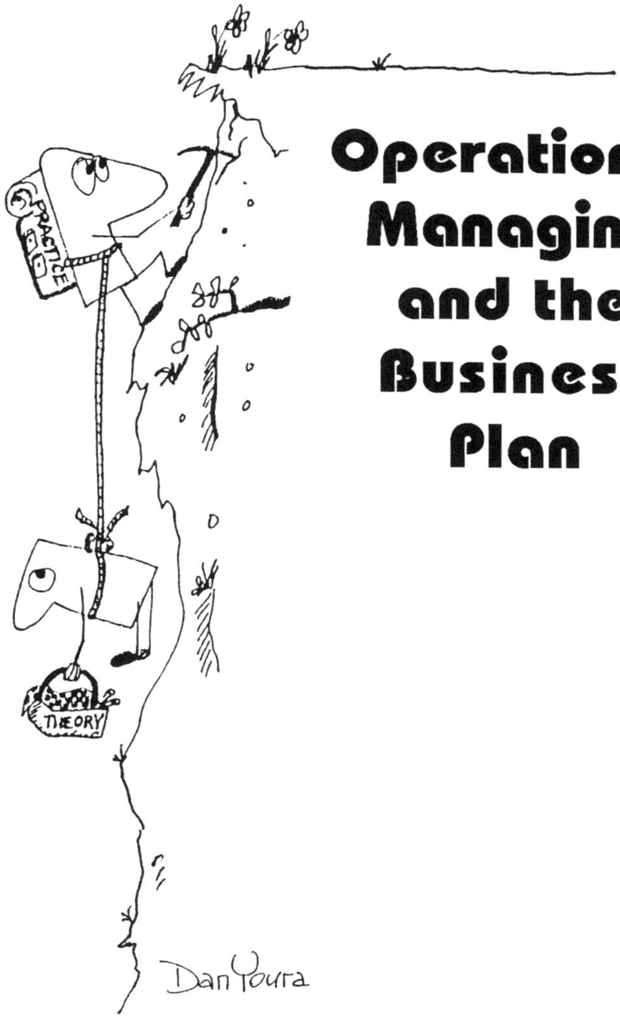

Operational Managing and the Business Plan

Chapter 9

Operational Managing and the Business Plan

Do not keep talking so proudly or let your mouth speak such arrogance, for the Lord is a God who knows, and by Him deeds are weighed.
—I Samuel 2:3

THE OPERATIONAL ARENA

The OPERATIONAL ARENA has more focused managing activities that move the organization from strategic (intent) managing to COMMITMENT and from there into EXECUTION.

To say it another way, the hope, excitement, visions and energy generated in the STRATEGIC ARENA are in constant dynamic tension (through the iterative process) with the everyday realities of the OPERATIONAL ARENA.

The OPERATIONAL ARENA itself has an ongoing dynamic tension (through the iterative process) between its Commitment unit of work and Execution unit of work.

Each unit of work (Commitment and Execution) is made up of the five functions of managing discussed at the out set of this section in the introduction. Those being PLANNING, ORGANIZING, DIRECTING, LEADING, AND CONTROLLING.

The Managing System matrix chart reflects the combined matrix of the Strategic Arena, (which we have already covered in some detail), the completed matrix with the OPERATIONAL ARENA and the related units of work under Commitment and Execution.

Operational Managing is the process of keeping the current business plan updated, alive, and well with the action being experienced in today's field of play. While this is happening, Operational Managing keeps the intent of the Strategic Plan in the forefront of current year operating plans. This means that neither the Strategic nor the Current year plans are static. Both need to keep current with each other. A dusty strategic plan is clear evidence of an unhealthy relationship between the STRATEGIC AND OPERATIONAL ARENA.

If the current operating plan is missing or dusty, the organization is already getting sick or in a terminal condition. Organizational health depends on actively performing strategic and operational managing chores. With that gentle bit of TRUTH AS WE SEE IT, lets take a look at each of the units of work (Commitment and Execution) separately and their relationship to each other.

COMMITMENT

When functioning in the Commitment unit of work, managers build operating plans, make commitments of organizational resources to accomplish those plans, and establish commitments to design organizational systems. Accomplishment of operational plans is monitored, and feedback is provided to evaluate strategic and operational plans.

During this Commitment work, the attention paid to each of the six organizational effectiveness systems is very important. Once again those systems are: PRODUCTION SYSTEM, RESOURCE SYSTEM, INFORMATION SYSTEM, ADMINISTRATIVE SYSTEM, SOCIAL SYSTEM AND THE MANAGING SYSTEM (which is the system we find our selves in as we are discussing Commitment and Execution units of work).

Remember the Commitment unit of work gives the marching orders to the Execution unit of work. Those who pay attention to the interdependent functions of each of the six systems that make an organization effective, will succeed in having those marching orders carried out with complete UNDERSTANDING, ACCEPTANCE, AND SUPPORT. THIS WILL ASSURE SUCCESS!

We now turn to an exposition of the Commitment unit of work and its relationship to the five management functions.

COMMITMENT PLANNING

The source document for Commitment managing is the OPERATIONAL PLAN sometimes referred to as the "operating business plan." This plan is the written road map that guides the enterprise toward accomplishing its strategic plans. It is the formal vehicle for committing time and resources to the vital few current activities necessary to succeed.

The time horizon for the operating plan is usually shorter than for the strategic plan; six-month to one-year operating plans are most common. The operational planning cycle usually determines (or is determined by) the budgeting cycle.

The centerpiece of the operational plan is the OPERATIONAL OBJECTIVE. Operational objectives are measurable steps toward accomplishing strategic goals. They define outcomes that the enterprise is committed to achieving. Each operational objective should relate to the accomplishment of one or more strategic goals.

The OPERATING PLAN also articulates the commitment of resources by the enterprise to achieve the plans. This commitment of resources is most commonly expressed in the form of budgets. Once again, budgets represent **the price of the plan, not a licence to spend.** Some of the more common types of budgets are income, expense, cash flow, personnel, and capital budgets.

In developing an operating plan, it is necessary to test the validity of the strategic plan at the operating level.

- How realistic are the strategic goals in light of the resources available to the enterprise?

- What changes do they need?

- What immediate-term factors in the enterprise or in its environment affect the direction of the enterprise?

- What are the limiting factors that were not anticipated in the strategic plan? What new opportunities have presented themselves?

- What changes need to be made to the strategic plan?

It is unrealistic to expect all systems to be completely satisfied in the operating plan. This is where the art of creative compromise and win-win interdependent action is required, particularly where resources are limited.

The following illustrates some activities that fall under

COMMITMENT PLANNING:

- Developing and approving annual, project, program budgets

- Establishing key objectives related to strategic goals

- Developing project management plans,, including PERT, CPM, or other project management technology

- Scheduling work

COMMITMENT ORGANIZING

Designing and committing to organizational systems are the principle activities of Commitment organizing. Here, specific commitments to a division of labor into departments and work groups are made. Detailed organizational structure is designed, staffing levels are set, and programs of work are assigned to departments and work groups.

One of the most unpleasant experiences in organizing is when work is assigned that is confusing, unclear, or for which there is little or no commitment of resources to back it up. We have seen many situations in which the key managers were unclear about what needed to be done. Still they had the audacity to find fault and pin blame with what was done.

Sometimes it is simply true that what needs to be done is not entirely clear. In these cases, it is appropriate for the manager to acknowledge this and then work with the people to develop more specific work assignments. By having UNDERSTANDING, ACCEPTANCE, AND SUPPORT for the present unclear situation people have a better chance of behaving in ways that value each other as they strive for more clarification.

The SOCIAL SYSTEM has a number of tools that help improve the work being performed under uncertain environments. Take time out to review the Social System and ask " How well are we doing in this area?"

Probably the most common error in organizing and delegating work is the failure to assign work and corresponding decision making authority to the closest point of action in the organization.

It is important to organize work in a manner that affords people the opportunity to be challenged (but not overwhelmed) in terms of their abilities, skills, and experiences. Reasonable challenges build "creative tension" and provide opportunities for achievement, recognition, and growth. In short, most people are motivated by being challenged and then given the resources and support necessary to succeed.

Here are some examples of Commitment organizing activities:

COMMITMENT ORGANIZING

- Setting staffing levels for departments or project teams
- Conducting wage and salary comparison studies
- Setting compensation levels for various positions in the organization;
- Classifying jobs for wage and salary administration purposes
- Negotiating and making contracts with labor unions
- Establishing a project team
- Setting a budget for a family vacation
- Establishing and committing to a specific investment plan for sending the kids to college
- Developing and approving expense, cash, personnel, capital, or other budgets
- Assigning areas of work to departments or work groups
- Establishing personnel ceilings

COMMITMENT DIRECTING

Tactical Commitment directing provides a situational management focus on overall work direction, enabling support to accomplish the operating plan.

BY SITUATIONAL MANAGEMENT we are referring to the different ways a particular problem, opportunity, idea, issue, person is worked with. One group of circumstances may call for a very direct, forceful approach. Another, a more questioning, open-ended and less game ending approach. While still another, an even more "let it happen" and see what comes out manner.

The situation dictates the way we go about handling our work. Each of us has the capacity to operate in many different ways to be successful.

This situational management focus is on the operating plans, on assuring availability and continuity of needed resources, and on ways of working together that will enable the department, work group and/or entire enterprise to successfully achieve those plans.

It is in this third area, ways of working together successfully, that managers are most frequently weak. This is probably due primarily to the fact that these things fall in that most nebulous of systems, the social system.

We continue to emphasize the need to become skilled at using the SOCIAL SYSTEM practical tools and principles to enable people to act more effectively in this arena.

It is also important to build and maintain effective working relationships within and among organizational entities. And for all of these, it is necessary to build understanding, acceptance, and support among the people involved.

Some of the kinds of activities that occur in the Commitment directing function are:

COMMITMENT DIRECTING

- Discussing and building a "behavior charter" for how people intend to work together on a day to day basis. The ***Working Guidelines*** are examples of such a charter.

- Making a commitment to operating as a team.

- Setting work direction for a project team or work group.

- Working with other groups or units to build, maintain, or improve working relationships

- Designing and committing to formal incentive or reward systems.

- Discussing and recording conditions necessary for success.

COMMITMENT LEADING

Leading in the Commitment unit of work includes those visions that provide hope, excitement, and energy for the present work. They are clear, and have resources committed to become real. They haven't happened yet. That occurs in the execution work unit.

Working philosophies like:

"meanings are in people not in words,"

"change starts from within,"

"we never get a second chance at a first impression,"

"your actions speak so loud I can't hear a word you are saying,"

find their truth in how they influence the present decisions we make about ourselves and others. These philosophies have stood the test of time and impact our behavior.

Leading in the present means behaving in ways that influence others to accomplish what we believe the organization must have in order to be successful. Here each of us displays our own BELIEFS about work and working with others. **Here teams of people can make statements of belief that are commonly understood, accepted, and supported and become known as CORPORATE BELIEFS.**

As stated earlier "BIG BLUE" IBM has three universally known corporate beliefs—one is a belief in the integrity of the individual.

When corporations begin violating the beliefs about people that made them successful generally marks the beginning of their downfall. This maybe true for families and countries as well.

Then Jesus said to the centurion:
"Go! It will be done just as you believed it would,
(and his servant was healed at that very hour)"
—Matthew 8:13

When individuals share their beliefs about work and working with others some magic generally occurs. Where this is done in valuing ways people say " I didn't know you believed that, now I know how I can help better." They also say "I can see why you and I are having our problems. Lets set aside some time and figure out a way for you to be you and me to be me and still do what each of us was hired to do." One of our beliefs is **"What I permit I promote."** If we see something going well we should affirm it, where the opposite is true–to do nothing is to say continue doing these bad things.

We know that a work group, department, or enterprise is strengthened to the extent that people are willing and able to examine and articulate their working beliefs, working philosophy, and beliefs about what conditions are necessary for the group or entity to succeed.

CONDITIONS FOR SUCCESS is a valuable tool because it openly articulates a level of TRUST that means I am willing to take a RISK and state needs and conditions from others. I am not able to do it all by myself. At the same time, it states my position and exposes me and my vulnerabilities. A working culture and climate of openness and trust increases the flow of useful information in valuing ways to all our advantage.

Leading in the present is a vital act of commitment. The proof of the pudding still remains to be seen—when we do as we say in the execution unit of work. We need to commit this effort here in our physical and psychological beings, visualize it as already happening and then do it. Not doing this results in generally a guess and b'gosh end result.

Some kinds of activities that occur in the Tactical Commitment leading function are:

COMMITMENT LEADING

- Discussing and recording shared working beliefs and philosophies about how to get work done.

- Team building.

Establish written corporate beliefs in a manner that clearly defines the culture that fits for us as a SUCCESSFUL organization. That may differ drastically from what our present culture is even though we're financially successful today. For some organizations, their product line and technical competitive edge keep them profit wise and sound foolish when it comes to their quality of life in their world of work.

Check it out. When the profit margins begin to slip so do the people who have been misused. ***Have our culture checked.*** Preferably by an outside, independent observer that can help us keep our organizational health in condition to weather the tough times as well as the good times.

Keep updating our picture with the visions from the strategic well of great ideas. Let them roll around during our iterative process. Commit to them when the timing is right and the completed staff work is done.

COMMITMENT CONTROLLING

Commitment controlling involves assuring that the committed work of the enterprise is in accordance with stated goals, objectives, policies, procedures, and practices.

It also involves making commitments to specific quality assurance systems, including activities, measurable outcomes, standards of performance, and commitments of resources.

This managing work unit can be best described by presenting examples of operational controlling activities.

COMMITMENT CONTROLLING

- **Conducting budget analysis;** comparing actual expenditures to planned (budgeted), analyzing deviations, and making necessary corrections to budgets or to practice.

- Planning, developing, and implementing **management information systems** (MIS) that provide ongoing information about progress in meeting operating objectives.

- **Attainment reporting** (outcomes in relation to plans).

- ***Building and committing resources*** to a quality assurance system.

- Conducting management reviews, project **reviews, or program reviews.**

- Designing and implementing performance **appraisal systems**.

The Commitment work unit establishes the priorities and momentum for the enterprise. Regardless of how well this is done, there will be unforeseen problems. To overcome them, it is important that there be an understood, accepted, and supported method for problem analysis, potential problem analysis, and decision making.

Families also need to have this same kind of understanding. Without this common commitment, people are hurt unnecessarily. When time isn't taken to distinguish between what is intended and what actual commitments have been made, confusion, disappointment, and conflict frequently result.

As an opportunity , we suggest spending some time with the family and/or work colleagues and discuss such things as beliefs, working philosophies, and mutual behavior commitments.

- What are some of our shared beliefs?
- What do we see as some necessary conditions for success of our family?
- Of our work group?

By the way, we realize that it is unlikely that families, or even established business or government enterprises will follow all of the steps of strategic managing and Commitment all of the time. This doesn't mean that people are bad or incompetent; it simply means that people are people.

Furthermore, life is such that there are times when it is necessary to drop the formalities of managing and just "wing it." These times are relatively rare, though, and it is our hope that by developing skills within a conceptual orientation to managing, people will improve their batting averages, with concomitant improvement in the quality and success of their work/life.

We will now go to the Execution work unit and tie the whole matrix of the OPERATIONAL ARENA together with the STRATEGIC ARENA, closing the loop with the managing system.

Chapter 10

Operational Managing:
The Task of Doing the Work

Chapter 10

Operational Managing: The Task of Doing the Work

When I was a child, I talked like a child,
I thought like a child, I reasoned like a child.
When I became a man, I put childish ways behind me.
–I Corinthians 13:11

We need to take the business of getting results seriously. Many *total quality* experts are so enamored with the process of doing work that the hope for the future is lost because there is little visualizing of the preferred future. The process of working eats up the energy necessary for weathering tough times because there is no vision. Where there is no vision people perish. When in fact we should focus on end results recognizing that process of the how to get there.

This part of the Managing System and work unit of the Operational Arena focuses on doing **all the work that directly makes the products and delivers the services to the customers.** This is where the rubber meets the road and where perspiration and inspiration finally meet.

This is where the MISSION, both personal and corporate, join in the reality of sales, flow of useful information, wise use of money, facilities, tools, equipment, time, and the continuity of policies, practices, procedures.

In addition this is where people behave in ways that value each other, provide criticism without blame, and validation. Where change is happening for all the right reasons and visions, hope, and excitement are obvious to everyone. Where profit is acquiring wealth and health for customers, families, employees, and stockholders.

This is where we practice our beliefs, both corporate and personal in ways that allow us to be ourselves in concert with the harmonious ideal of working and living interdependently together. Recognizing that we may lower our batting average once in a while, with our VALUING SPIRIT OF INTENT we will not let that change our commitment to forgive and MOVE ON TO THE NEXT DEAL!

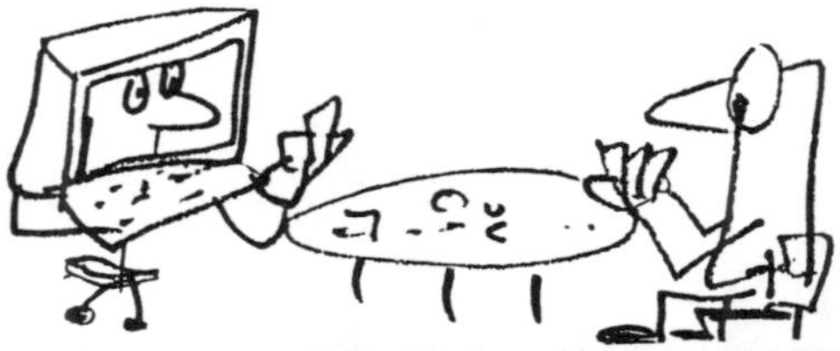

The Execution work unit of the Operational Arena takes the enterprise from the level of intent and commitment to the level of implementation. This is where the actual work of the enterprise is managed, specific day-to-day work is defined and carried out.

Execution responsibility in traditional hierarchical organizations falls primarily at the levels of first line management and operative employees. In small organizations or families, everyone usually shares commitment responsibilities.

Let's turn to an exposition of the Execution work unit and its relation to the five management functions. PLANNING, ORGANIZING, DIRECTING, LEADING, & CONTROLLING.

The focus of the Execution work unit planning is on TASKS.* Tasks represent the actual things that people do in order to meet operating objectives. Once again, recall the gap between the Tactical Commitment and Execution work units in the managing system matrix. This gap reflects the almost menacing certainty that day- to-day events are not likely to conform to our best laid plans. (Although think about how dull life would be if they did!)

The changing and emerging situation requires a continuing and disciplined attention to the process of planning and executing the most vital work and eliminating as much "trivial" work as possible.

We have found that most work is either assigned verbally, or is not assigned at all. When we ask people how they know what the most important work they should be doing is, they frequently tell us that they just know based on their experience. We acknowledge that this may be true in many cases, but we also see this phenomenon creating weak or nonexistent links between the overall plans of the enterprises and what people are actually doing.

Ongoing work becomes a matter of habit and tradition rather than an effort that is coordinated and oriented to fulfilling a larger plan.

A further consequence of working by habit or tradition is that individuals become isolated and do not see how what they do fits into the bigger picture. For many, this is demotivating; the work amounts to a monotonous daily routine, or, in some cases, a matter of fighting one "brush fire" after another, with little or no consistency or direction to the work.

For these reasons, we strongly recommend that the vital few tasks that relate to the strategic and operational plans of the enterprise be planned in writing, using a framework such as we describe in the ***Working Agreement*** chapters. This enables clear communication about what is being done and a broader sense of purpose for the specific work of individuals. Also, as we shall explain under ***Execution*** work unit controlling, it provides for a meaningful, motivating, collaborative appraisal of performance based on the actual work that people do.

Finally, this TASK PLANNING PROCESS is the most effective way we know of building understanding, acceptance, and support for the work that has to be done. Failure to achieve understanding often results in someone going off and doing something quite different than his/her supervisor or work colleagues expected.

Has this ever happened ?
What about with children or other family members?

*(*In 1972 Richard Gillespie was responsible for developing a program called "Approach to the 70s" where "THE TASK" was featured as the primary organizing principle for getting the work done, over and above traditional structure.*

Failure to achieve acceptance and support can result in non-action, or even sabotage, subterfuge, or other counterproductive actions, all of which are costly.

The chart that follows illustrates some tactical planning activities.

EXECUTION WORK UNIT PLANNING

- **Designing specific tasks**
- **Assigning specific work to individuals or project teams**

- **Developing and implementing specific policies, practices, procedures, or rules that apply to ongoing work**
- **Taking accountability for specific work**
- **Coordinating task assignments with other individuals or work groups**
- **Building individual/group work plans**
- **Sharing individual work plans with other interested or affected individuals**

- **Coordinating individual work plans with operating plans of the enterprise**

- **Taking responsibility for specific tasks in maintaining a household.**

EXECUTION WORK UNIT ORGANIZING

The Working Agreement is a format that encompasses the vital few elements for defining what a person is hired to do, what results are expected, and how that work will be measured before it is started.

The philosophy behind the Working Agreement is to put the person(s) into the job, not just the work into a job as so many job descriptions do. How a person functions in his/her work is critical to the ultimate results.

Frequently we hear people say, "I need to get organized!" Many times this means they are unsure of priorities, what the outcomes should be, how long it is going to take, how much money is required, who else should really be involved, etc. The fact is this work must be done, not just promised for tomorrow. Procrastination, in this case, is a thief of time.

More good ideas are lost because of poor presentation, than for being a poor idea. When ideas are clearly presented the receiver understands, accepts, and supports (takes action) on the idea.

Organizing takes the many tools of the social system and blends them into processes that "lay out" sequential steps for people to participate at their level of competency. These processes need to have a clear notion of the functions to be accomplished and then attach a sense of structure that best helps these functions to work.

Sometimes people decide to change the structure because they don't want to deal with a particular people problem. In other cases people are promoted outside of a unit to get rid of a people problem. The deserving person is denied the promotion because the boss likes this excellent worker close at hand. Hence a headhunter gets an opportunity to confidentially get the deserving person another job, and the company loses a valuable resource. Headhunters exist because good people aren't being treated and/or tested to their highest potential. Good people need to be stretched and want a chance to accomplish their beatable achievable visions.

Execution work unit organizing is done concurrently with the planning noted above. This is the process of creating a specific division of labor among individuals, work groups, and project teams and recruiting, hiring, and retaining qualified individuals to meet the staffing responsibilities of the enterprise.

Examples of tactical organizing activities are presented in the following chart:

EXECUTION WORK UNIT ORGANIZING

- **Assigning specific work to individuals or work teams**
- **Dividing household work among family members**
- **Establishing selection criteria**
- **Recruiting, interviewing, selecting, hiring, promoting, training, transferring, and if necessary, firing people**
- **Writing position descriptions**
- **Setting up trade show presentations and booths**
- **Making travel arrangements**
- **Keeping various phases of research, production, and sales on schedule and updated**
- **Gearing up for board, sales, staff, and product meetings of all sorts**

And the organizing list goes on, and on , and on—

EXECUTION WORK UNIT DIRECTING

We are who we are , who we are—the extent to which any of us see ourselves as others see us (paraphrased from the Scottish poet Robert Burns) will greatly enhance our opportunities to act in ways that meet any particular situation with sensitivity, candor, and resolve to get the job done.

Doing the directing work requires sound experience in the fundamentals of problem analyses, decision making, potential problem / possibility analyses, situational analyses, establishing expectations, and implementing and maintaining the plans geared for being profitable.

DIRECTING is the work that pursues the target with vigor, and clear purpose for outputs. There are times when a sense of "single mindedness" is criteria toward persons and corporate success. For a short period of time, at the exclusion of all else except faith and family.

We need people who are willing to be driven by a vision (mission) where worthy results benefit us all. We should see that person as *gifted.*

The extensive strategic and commitment work has the road for action mapped out with stakes in the ground to measure progress. Directing sees to it that it gets done.

This action phase constantly checks back with the stated direction and movement laid out in the planning phases using the iterative process. This means that where new information occurs during the "doing" phase, both plus and minus impacts are considered and kept in dynamic tension with the targeted outputs.

The outputs are the flag at the end of the furrow that keeps the furrow straight. Once the eye loses contact with the flag the furrow gets crooked, and difficult to straighten out. Consequently the land doesn't get worked right and the crops suffer.

Once we lose sight of our outputs, a lot of resources are wasted, the outputs suffer, and scarce resources are wasted. Directing keeps the work on track, straight to the point knowing how to handle the rocks that get in the way.

The question of "style" comes up here. Our job is not to recapitulate the vast literature that has been developed around the topic of managing styles, but rather to highlight a couple of things.

First, it is true that most people come into managing positions or situations **with their own personal theories of effective managing and with their own "natural," or preferred, or habitual ways of managing**. It has also been aptly demonstrated that different situations require different kinds of managing in order to be effective.

Some management theorists argue that an individual's habitual or preferred style is unlikely to change. Therefore it is important to select people for influential positions based on appropriately matching their personal styles to the work situation (e.g., select an "autocrat" to be a military drill sergeant). Others argue that people can change their approaches based on the situation they are in. **Therefore the task is to train leaders to recognize different kinds of situations and to behave appropriately in those varying situations.**

The truth is probably somewhere in between. We have observed people who are willing and able to be autocratic when they need to be and to encourage shared leadership and self-regulation when the task can be most effectively approached in that way.

We have also experienced individuals who believe "My way or the highway". For these people it is important to place them in work situations that require their particular orientations.

EXECUTION WORK UNIT DIRECTING

- **Providing individual work direction**
- **Providing individual counseling for employees or co-workers**
- **Involving people meaningfully in planning their work and the work of the organization or unit**
- **Providing encouragement, support, ideas, or resources**
- **Providing orientation to new employees**
- **Displaying and encouraging valuing behavior**
- **Providing appropriate and timely validations**
- **Providing Criticism Without Blame where it is appropriate and helpful**
- **Modeling effective ways of doing the work**

- **Building trust and encouraging openness**

- **Encouraging appropriate levels of risk taking**

- **Appropriately using formal reward systems.**

EXECUTION WORK UNIT LEADING

Have them serve as judges for the people at all times,
but have them bring every difficult case to you,
the simple cases they can decide for themselves.
That will make your load lighter, because they will share it with
you. If you do this and God so commands,
you will be able to stand the strain,
and all these people will go home satisfied.
Jethro to Moses —Exodus 18:22&23

Leading carries a lot of unknown freight like charisma, mysticism, poise, confidence, power, wisdom and generally right. **Another way of looking at leading is to consider serving, giving, doing for others without strings attached,** courageous, forgiving, encouraging, thanking, and unassuming. None of these suggests weakness, selfishness, or taking advantage of someone else.

We are not using the *noun* "leader" because in the managing system **we believe that all people have a responsibility to take a leading role in the work they are hired to do** whatever the Focus and depth of that work. In the leading function, the action is measured by how we go about influencing and empowering others to be as great as they can possibly be.

Here our visions take shape in the hope, excitement, and energy we display even when the tough times occur. **When we are broken down we are broken open to the possibilities of the future.** Without visions we are dwelling in the quagmire of disappointment and self doubt.

When in doubt TAKE A VISION TO LUNCH. Chew on it, digest it, and feel the body and spirit glow with energy and renewed commitment.

This action phase of LEADING means carrying the standard pointed at the critical work to be done in a way that suggests being able to take a direct hit in place of someone else and at the same time not take the credit if the job is done beyond anyones highest expectations.

All people, regardless of where they are at in the organization have unique opportunities to influence others in ways that trigger hope, excitement, and energy. Here are some real examples:

A college president routinely welcomed the opportunity to visit with the janitor who cleaned his office. Their discussions added a level of understanding to the president that reflected a feel for the dedication and wisdom of many support staff. The janitor, in turn, gained a sense of commitment from the president for the whole team and the importance of each role. This *mutual spirit of cooperation* was informally passed on to people that both came in contact with during their normal work activities.

An executive manager was having difficulty with a secretary in the area of productivity and cooperation with support staff. In frustration he discussed this with the Executive Assistant to the President and Chief Operating Officer whom he greatly respected for her professionalism, productivity, and concern for people. The result was a low profile enabling opportunity by the Executive Assistant to help both the secretary and the executive focus on the issues, situations, and tasks that needed to be done. In addition they were given some valuing feedback on how to help each other when things weren't going well.

This leading effort didn't happen by chance. The Executive Assistant was prepared to help because of her competency.

Competency is where intelligence, knowledge, and experience meet in successful results. Many people have opportunities to lead and miss them because they are not prepared.

Motivation Leading to Success

Perhaps the center of LEADING is fueled by people's motivation to succeed. Motivation is that intrinsic desire to accomplish something specific that adds value and meaning to personal and corporate life.

During this execution phase motivation takes on a very tangible form. This tangible form is in the behavior of people which is critical toward gaining the trust and confidence of others. Behaving in ways that trigger opportunities for people to "be motivated" to help each other.

Motivated people seek ways to accomplish the work and get the results that have a direct value to them. Operational managing through leading works at finding ways for people to buy into the results as their personal agenda. This means paying enough attention to what's going on in a manner that keeps the "spirit" of the people working in harmony even when tough times are the norm.

The CURRENT CULTURE of the enterprise is that accumulation of beliefs, behaviors, values, attitudes, and visions that people have as they go about doing their work. All of these elements can be influenced by those who have the strong desire to set the pace whether they be right or wrong. A disgruntled employee, left in place over a long period of time will have a direct affect on the immediate working climate.

Management is responsible for determining the type of working climate that best fits. Management is equally responsible for being the best example by doing and acting as if that is the only "acceptable working climate in town." That working climate should always be a valuing one. Obviously involving others to articulate and implement the "acceptable working climate" is critical. **"Asking and sharing gets ownership–and persuading gets resistance".**

EXECUTION WORK UNIT LEADING

- **Be clear about the type of work environment and see that it stays that way to everyone's advantage.**

- **The continuous signs of hope, excitement, and energy are indicators of leading that is working even in tough times.**

- **Differences are important in all enterprises when they are handled in valuing ways.**

- **Leading is everyone's opportunity. Intelligence, knowledge, and experience insure success at taking advantage of that opportunity.**
- **Paying attention to detail helps maintain a sense of reality so that people know that the link with the future has a solid base of understanding in the present.**

- **Handling today's tough issues adds credibility to the potential of tomorrow.**

- **Leading recognizes that LUCK IS WHERE PREPARATION MEETS OPPORTUNITY.**

EXECUTION WORK UNIT CONTROLLING

Whatever you have learned or received or heard from me, or seen in me–put it into practice.
Philippians 4:9

This last cell of the managing system matrix is one of the most important and probably the most difficult managing area for many people. It is here that the formal tracking and informal sensing of the ongoing work of the enterprise are conducted.

IT HAS BEEN SAID THAT MORE TOP EXECUTIVES HAVE LOST THEIR JOBS BECAUSE THEY WERE NOT ABLE TO MAINTAIN THE DISCIPLINE NECESSARY TO HAVE THEIR OWN SENSE OF WHAT WAS GOING ON.

President Reagan's and Admiral Poindexter's lack of attention to detail, are classical dilemmas experienced routinely in business. When subordinates run amuck its because this function of control was left unattended.

CAUTION: This doesn't mean that over control is desirable. Rarely should there be a heavy emphasis on control. What there needs to be is a consistent effort to stay in touch with the tough realities that expose the enterprise to unnecessary RISKS. Once again it is important to take KNOWLEDGEABLE RISKS, NOT GAMBLERS RISKS!

Balance between the functions is critical. Sometimes the leading function has a vision, desire, hope so strong that it consumes the caution flags of good judgement. These built in sensors deserve to be considered whenever they rise to the surface of our consciousness. They are the keepers of our historical perspective, and valuable members of our personal effectiveness team. Bench this team without a reasonable amount of playing time and sooner or later we are going to foul up and possibly foul out.

Formal tracking is intended to compare observations and measurements of what has occurred against standards, policies, practices, procedures, plans, and directions. Deviations are analyzed and appropriate responses are undertaken. Some possible responses to deviations are to change the work activity, re-direct the work, change the approach to the work, or change the plans.

When deviations are found, a common reaction in organizations is to go on a **"which hunt" ("which one of 'em did it")** in order to identify who is at fault and whom to blame. This orientation is one of the many things that causes people to have negative reactions to the controlling function.

Informal sensing is an important role for all managers and non-managers alike. Visiting people in the work place, keeping one's eyes and ears open, being aware of the "feeling" (or smell) of the organizational climate, and being alert to signals about what is going well and what might not be going well provide vital opportunities to correct problems in their early stages and to keep the enterprise on course. In the late 1800's Patterson, the founder of NCR practiced this and taught it to one of his chief salesmen, T.J.Watson, who founded IBM. Mr. Watson made walking around management one of his hallmarks as did his son, T.J. Watson Jr. I know because I worked for IBM from 1956–1969; and met Mr. T.J. Watson Jr. MBWA is not new–and it is important.

Informal sensing is not "spying," but rather a useful way of staying informed and sharing in the excitement of enabling the enterprise to succeed.

One formal controlling activity is the PERFORMANCE APPRAISAL PROCESS. One of the major barriers to productivity in organizations is de-motivating performance appraisal systems.

At best, many appraisal systems make the job of wage and salary administration a bit easier. At worst, they build distrust and create conflicts and misunderstandings between managers and those they manage. These negative consequences are due primarily to one or more of three factors: poor or inappropriate appraisal systems, lack of skill in conducting appraisals, or unclear purposes for doing appraisal in the first place.

APPRAISAL SYSTEMS

One of the most inappropriate forms of performance appraisal is the trait-rating system. In this system, managers are asked, once or twice a year, to rate their employees on a series of traits (e.g., attitude, honesty, industriousness, loyalty, leadership). This puts managers in a position of having to make judgments or inferences for which

1. they are not qualified to make
2. typically have little or no bearing on the person's contribution to the enterprise.

As a result, the ratings tend to reflect the rater's personal attitudes about the individual being rated. We can see questionable benefit to the people involved nor to the enterprise from this approach.

Behavioral approaches to performance appraisal are a fairly recent invention. For this approach, observations of critical incidents of effective and ineffective performance are made, and then performance rating scales are built around behaviors that are found to be related to effective and ineffective performance. To conduct an appraisal, the supervisors (or in some cases, co-workers) rate their observations of the person's behavior on each of the behavior scales. If the person is observed as having done a lot of the "effective" behaviors and not very many of the "ineffective" behaviors, the performance rating is high.

The behavioral approach has severe practical limitations. First, it is a very costly process. Usually a trained psychologist is required to develop the behavior observation scales and to train raters to use them. Second, a separate scale has to be constructed for each job. Finally, it requires that people learn to be "objective" observers of the behavior of others.

The most effective appraisal systems are based on the actual work that is done. In the next chapter, we will describe a system of work planning, management and evaluation that makes it possible to evaluate people's performance based on mutually planned, agreed-upon work.

Appraisal Process

One of the most common misconceptions about performance appraisal is that it is something that should happen once or twice a year. This point of view causes people to see an appraisal as an event which at best is a silly exercise to be endured by managers and employees alike, and at worst an ordeal to be dreaded, endured, and gotten past with as little pain as possible.

If performance appraisal is to be both a helpful and motivating experience, then it must be recognized as an ongoing responsibility of supervisors and those being supervised. People deserve regular feedback about how they are doing, what is going well, and what opportunities there are for improvement. Furthermore, this activity is much more effective to the extent that it is seen by the supervisor and the person being supervised as a mutual responsibility; as an opportunity to collaborate in order to strengthen both of them in the process of doing work. Finally, this ongoing appraisal effort must focus on actual work, issues and situations surrounding that work, not on traits of the individual.

In order to enhance the questionable benefits of the appraisal process, we suggest the following:

1. **Plan and schedule regular meetings to review performance.**

2. **Focus the conversations around planned tasks that have been previously agreed upon. It is most helpful to use a task planning process like the one described in Chapter 8.**

3. **Identify and celebrate successes; the things that have gone well.**

4. **Have it go both ways. The employee should have the opportunity to comment on things the supervisor has done that have been helpful as well as on things he would like the supervisor to do differently.**

5. **Keep a running, written record of performance on completed tasks, so if the organization requires an annual formal appraisal, it can be a mere compilation of what has been discussed throughout the year, with no surprises.**

QUALITY CONTROL

The other formal controlling device that we will discuss is QUALITY CONTROL. In contrast to quality assurance, QUALITY CONTROL is a process of inspecting or tracking progress according to previously determined standards. It is usually done by a third party not performing the work being inspected. Exceptions to this include situations in which test equipment, tools, and fixtures are certified to ensure the quality of the product according to measurable criteria.

Quality inspection can be a built-in opportunity for conflict between the doers and the inspectors. A commitment to working together interdependently, including mutual development of and commitment to quality standards, and following the principles of the Working Guidelines, can minimize conflict and create opportunities for synergistic problem avoidance and problem solving.

The following are some examples of controlling activities.

EXECUTION CONTROLLING

- **Identifying and taking action on opportunities for improvement.**
- **Conducting ongoing reviews of performance**
- **Conducting formal performance appraisal**
- **Walking around and talking to people**
- **Conducting quality inspections**
- **Discussing or clarifying rules, regulations, or policies**
- **Conducting informal sensing meetings. Identifying and celebrating successes and well-done's**

Chapter 11

Working Agreement:
A Managing Framework for Assuring Success

Chapter 11

The Working Agreement: A Managing Framework for Assuring Success

His master replied, Well done, good and faithful servant!
You have been faithful with a few things;
I shall put you in charge of many things.
—Matthew 25:21

The ***Working Agreement*** is a tool of the Work/Life System (W/LS) designed to capture the vital work people are hired to do, the results/outputs expected, and subjective/objective measurement agreed to in advance of doing the work. Remember vital work is that work which gets the job done in an efficient and effective manner. This seems simple enough. We have shared our understanding of the vital ingredients which help an enterprise be successful.

This information is valuable when it is a part of the routine effort for doing the work. How do the W/LS philosophies, tools, concepts, and beliefs get implemented? One way is to make sure that the philosophies of the ***Working Agreement*** are implemented in a format that best fits the individual, function, and enterprise.

The *Working Agreement (WA) System* consists of a CONCEPTUAL FRAMEWORK for developing the Working Agreement founded on the W/LSI philosophies, tools, and implementation experience. The ***Working Agreement*** as a communication tool may vary in format but not in its basic elements for work tracking, sensing, job appraisal, and ongoing performance review, renewal, and updating.

The heart of an enterprise is its mission, which provides identity and purpose. For an individual the heart is the work which identifies where the "fit," or turf, is and why it is important, this gives personal purpose and reasons for intrinsic motivation. Motivation comes from being needed, recognized for being needed, and actually getting the *right job done and the right job done right.*

The ***Working Agreement*** principals strengthen the odds in everyone's favor for maximizing peoples desire to be successful and seeing that they get rewarded for their outputs as individuals and interdependent teams.

Motivation is further increased when the vital few work is VISIBLE between and among people responsible for each others success. Once again the KEY IS VISIBILITY OF THE VITAL WORK WHICH PROPELS THE ENTERPRISE AND INDIVIDUAL INTO CONTINUOUS CYCLES OF GROWTH AND PROSPERITY.

Visibility means that this valuable information is constantly reviewed, massaged, updated, renewed, shared, challenged and dealt with in both tough times and periods of success.

Other sources for work definition such as job descriptions, program plans, budgets, and future strategies all add value toward linking individual, unit, and enterprise work together. The ***Working Agreement*** synthesizes these source documents into an intelligible, brief, and dynamic system that works for the people, by the people, and with the people to their advantage. (Some tracking systems take on a life of their own and eat up a lot of precious energy only for the sake of continuity, control, and self protection.)

In doing a ***Working Agreement, It is necessary*** to fulfill an individuals creative discipline to ensure an ongoing assessment of performance to plan and flexibility of the plan to meet legitimate changes for getting results.

Work is an honorable endeavor, a blessing for which we can be thankful. Work provides an opportunity to use the gifts that each of us has been given. Each of us deserves to seek out that which best fulfills our visions and motivations to achieve something. Each of us have the unique opportunity to be a part of helping people to improve the quality of their work/home lives.

The principles and tools of the ***Work/Life System*** have been designed to accomplish the merger of work and home life. Everything we have talked about so far in this book has been shown in many settings to be helpful to people in improving the effectiveness and quality of their work /home lives. We will find a practical use for the ***Working Agreement*** at home with children as well as a guide for vital few family tracking decisions.

The ***Working Agreement*** offers some specific ways to help put many of the other ideas into practice. The ***Working Agreement*** is an operational tool for planning, managing, and evaluating work. It is a written document that can be successfully used to establish continuity between the work of individuals, functional groups, and project teams with the strategies and operating plans of the enterprise. Properly used, the ***Working Agreement:***

- identifies the highest priority work of the enterprise;

- enables individuals and groups to coordinate their work with one another and with the plans of the enterprise;

- fosters effective delegation of meaningful work;

- allows for flexible work planning;
- enables effective communication about work assignments, responsibilities, and authorities;

- provides a mechanism for motivating, work related performance appraisal;

One of the more important values of the ***Working Agreement* is that it enables people to effectively plan and manage not only their technical work, but also the managerial behavioral aspects of work.**

It serves as a way to recognize and acknowledge that the care and feeding of the social system is a legitimate part of the work of the enterprise.

It provides the technology for planning, managing, and evaluating work that focuses on achieving subjective, and intangible outcomes (which is true for most work in the social system).

We have found that the ***Working Agreement*** process is threatening to some people, particularly those:

- who are "retired at their desk,"

- who have managed to build their own independent enterprise within the larger enterprise

- who do not have the skills to effectively carry out their present work

- who are very unclear about what work they are supposed to be doing.

Fortunately, for most of these individuals, entering into the *Working Agreement* process has given them a new lease on their work life.

One individual, for example, held the position of Financial Vice President for a medium-sized manufacturing company. For several years, the President had been dissatisfied with the work of the individual, but had not dealt effectively with the situation. By going through the ***Working Agreement*** process, the individual realized on his own that he did not have the skills required to do the Financial V.P. job for that company. He submitted his resignation and reported back that two weeks later, he had found another job that was ideally suited for his skills and interests and with higher pay! That was a win-win situation for the person and for both companies.

We initially developed the ***Working Agreement*** as a tool for managing the work of individuals. We have subsequently expanded the application of the ***Working Agreement*** to functional groups, projects, and proposals. We'll discuss each of these in turn.

INDIVIDUAL WORKING AGREEMENTS

The individual ***Working Agreement*** ties the work of the individual to the plans of the enterprise. **It is a written document that establishes understanding, acceptance, and support between a person and his or her manager, or among work colleagues, for the important work that person will do.**

In a traditional hierarchical organization, the president, or chief executive manager would have a ***Working Agreement*** with the board of directors that would broadly state his/her priority responsibilities in light of the mission, strategy, and operating plans of the enterprise.

The next level managers who report to this key manager would each have ***Working Agreements*** that identify their roles as members of the executive managing team and their more narrow pieces of the work in the enterprise. This partitioning of the work is continued through the levels of the organization.

A frequent occurrence in organizations is that as the work is partitioned, various departments or divisions lose sight of their interdependence or of being part of the whole.

In his pioneering work on organizational theory, Rensis Likert developed his "linking pin" concept that offers a conceptual solution to this problem of independence of organizational units. Likert asserted that each manager is a "linking pin" that ties his or her part of the organization vertically to the next level of the organization. Instead of being a representative of work group to higher management or vice versa, the manager is a fully functioning member of both groups. There **is no question about the notion that people other than the "manager" can /should be the hear of a particular task team. Mistakes occur when the assumption is made that *teams* hire, fire, counsel or promote people. Teams recommend and supervisors execute!**

The manager is the head of one team of people and is a staff member of the next above managing team. The responsibility of all managers, then, is to build effective, functioning work teams and link them together interdependently and BE AN EFFECTIVE STAFF MEMBER OF THE NEXT ABOVE MANAGEMENT TEAM.

The ***Working Agreement*** is a very effective tool for identifying and implementing this linking pin role for managers. Incidentally, managers and non-managers can also serve as horizontal linking pins in an organization. These roles tie work groups together around common tasks or points at which work needs to be coordinated.

The *Working Agreement* differs from a position description in that it puts the particular individual into the work, whereas a position description only focuses on responsibilities; it does not provide for the unique nature of the individual.

The ***Working Agreement*** is designed to focus on only the vital, high priority aspects of the job. The more routine responsibilities are accounted for in the position description. Therefore we do not recommend eliminating position descriptions; they are useful for job classification and personnel selection functions.

When a new person comes into an organization, the ***Working Agreement*** provides an important bridge to help that person become oriented to the enterprise. By reading the ***Working Agreements*** of not only the person she/he replaces, but also of those with whom she/he will be working, the new employee can quickly "get up to speed."

The ***Working Agreement*** document has five sections: Overview, Focus, Tasks, Visions, and Working Beliefs. These sections are designed to plan the work and to integrate the individual into the job.

OVERVIEW

The Overview section provides an opportunity to briefly describe the identity and purpose of the job. Just as the enterprise as a whole has an identity and purpose (mission), so does each individual job.

The Overview section answers the question, "What are you hired to do? What are your general responsibilities?" Completing the Overview section simply requires a list of brief statements of the person's major responsibilities.

FOCUS

This section begins the process of bringing direction and movement to the work within a specified time frame. A time frame for the ***Working Agreement*** is stated (usually one year, but this varies with the nature of the work), followed by a list of goals toward which the individual will focus work during the specified time period.

These goals are taken from the operating business plans for the enterprise and therefore provide the point at which the work of the individual corresponds to organizational plans. This is a clear linking point at which individuals are able to take accountability for their part in fulfilling the plans of the enterprise. We will show how to write these goals in a way that adds commitment and clarity in Chap-ter 13.

This section also provides an opportunity for managers to identify work for which they will take LEAD (execution) RESPONSIBILITY and work for which lead responsibility will be delegated to others.

Goals in the Focus section should focus on the person's technical, managerial, and behavioral work as appropriate.

- For example, a manager might recognize problems or opportunities in the ways that people in his department are working together. He may choose to have as a goal in his ***Working Agreement*** something like, "to have our department working together more effectively as a team, where the flow of useful information is creating trust and effective completions of results."

- An example of a goal that focuses on managerial work is, "to have a more timely and relevant operational planning and budgeting process in our department." This point must be stressed: By including a goal which ensures the effective utilizations of resources to meet our __% return on investment in the Focus section, the person establishes intent to do something toward accomplishing that outcome during the time period of the ***Working Agreement.*** The "how to"–How to's must not be in the focus section! For fulfilling that intent is provided in the Task section.

Conditions for success may be added in the FOCUS section to add pertinent information that is necessary to ensure success. One condition for success in our own business is maintaining the discipline to schedule time for marketing at routine intervals each month. (The tendency for us is to fill all available time with billable time. This doesn't leave much time for new clients)

TASKS

Tasks are in the (execution) how to phase, the work that is actually done to achieve the objectives of the enterprise. In this section, the individual describes the important tasks that will be done to achieve the outcomes described in the Focus section. Each task must relate back to one or more goals in the Focus section.

Furthermore, there must be at least one task that pertains to each of the goals for which the individual is taking lead responsibility. (For delegated goals, the person to whom the work is delegated develops and carries out specific tasks.) For some work there are very detailed, clear, and well laid out tasks through other established tracking systems. In these cases the following task elements serve as a check list for reference purposes. The important point is that these elements are complete and mutually understood, accepted, and supported by all people involved.

Each task statement describes the specific objective(s), the ***activities that will be done*** to accomplish the objective(s), the ***value to the enterprise*** and to the individual of doing that task, ***the conditions necessary for success*** in accomplishing the task and ***the measurement criteria for evaluating*** performance on the task. A scale is also provided for rating the performance, and space is provided to record running comments about progress in the task, problems that occur along the way, and narrative comments about effectiveness in doing the work.

The value of specifying important tasks in this way is that it enables people to communicate effectively up front about what will be done, how it will be accomplished, and how that accomplishment will be measured. This helps to avoid conflicts later about expectations or different points of view in evaluating performance. Remember the convenient loss of memory habit (CLM) . The Working Agreement helps eliminate CLM. Also keep in mind its been said that what we only hear is retained at the 2% level in 72 hours. What we do, write, participate in is in the high 80's in 72 hours! It also makes ongoing, work-related performance appraisal possible and makes delegation much more effective than it normally is.

VISIONS

In this section, the person writes some brief statements describing his or her personal visions and visions for the future of the enterprise. Writing and sharing these visions becomes contagious and soon, people are interdependently working to see that those visions become a part of the strategic and operational efforts of the enterprise.

Many times, visions for the future serve as a source of inspiration for strategic direction of the enterprise. They can also help individuals focus on more meaningful, exciting aspects of their work within the context of the work of the enterprise.

We had a case in which an executive manager, after completing the ***Working Agreement,*** looked it over and exclaimed, "What my boss and I really want me to be doing are those things I have listed in my VISIONS." This was said with great colorful action and emotion. The marking pen he had been using on the easel to write his ***Working Agreement*** went sailing across the room and hit the vision sheet square on the word VISIONS. The pen hit so hard it took on a life of its own and almost claimed one of us as its victim. It was worth it to see such excitement and learning happen all at the same time.

He went on to say "With this ***Working Agreement,*** I will be able to clearly delegate more important work to my staff and get about doing those things that I really should be doing."

A year later this same person gave a testimonial about the ***Working Agreement*** and how it had helped him do many of the things he had been training others to do and how it helped him implement what he had learned in his graduate program at the university. There was clear evidence of moisture in his eyes as he emphasized the importance of visions and the hope and energy they add to everyday work.

We should take an opportunity to think about and write down our visions for our own personal future and then shared them with significant others in our life?

What about visions for the future of our family? For the future of other enterprises of which we are a part? If not, we may owe ourself the treat of doing so. If we have done so in the past, maybe it's time to revisit those visions.

WORKING BELIEFS

The Visions and Working Beliefs sections of the ***Working Agreement*** are designed to put the person into the job. In the Working Beliefs section, the individual writes the more important beliefs that affect working with others. Beliefs can focus on such areas as management, organization, people, and conditions for success. When written in a ***Working Agreement*** and shared with others, beliefs are important sources of information that help build confidence and understanding of why people behave in similar and different ways in the same situation.

Beliefs also provide an opportunity for stating certain conditions that are necessary for people to be successful in their work.

For us one of these is that people who work with us must recognize that we are unable to do all the things we say ought to be done. We work on improving our **batting averages** at following the principles of the Work/Life Management System. To let others believe that we can do all this 100% of the time would be setting ourselves up for failure, and would contribute to others being skeptical about our honesty!

The chart on the following page recapitulates the general form of the ***Working Agreement.*** It is important to affirm that this is only a general form.

To be useful, any tool must serve the needs of the user, not the other way around. This is also true for the ***Working Agreement.*** Mold the particular form of the ***Working Agreement*** to fit our particular situation. Many of our clients have modified the ***Working Agreement*** to serve them. Some of our clients have focused primarily on the Tasks section. Others, for whom the tasks are routine, repetitive, and well understood, have eliminated the Tasks section and focused their attention on discovering the shared visions and beliefs of people who work together.

The ***Working Agreement*** is primarily a communication device. It is a method of clearly communicating with one another about the complex world of work.

It is also designed to be flexible. As new information becomes available that requires changes in the work, it is possible to make changes by adding, modifying, or deleting goals, key objectives, and tasks. These changes then can be communicated to others who are affected.

In Chapter 12 we provide a standard form of the ***Working Agreement*** in the form of a questionnaire. By simply working through the form, we can develop a first-cut ***Working Agreement*** for ourself. If our work is very clear, it shouldn't take very long. If, on the other hand, our work is not clear, the time it takes to complete the ***Working Agreement*** is an excellent investment.

WORKING AGREEMENT OVERVIEW

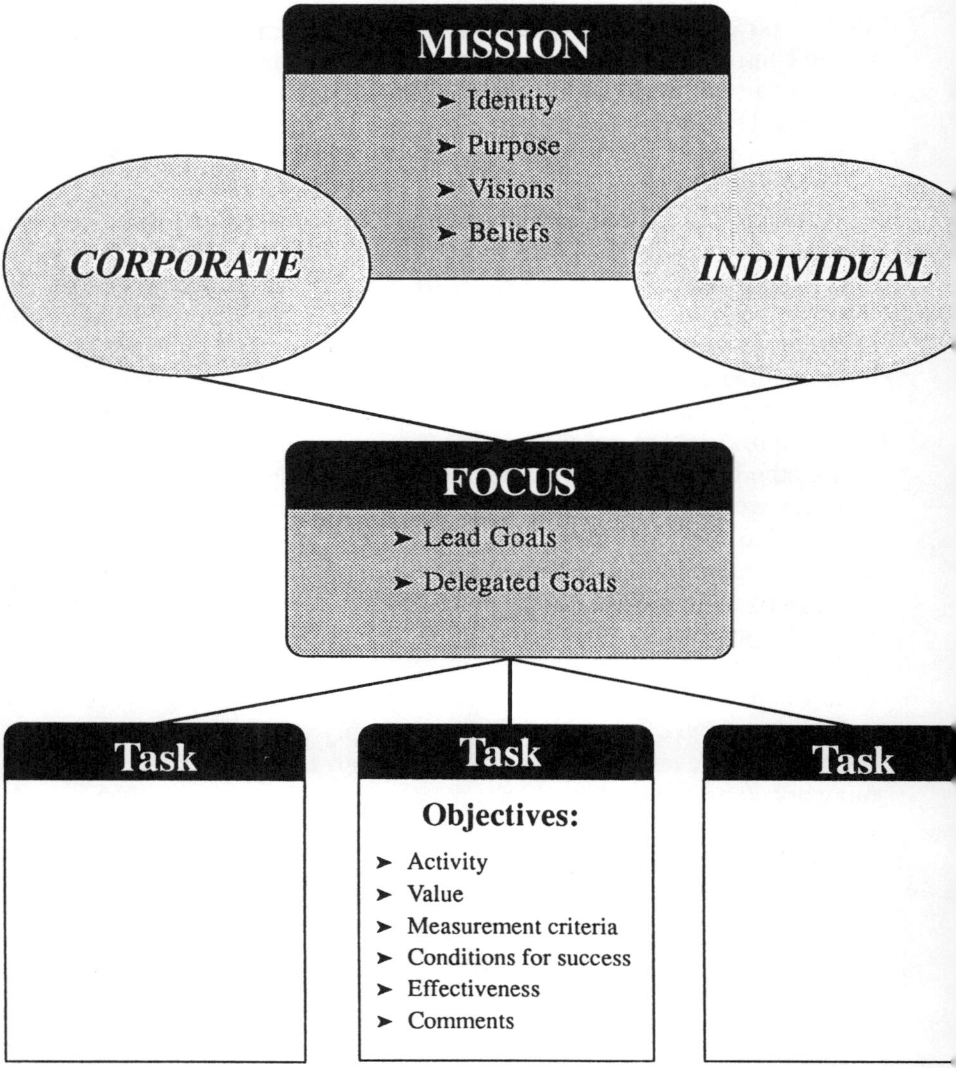

GENERAL FORM OF THE WORKING AGREEMENT

- ***OVERVIEW***
  Brief statements describing the identity and purpose of the job in the form of responsibilities.

- ***FOCUS***
  Statement of the time period for the ***Working Agreement.***
  A list of goals or key objectives for the work of the person with delegated work and work for which the person will take lead tactical responsibility identified as appropriate.

- ***TASKS***
  A complete description of each task the person will perform to accomplish the goals and key objectives in the Focus section.

- ***VISIONS***
  A list of the person's visions for himself and for the enterprise.

- ***WORKING BELIEFS***
  A list of the person's more important working beliefs or values about such things as managing, people, behavior, organizations, or conditions for success.

FUNCTIONAL WORKING AGREEMENT

This variation of the ***Working Agreement*** focuses on a functional work group rather than on an individual. We use this kind of ***Working Agreement*** for managing partnerships. We have also seen it applied effectively to a sales department.

The functional ***Working Agreement*** is most valuable when a functional group of people are working closely together to accomplish some very clear, mutual goals and objectives. In this case, the Overview and

Focus sections apply to the group as a whole. The Overview describes the responsibilities of the functional area, and the Focus lists the goals or broad objectives on which the group is working.

It is also valuable for the group as a whole to develop sections that describe their shared Visions and Working Beliefs.

This is an extraordinarily useful team building exercise. The work is then partitioned among the individual members of the group by assigning particular goals or key objectives to individuals.

The individuals then develop Task plans to achieve those goals or key objectives.

Individuals are also encouraged to develop their own personal Visions and Working Beliefs sections.

The Tasks and personal Visions and Working Beliefs are shared among the group members to assure consistency and completeness and to identify opportunities to support one another interdependently.

PROJECT WORKING AGREEMENT

The project ***Working Agreement*** is designed very similarly to the Functional Working Agreement. The difference is that a project team is usually an ad-hoc group made of people from different functional areas, who are together only for the purpose of completing the project. After the project is completed, they return to their functional assignments. At least three challenges immediately face a project team. First, the people may have never worked together before. They are therefore starting at the first step of developing effective working relationships. Many project teams fail to devote time and energy at the beginning to develop a good working team. This often results in costly communication and working relationship problems later. In developing a Project ***Working Agreement,*** team members have the opportunity to:

- Jointly plan the work of the project
- Discuss their shared beliefs and values about how to work together

- Build a behavior charter (Working Guidelines) for how they will work together

- Establish legitimate goals and tasks that focus on the behavioral (social system) aspects of their project work

Second, when formal performance appraisal time comes, it is difficult for a functional manager to fairly appraise the work of people who have spent much of their time away doing project work. There needs to be a useful way for the project manager to convey performance-related information about individuals to their functional managers. The built-in appraisal mechanism in the Task section of the ***Working Agreement*** makes this communication possible.

Third, there is the question of how the actual project work will be divided among team members. The ***Working Agreement*** offers a way to clearly divide the work while minimizing overlapping or underlapping responsibilities.

PROPOSAL WORKING AGREEMENT

By using the ***Working Agreement*** form for proposals to prospective clients, it enables us to clearly communicate what our role will be, what we intend to accomplish, and how we intend to accomplish it. It also enables us to share some of our exciting visions for the work we do together as well as our most important beliefs and values about how we work with clients. It establishes benchmarks by which we can work with the client to monitor progress along the way and to make changes in our agreement as they become necessary. Describing our proposed work in ***Working Agreement*** format enables clients to develop understanding, acceptance, and support for the proposed work.

SUMMARY

We have described the ***Working Agreement*** as a useful tool for planning, managing, and evaluating work. The format may vary as long as the basic philosophy remains intact. People deserve to know what is expected of them, how they are going to be measured, and to be given every opportunity to succeed, whether it be at work, at home, or in other endeavors.

Furthermore, people deserve to have the opportunity to share their visions and beliefs about the enterprise.

Finally, the ***Working Agreement*** is a tool to be used to the advantage of people, not to be cumbersome and have a life of its own.

Documenting work planning in writing is not for covering one's tracks! It is to make some tracks to maintain direction, maximize efficiency, and result in improved effectiveness.

Families may apply the principles of the ***Working Agreement*** (if not all of the detail) to their own work planning. This is particularly true for single parent families or families in which both parents work outside the home, and it is necessary for older children to pick up some of the work load. When the whole family is together on the identity of the family, and their individual and collective desired outcomes, there is a much better chance for everyone to be successful. The house gets cleaned, dishes are done, time is allotted for fun together, and all share in the improved quality of life at home. Remember ***The Working Agreement System*** :

- Is flexible
- Links personal and corporate planning
- Uses a common and interrelated vocabulary
- Realistically identifies expected results
- Helps people focus on the "vital few" top priorities
- Legitimizes the effort to prevent "filling up the calendar" and encourages planned "dwell time"
- Fosters delegation

- Helpfully assures accountability

- Places a specific person into the work as well as defining the work of the position or job

- Responsibly involves others in complicated work at their level of competency (delegating to others while maintaining a review, monitor, and approval role)

- Enables people to take on more challenging work or realize that the job is too much for them (either work load, or not qualified for it)

- Divides complicated work into manageable parts

- Clearly focuses on what a person is hired to do

- Allows for subjective, objective, tangible, and intangible measurement

- Facilitates delegating critical, challenging, meaningful work, even to the extent of taking knowledgeable risks, with appropriate sensing and tracking

- Improves communication about the work itself

- Provides for planned criticism without blame

- Provides written tracking / sensing (audit trail)

Chapter 12

Making the Working Agreement Be a Vital Part of Today's Reality

Chapter 12

Making the Working Agreement Be a Vital Part of Today's Reality

This book is an overview and presentation of the W/LS tools and concepts that we have and are currently using with our customers. In some ways the ***Working Agreement*** represents the opportunity for all of us to give visible evidence to ourselves and others that we are serious about implementing the W/LS AND test out our commitment to the notion that **" Managing is Everybody's Business."**

Whether we are at work or at home, it takes special effort to make visible the vital information that establishes where we see our selves in the future, where we are now, what it is going to take for us to realize our future, and how do we and others know that we are on course.

As we will discuss in the chapter on change, current habits can either help us or get in the way. When we are disciplined in the "art of visioning" and making those visions visible for ourselves and others, we open up the opportunity for synergy to occur.

Sharing our vital thoughts opens us up to comments that may or may not agree with us. The INVITATION to others must be real and open for feedback as an opportunity not a threat. As we also note in the change chapter, the decision is ours to let others influence us. Following the working guidelines helps keep the flow of useful information open and exhibits confidence in ourselves and in others.

When writing our own Working Agreements we have often resisted the process because we didn't like the output. This means that where we thought we were clear about where we were headed, when it was written down it didn't make a whole lot of sense. It is exasperating to know that we failed to practice, practice, and practice what we ask our customers to do to increase their effectiveness and efficiency. It is the old story, the tailor's kids go with worn out clothes, and the cobbler's kids without shoes.

THIS DOESN'T NEED TO BE THE RULE! We are in charge of our lives and are changing our habits of keeping the ***Working Agreement*** up to date. WHY? Because success still comes from the old fashioned way—we need to earn it. The discipline of following the principals of the ***Working Agreement*** pays off in performance.

Take up the HABIT of care and feeding of the ***Working Agreement.*** Stare it in the eye without wavering. Keep the picture clear. Keep it alive by celebrating the successes and handling the things that are getting in the way. Above all keep it visible. Remember, out of sight out of mind.

As we've stated before an idea doesn't care who has it as long as it is used. Imprint the basics of the ***Working Agreement*** in all aspects of life and using them will be as natural and real as breathing and other bodily functions.

If we are a one person family, business, or committee seek out a listening ear and share your ***Working Agreement.*** Sometimes just hearing our own story as well as seeing it greatly increases our retention and commitment to action.

As we have said before within 72 hours after we have heard something, we will retain only 2%. On the other hand if we talk about something, and do what we talk about, we have the possibility of retaining 85%+ within 72 hours. The ***Working Agreement*** is an opportunity to capture those vital few things that we want do and be in a way that increases the possibility of success.

The physical drafting of the ***Working Agreement*** takes on many forms and sequences. The individual, functional, and proposal ***Working Agreement*** all have different audiences. For some it is easier to start with the OVERVIEW, for others it is easier to start with VISIONS and BELIEFS.

For some people it is just difficult to get started period! There is the fear of writing! It is common knowledge that many people at ALL levels of the organization, years of education, ages, and experience just have difficulty composing the written word.

For some it is spelling, others its sentence construction and grammar, and others handwriting. We know of people who get cramps in their fingers holding the pencil so tight because of their fear of writing. We take all this pressure off the ***Working Agreement.*** Here is how we do it:

1. The ***Working Agreement*** is very friendly. It doesn't care whether every word is "speld properle or knot." It does want to make sure that everyone involved has understanding, acceptance and support. If grammar, spelling, and composition are an issue, delegate that out of a friend. In our case the word processor has a spell checker. We hit a button and it procedes to give us feedback options for spelling.

2. Many of us think out loud with others more frequently than we do with our selves (remember above the line and below the line?). We find it helpful to have another person capture our thoughts on an easel pad. This person acts as a scribe and may even help us formulate how to say what it is we want to say. This provides additional help for the dilemma of spelling, composition, and grammar.

3. Think of the ***Working Agreement*** as an ongoing discussion draft, constantly open to new information, review, and updating. IT IS FINISHED are three words Jesus uttered when he died on the cross. We don't want the ***Working Agreement*** to die. Keep in mind that it is a live, dynamic force for ensuring success, growth and prosperity. KEEP IT LOOSE—AND ACCURATE!

4. Keep it simple. Make sure it says what you want it to say in your own words. We don't worry about adverbs, adjectives, verbs, nouns, predicates, or dangling participles.

5. The only time a person needs to worry about exposure is if the exposure is illegal, immoral, or highly confidential. Fear of not having a meaningful job and clear assignment is resolved during the process of developing the ***Working Agreement,*** not documenting that in the ***Working Agreement.*** Keep in mind that if a job isn't meaningful, now there is common knowledge about that and the thing to do is get it resolved, pronto!

6. When the working climate is predominately one of valuing behavior, openness and trust, people willingly seek to help each other be successful. The W/LS principals and communication tools encourage behavior that respects the integrity of the individual. Taking personal responsibility to use them means that each of us is able to be in control of how we behave whether others do the same or not.

7. Remember the ***Working Agreement*** is a system that has a planned cycle to it. This cycle involves initiating the ***Working Agreement***, periodic sensing, tracking, through periodic and annual review and renewal. This cycle is an ongoing process of basic managing for all of us.

We believe that keeping the seven items listed above in mind takes the pressure off the ***Working Agreement*** and on our responsibilities to be clear about what we have been hired to do, the results expected, and how they are being measured.

The ***Working Agreement*** isn't designed to replace the job description, corporate business plan, or detailed work assignments. It is a quick ready, reference for the vital few elements that must be done, a glimpse into the future through personal and corporate visions, and a profile of our managing beliefs to increase our understanding about how we are working together.

Let's look at the elements of the ***Working Agreement*** from the cover page through annual review and renewal.

COVER PAGE

WORKING AGREEMENT

FOR:

POSITION TITLE:

DATE INITIATED:

REVISION DATE:

AGREED TO BY:

MANAGER:

GENERAL PROCESS COMMENTS

The initial ***Working Agreement*** is drafted by the employee, and a "discussion draft" is presented to the supervisor. The two discuss it, negotiate any changes following the W/LS principals, and gain UAS. (UNDERSTANDING, ACCEPTANCE, AND SUPPORT)

The final is signed by both parties. On many occasions the discussion draft is shared with peers within the department and among key "internal" associates who are impacted by the that person's work. This process gains the wisdom of others and helps to assure a common sense of priorities. UAS by those who are served adds value and commitment.

On occasion there are some elements of the ***Working Agreement*** that are of a personal and private performance nature. These situations are made as an addendum to the public ***Working Agreement*** and held in closed personnel files. The same may also be true for highly confidential company information for selected people on a need to know basis.

When people know their job, it takes from two hours to four hours to fill out the ***Working Agreement.*** We've seen it take three days for some executives to complete it because of the complexity and unclear UAS with their peers and supervisor. The tremendous value of doing the ***Working Agreement*** is obvious.

OVERVIEW

Consists of a set of descriptive statements that give a general overview of what the specific individual is hired to do:

- Begin with the phrase: "As (position title), responsible for:"

- Write a series of concise, bulleted statements (complete sentences are not needed) that clearly describe the major areas of responsibility.

This section describes the person's "turf" as he or she sees it in light of what the position description outlines and what specifically is brought to the job by the individual in addition to informal understandings unique to the relationship with the immediate supervisor.

This section is the broad mosaic of the person's job which on quick review provides individual identity and purpose within the context of the work of the unit, function, and enterprise. It differs from the position description in that it places the PERSON into the job vs the work into the job that could be generic to anyone filling it.

The magnitude of the job must be captured to include the vital elements. Where subordinates are involved, they must be able to find their piece of the action, in a broad way from the supervisors OVERVIEW. This ensures a tracking system of vital work throughout the enterprise from overall mission through execution at all levels. Areas to include: technical, supervisory, public relations, special committees, projects, advisory relationships, and the contribution toward working behavior.

The President's OVERVIEW generally covers the overall mission of the company. Subsequently everyone, at their level of responsibility, works to help carry that out. There are some things that everyone has a responsibility to work on and that is to work in valuing ways. This section is used as a tool to keep important work visible, not to cover all the foreseen and unforeseen duties as a self protection device for the individual and / or supervisor.

Developing the OVERVIEW, and for that matter the whole ***Working Agreement*** is an **ITERATIVE** approach. We discussed the iterative process in the MANAGING SYSTEM. ***Basically it means an ongoing process of developing and maintaining understanding, acceptance and support. (UAS).*** It is a "back and forth" dialogue that seeks clarity because meanings are in people not in words.

Many jobs have a more common broad general focus, like sales, on line assembly, clerical, secretarial, computer programmer, warehouse/ stock attendants, police officers, teachers, nautical chart technicians etc. Sometimes a like group will get together and mutually develop a basic overview and add their particular "place" into it. This still provides individuality plus a sense of continuity with multiple common jobs.

There are times when a blanket statement is made like "and other duties as assigned." When this occurs add the word "LIKE"and give some possible examples of those vital few possibilities.

FOCUS

The format for the FOCUS is:

This *Working Agreement* is for the period through , and focuses on!

Use bulleted statements which more specifically delineate what the VITAL FEW assigned elements are for this period of time. These statements are written as goals that are being accomplished or need to be accomplished. They describe the areas in which time, energy, physical, financial, and human resources are utilized to accomplish specific outputs. To write these goals consider the following:

- **Visualize what the situation is like once the goal is completed.** Consider how it feels to be successful at accomplishing that goal and living with that success.
- To help do this, review the chapter on change and KEEP IN MIND THAT FEELINGS ARE A VITAL PART OF DECISION MAKING. The stronger, more clear the visual picture, the better the possibility for anticipating success AND feeling confident about doing the work.
- Most tough situations are realistically dealt with when there is a clear sense of the benefits for handling it and a commitment to specific EXECUTION. How many times have we heard the statement "I know what to do, I've been through this before, but I just can't seem to get it done?" This lack of results is directly related to a lack of specific FOCUS!
  Here is an idea worth pursuing.

1. Take a pen, take a piece of paper, or word processor, and write down the beatable/achievable end results that are vital to the work.
2. Now that we have done that turn up our logical valve and describe what the situation looks like as specifically as possible, in technicolor if possible, who is involved, what they look like, how they feel, why it is beneficial, where it goes from here, and what our part of it is.
3. Now list how we FEEL about getting that job done. Worthwhile work promotes worthwhile feelings of satisfaction. When

work has a positive contribution toward accomplishing the identity and purpose of each person then productivity increases, possibilities happen, and **people/enterprises grow and prosper**.

What happens when there is little evidence of a contribution adding value to the individual and collective work? The obvious—boredom, waste, loss of energy, and a devaluing work environment. People say "I work here because I have to and I've too much time invested in this enterprise to start over."

Meaningful goals, desires, outcomes, expectations, targets have their source in meaningful work described in the overview and a working environment that fosters interdependence, trust, and job results.

The goals in the FOCUS section are divided into two categories: LEAD goals and DELEGATED goals. Let's look at them individually.

LEAD goals are the responsibility of the person making out this individual ***Working Agreement***. They reflect vital few work that requires direct initiative, time, energy, and commitment to accomplish as the primary source for end results. The buck stops here on this work, even though others may also be involved.

Personal accountability is seen as integral to the physical, financial, and psychological well being of the person with lead responsibility. This is where the specific division of labor takes on personal significance. That is why the time spent on this section is so critical, because it sets the stage for action.

Gaining UAS is critical with all people vitally involved in accomplishing LEAD GOALS. Notice the word VISION, in DIVISION. Where there is clear, exciting, realistic VISION in the division of labor, everyone wins.

DELEGATED goals are goals for which the individual who has some supervisory responsibility for others involves them to carry out the lead responsibility.

The trail of delegation from top management may include three or four different points of action for delegation before the assignment of LEAD responsibility takes place. THIS IS ONE OF THE PRIMARY REASONS FOR COMPLETING A ***WORKING AGREEMENT***—to insure tracking the vital few work, in a way that values peoples to get the job done with a minimum loss of UAS between the upper management level and final LEAD EXECUTION! REMEMBER—

MEANINGS ARE IN PEOPLE NOT IN WORDS.

List the goals with the same precision noted in the LEAD section. Seek UAS USING THE ITERATIVE PROCESS with the person to whom the work is being delegated. When UAS is achieved as mutually decided, add this to the delegated section under focus, and enter the person's name after the delegated goal. Obviously upper management will have more delegated work and less LEAD work. People without supervisory assignments will have only LEAD RESPONSIBILITY work, unless they are team project leaders.

It takes time to effectively delegate important work. Delegation requires critically following the WORKING GUIDELINES as a means for gaining UAS before the delegating is complete.

People receiving delegated work have a responsibility to regularly determine to what extent the delegated work matches their OVERVIEW. Sometimes, in the heat and flurry of crises, work is received in an effort to please a top manager who may not have in depth knowledge of a persons competency to carry out a "hot" assignment.

The working environment must foster the legitimate response by a person closer to the point of action to decline the job and steer the delegator to another delegatee. THE W/LS TOOLS AND PRINCIPALS CLEARLY PROVIDES HELP SO THAT THIS TYPE OF INTERCHANGE OCCURS WITH CREDIT TO BOTH PEOPLE.

Delegating is a two way street. There is an old adage that says sewage runs down hill, as does delegation. For years this had a lot of truth. Many times supervisors don't know what they want done so they delegate fertilization. When queried by the receiver the response is often "That's what I hired you for" or "Just do it." I will know what it looks like when I see your results." The sad point here is this is all too prevalent in today's work place. We should delegate with integrity, interdependence, humility, and knowledgeable risk. Enjoy the opportunity to iteratively ascertain the vital few work necessary to track people doing something right.

Conditions for success may be added in this FOCUS section as a means for highlighting those areas where interdependent work, sufficient physical and financial resources and timing factors dynamically impact the success of the work.

To add Conditions for Success, simply state them in bulletted form and the phrase "VISUALIZING WHAT IT IS LIKE WHEN........ " then itemize each condition describing the "when" situation.

For example: as conditions for success in our following this ***Working Agreement*** tool **we visualize our having a routine where we are updating our *Working Agreement,* sharing it with those who have**

a need to know, and are feeling confident about what we are hired to do, what results are expected, and how we are going to be measured and rewarded.

The conditions for success are having a routine for updating and sharing in a way that feels good to us, and that we feel confident about.

TASKS

Tasks represent the day to day work that will be done to accomplish the vital few goals. Each task must derive from one or more LEAD goals noted in the FOCUS section.

In some situations the present work documentation systems may satisfactorily accomplish all the elements in this TASK section. The important point here is THE ELEMENTS FOUND IN THIS SECTION MUST BE DONE WHETHER WE USE THIS EXACT FORMAT OR NOT!

We recommend that the following elements be used as a guide for outlining vital few work for formal tracking and sensing effort by individuals and supervisors. Keep in mind that the iterative process, UAS, working guidelines, and meanings are in people all apply here as well.

TASK STATEMENT

Tie in the outputs noted in the referenced goal. Sometimes the goals in the FOCUS section are numbered. This helps to tie in goals and tasks. There are times when one task may cover more than when goal. When that occurs, reference all the goals in the TASK statement.

ACTIVITY

In bulleted statements list the vital few primary work to be tracked. We may include time, quantity, quality, dollars, who, where, completion date. The importance here is to describe the overall elements that, when accomplished, will ensure success. On occasion there will be an activity which requires working on a particular behavior to get others involved and gain UAS. There may be a statement that says: Plan for implementation to be completed by— with UAS FROM——— and others. Another statement may say: The activities pertaining to financial review are ONGOING.

VALUE

This includes a description of the VALUE to the enterprise and to the individual. It answers why the work is being done, and gives credence to the goal established in the FOCUS section. It must be clear that this work is worth doing. Being clear about the OUTPUTS results in a clear understanding of value to the enterprise and the person. This information helps to decide wether or not the task is worthwhile. If it comes up short on value the work may have to be cancelled, expanded, delayed, or reassigned. Value to an individual reflects some of the primary sources of motivation resulting in a strong commitment to quality, cost, time, and productivity goals.

MEASUREMENT

Measurement must achieve UAS before the work starts. When this occurs it :

- helps to further clarify expectations for what is to be done, which decreases the incidence of unclear or misunderstood work assignments
- minimizes conflicts of understanding at appraisal time
- promotes confidence, fairness, and commitment to results.

A great deal of work is directed toward the intangible outcomes (improved working relationships, higher morale, increasing trust, gaining people's UAS) FOR WHICH JUDGEMENT IS SUBJECTIVE. Measuring the intangible is best done when people agree in advance what the criteria is. For intangible measurement the criteria can center on "evidence of" the desired outcomes occurring:

- through discussion with others (name some of them)
- through observation by the supervisor
- through feedback from those being served or affected
- through reports of feelings or value
- through comments of employees being measured

Objective measurement is preferred. It could be argued that if all the objective measurements are met within profit targets then the enterprise is successful. We know that may be true in the short run but human profitability must also be measured in turnover, burnout, sickness, accident, and general quality of work life. If this isn't done, sooner or later good people leave and the enterprise pays a residual price for someone else's short lived success.

Where is that guy who sold out our human resources for quick profit, left for a bigger job at another company and left us holding the bag? Measurement can be tangible, intangible, objective and subjective. Let's measure for long term success, to value all people, and track our growth and prosperity.

CONDITIONS FOR SUCCESS

Conditions for success may be entered here for the same reasons mentioned in the FOCUS section. They will help ensure the UAS for commitment to interdependent action and the need for upfront clarity of possible glitches.

PRIORITY (OPTIONAL)

This specifies the relative importance to the enterprise of doing the task. It could be said that all vital few work listed in the ***Working Agreement*** have priority. Why have this scale? We find that there are times when discerning between tasks helps gain UAS for what comes first when times are tough and resources scarce . Although all are important, the bucket is full of work and we must decide what isn't going to be done now. We recommend a simple 1-10 numeric scale to indicate priority

1—2—3: Important/urgent Some influence and control

4—5—6—7: Important/not urgent. High influence and control

8—9—10: Important/urgent. High influence and control

The influence and control refers to the individual's delegated parameters and conditions for success as noted above. There are times to state in the FOCUS section and the TASK section what isn't going to get done. This provides for common UAS for risk decisions. It also eliminates serious surprises about tough work that just wasn't done because of scarce resources. We all own that decision.

SORTING OUT AND PRIORITIZING

	Degree of Influence/Control		
	Virtually Complete Influence ↕ Control	Considerable Influence ↕ Some Control	Little Influence ↕ Virtually No Control
Urgent and Important ↔	A	A / B	C
Important and Less Urgent ↔	B / A	B	C
Less Important and Less Urgent ↔	C	C	C

EFFECTIVENESS

The evaluation of the work accomplished fills the "real time" performance element of the ***Working Agreement***, and is a cornerstone of a motivating performance appraisal process. We recommend a 12-point effectiveness rating scale:

(1—2)	(3—4)	(5—6—7—8)	(9—10)	(11—12)
PP	BSP	SP	ASP	OP

PP—Poor Performance
BSP—Below Standard Performance
SP—Standard Performance
ASP—Above Standard Performance
OP—Outstanding Performance

COMMENTS

This section provides room for both parties to document additional items of success and criticism without blame (CWB). Both are valuing ways to track continued performance.

VISION

Vision refers to an individual's look to the future, for self and for the enterprise. Refer back to the chapter on change and note that motivation is directly related to a person's vision of private life and work life direction. Everyone benefits when visions are identified and shared with others affected by our work. Visions promote:

- inspiration
- energy
- creativity
- excitement
- hope for the future

Visions are written in clear, short statements; avoid flowery prose. Visions can include:

- ideas for mid and long term plans
- ways to explore making a job, department, or enterprise more effective
- areas that cannot be addressed in the present ***Working Agreement***, but may be addressed in the future.

A vision section can be a source for future goals. As we see and experience it, MOST PEOPLE GO THROUGH LIFE RIDING ON OTHER PEOPLE'S VISIONS. When they start writing their own visions there is a fear. We have seen people actually break out in perspiration struggling to articulate realistic visions for the future. In some cases people have sat in silence to the point of tears rolling down their cheeks and stated **"I've followed so long I don't have a vision."** This happens at ALL LEVELS IN THE ENTERPRISE. Ask for help from another person to write as we think out loud about the future. Have some fun, spin a vision or two. As noted in the change chapter, the "Art of Visioning" is critical to all our growth and development. We have said before,**without visions the people parish**. So do enterprises.God has endowed us all with the wonderful opportunity to influence our own future. All we have to do is seek it out and accept this unconditional extravagance. (For us this additionally means our CHRISTIAN FAITH).

WORKING BELIEFS

Working beliefs, when shared, help others more easily understand what influences positive and less positive work behavior.

For example we believe "what we permit we promote"; therefore our behavior is assertive when we want to ensure that expense accounts are filled out on time, that we are on time for meetings, and that we value people in the ways we work with them.

Working beliefs can also convey to others a person's own preferred way of working with others. For example; a person might say "I don't jump into discussions quickly, because I believe I can express my ideas more clearly if I take time to think them through." Some beliefs set clear parameters for managing; Once again IBM's 3 basic beliefs:

- Respect for the integrity of the individual
- Striving for excellence in the quality of products
- Providing the best possible customer service

Beliefs like these that are shared by all members of an enterprise can become part of the culture of the enterprise. They can be "corporate beliefs".

The W/LS principals could be adopted as WORKING BELIEFS. Once they are a part of the fiber of everyday work they become an integral part of work behavior. Review the working guidelines, the change chapter, the managing system and the information system. The entire W/LS is loaded with ideas about working beliefs that promote a healthy quality of work life.

Working beliefs should be written as clear concise statements. Writing beliefs is a meaningful event where people discover more about themselves and about others as these beliefs are shared in a group session with work associates.

During the sharing sessions people routinely say they learned new things about each other. they often think of ways to help each other understand why things go well sometimes and not others. As a result of sharing their past beliefs.

Writing beliefs is a very rewarding experience when we seek out help from others to articulate what we have in mind. This mutual thinking out loud and writing effort yields opportunities for planned change and feedback that increases our batting averages for improving the sharing of useful information.

TRACKING

The ***Working Agreement*** provides a responsible way for tracking the "vital few" work elements as well as the trivial mandatory items that are important and must be done as a part of the day-to-day work.

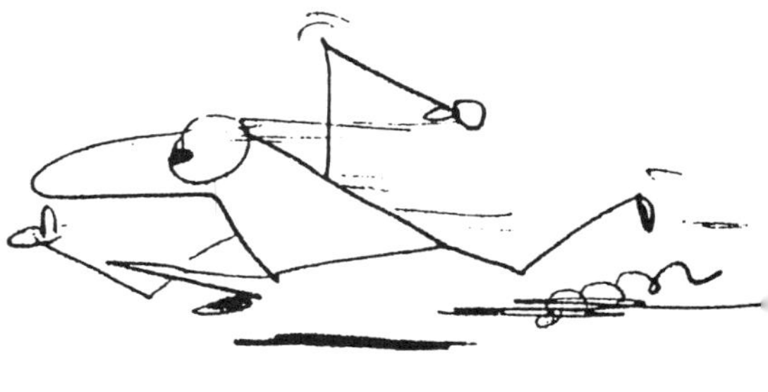

It takes discipline to set aside time for follow up, especially when schedules are full and people have additional tasks of their own to accomplish for their upper level supervisor. The delegated tasks seem a little further away when tough issues are chewing on the supervisor regarding lead responsibilities in need of immediate attention.

Tracking refers to a more formal way of keeping in touch with progress once there is "UAS" FOR THE WORK TO BE DONE. There are many ways for developing "tickler files" that insure follow up. Some of the simple ones are:

- Post notes as a reminder in the daily and monthly calendar.

- Establish schedules for review, weekly, monthly, and / or quarterly depending on the situation with each individual and the risks involved with their work.

- Note on word a processing calendar that flashes critical review meetings.

- Assistance from support services like administrative assistants, secretaries, and personnel for formal reviews.

Tracking will continue to occur to the extent that this function is seen as a vital part of every supervisor's responsibility. This is helped when the tracking:

- Focuses on vital few work.

- Allows for ongoing re-evaluation of work priorities.

- Provides opportunities to add, modify, or delete tasks, commensurate with changing situations.

- Insures ongoing appraisal of work as it is completed.

Tracking means valuing people for the work they are doing by showing interest in their progress in a manner that searches for what they are doing right and gives CRITICISM WITHOUT BLAME. It is an opportunity to "validate" those things that are going well as close as possible to the time they occur.

For tracking to be truly successful it is necessary to visualize people as succeeding in doing the vital few work. Assisting them is the supervisor's job. One way of doing this is formal tracking which builds confidence because people know they are a part of a team and have help available.

SENSING

Sensing is the work that follows a more informal effort . Sensing seeks understanding of how things are going in general, and includes looking at the trivial many, trivial mandatory, and the vital few. It is a way of letting people know that they are important without having a predetermined agenda or time schedule.

One form of sensing is to find out in more detail what people are working on at that time, and how they feel about their work, the enterprise, and their future. This is an open effort to get to know people at all levels.

There are times when people will bring up problems. It is important to ask enough questions about the situation and understand to what extent the person feels someone is handling the problem already. If not, have them bring it to the attention of their supervisor and give the supervisor the first chance to handle it. If they feel that no one is willing to handle it then let them know that additional people will get involved with that supervisor as an opportunity to help.

Finding things that are not going well is a common activity of sensing. The important point here is to work at valuing people at all levels and show how problems can be handled interdependently without resorting to devaluing behavior (pinning blame, etc).

Sensing provides an opportunity for people to "see" each other at a more personal level. There are no heavy agendas. Friendly conversation where both people are sharing things that are going well and are sharing things that are of concern builds a more solid ground for times when tough issues need to be handled.

As stated before both sensing and tracking are a part of formal performance review and appraisal. The effort of tracking and sensing gathers useful information for reviewing our own performance as well as that of others, whether we work for them, they for us, or we work together as peers.

PERFORMANCE REVIEW AND APPRAISAL

Performance review means taking time to give feedback to a person on the results of assigned work in both tangible and intangible categories. This review becomes meaningful when:

- There are previously UAS specific results that tie products and services to internal and external customers.
- Tracking and sensing functions are routinely carried out with the "spirit of intent" to catch people at doing something right.
- CRITICISM WITHOUT BLAME is the normal process for helping a situation move from unsatisfactory to satisfactory and beyond.
- The performance review is seen as a mutual responsibility of all people including peer, subordinate, supervisor, and self.
- The person performing the review seeks useful information from sources other than this one person's experience. A supervisor should seek information from the people being served; a subordinate should check out the experiences of others with that same supervisor; peers should check with others and, as an individual looking at my own work, I should check it out with others before making a final "judgement" on my performance.
- Validation is a vital part of celebrating the work that has met the requirements.
- The timing of the review is planned to provide opportunity for both people to prepare to give feedback on things that should continue happening and things that should be done differently.
- The location is private and convenient with easel and/or white board for sharing more complicated issues.

- The process includes following the working guidelines, valuing behavior, the SEA decision making process, and a commitment to future direction, target dates, conditions for success, and rewards for successful results.

- The ***Working Agreement*** is revised with UAS for the next focus period.

- Subordinates are given help with ways to communicate clearly with their supervisors, peers and self evaluation. The W/LS tools provide this type of help. Sometimes people may act as a sounding board to help employees articulate their situation in very critical situations before the formal review with a supervisor. In this case personnel people are acting as a consultant.

- Everyone remembers that there are four levels of information: Data, perception, interpretation, and evaluation. During the review all levels are in the realm of useful information.

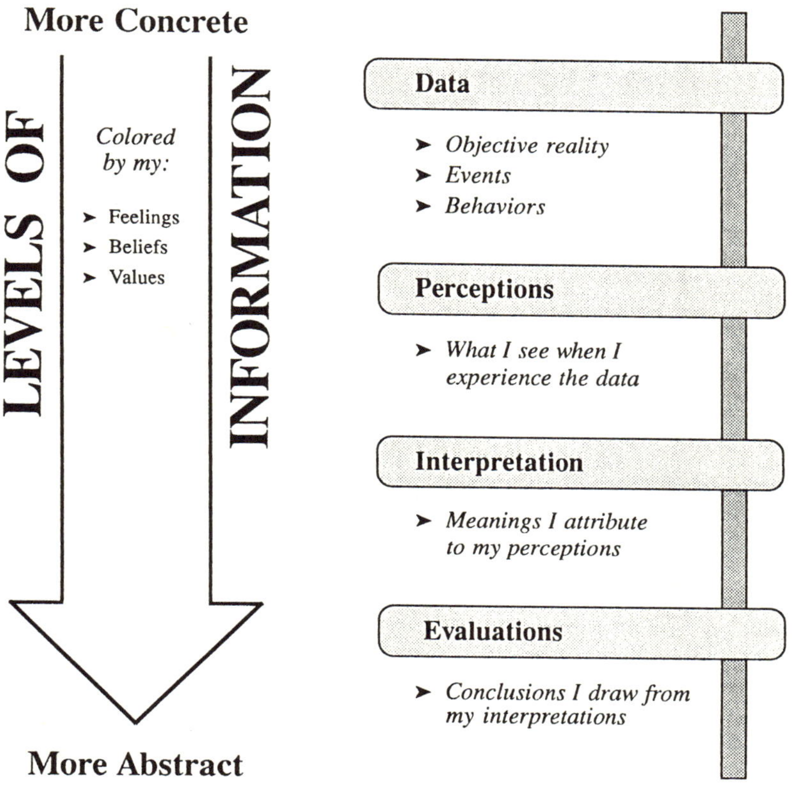

The formal performance review process includes an assessment of the person's combined effectiveness at the time of this review. For some enterprises there are five categories which serve as the APPRAISAL evaluation for this period of work. They are:

- OUTSTANDING PERFORMANCE (OP): Performance exceeds the requirements of the ***Working Agreement*** by a significant margin on a regular and consistent basis. Verification of this is confirmed by peers of the subordinate, peers of the supervisor rating the subordinate, and the supervisor's next level manager.

- ABOVE STANDARD PERFORMANCE (ASP): Performance often exceeds some of the requirements for the ***Working Agreement***,and is intermittently performing satisfactory on others.

- STANDARD PERFORMANCE (SP): Performance is satisfactorily according to the ***Working Agreement***.

- BELOW STANDARD PERFORMANCE (BSP): Performance is inconsistent according to the ***Working Agreement***, below minimum standards. CWB is given with a clear UAS FOR A PLAN TO IMPROVE CONSISTENTLY within a specified period.

- POOR PERFORMANCE (PP): Performance is unsatisfactory, CWB and the related plan are in effect with little evidence of improvement, the person is on probation with job in jeopardy.

These five categories are used to determine an individual's eligibility for merit increases, cost of living increases, bonuses, promotion, continuing and future employment. The process used to determine these ratings varies and so do the forms used to maintain some sense of continuity throughout the enterprise.

The ***Working Agreement*** provides a standard for defining the vital few work, conditions for success, and specific tasks in the more complicated work. It may also provide an opportunity to have some elements that are generic to all work that provides input to complete the APPRAISAL portion of the performance review. For example:

EMPLOYEE PERFORMANCE SUMMARY FOR THE PERIOD:

- Met the conditions for success required by associates for the team to accomplish its goals as well as own ***Working Agreement*** goals.

Comments

- Routinely works at valuing people, giving CWB, follows the working guidelines, and shares useful information as evidenced by:

Comments

WORKING AGREEMENT OVERALL APPRAISAL RATING

(1—2)	(3—4)	(5—6—7—8)	(9—10)	(11—12)
PP	BSP	SP	ASP	OP

SUPERVISOR'S ASSESSMENT OF EMPLOYEE

- Specific things to continue doing:

- Specifically things to do differently:

- Development needs and plans for improvement:

EMPLOYEE'S ASSESSMENT OF SUPERVISOR

- Specific things to continue doing:

- Specific things to do differently:

- Development needs and plans for keeping employee informed

CAREER PLANS:

Employee capacity and potential for advancement:

- Possible next assignment

- Preparation necessary for advancement

- Range and limits of the present assignment

Revised ***Working Agreement*** by————, based on this formal performance review.

- Employee Acknowledgement

- 1st Level Supervisor

- Reviewed by 2nd Level Supervisor

- Date of next review

Performance review and appraisal time are critical functions of every supervisor. Successful supervisors are pleased when the time for formal appraisal occurs. They have prepared for this time of celebration. They are able to celebrate because:

- There are no surprises for either the subordinate or themselves.
- Review has been an ongoing process of **serving** the subordinate, helping success occur even in tough times.
- Useful information is gathered from sources throughout the employees realm of influence and is helpful in determining a fair, clear, and meaningful review.
- The subordinate has routinely offered feedback during this performance period, and there is **vision congruence** on what is being done and what needs to be done.
- The corporate goals are being met and they have a vital part in formally preparing to meet those of the future as they update and renew the subordinates ***Working Agreement.***

It is important to help supervisors prepare for formal performance reviews. The supervisor's manager should "dry run" a review before it is given to the subordinate. After there is evidence of real success, the supervisor's manager should get a chance to review the written review before it is formally given—even if a dry run isn't necessary.

CONSISTENCY,
FAIRNESS, and
ACCURACY are significant attributes when evaluating performance. All too often managers fail to bite the bullet in formal performance reviews and problems continue year after year.

We routinely run into people problems only one supervisor leaves and another takes over a tough situation to discover mediocrity is rewarded with "exceeds requirements" appraisal ratings.

We also find the distribution of "exceeds requirements" and "outstanding" light years out of proportion to the actual accomplishments. Part of this is due to the lack of job definition.

Working Agreements quickly spell out who knows what their job is and whether or not they are able to do it.

Let's face it, supervisors are responsible for verifying work accomplishment per plan. When an enterprise is profitable, growing, and prospering with people who look forward to coming to work,

THEN EVERYONE HAS FUN AT APPRAISAL TIME
AND WELL DESERVED IT IS!

This overview of PERFORMANCE REVIEW and APPRAISAL is always supplemented with the principles of the W/LS. The chapter on change clearly points out the need to consider habits, memories, beliefs, and labeling as positive tools for influencing both strengths and developing ways of doing things differently.

Valuing people is critical when an appraisal of less than satisfactory has future financial and career limiting implications . Change works best when there is a mutually UAS common base of current performance and future opportunities.

There are times when people's behavior prevents obtaining a common UAS. When these situations occur, seek out a neutral person to listen to each side and reflect what is being said. Remember a whole lot of conflict is due to misunderstanding.

SEEK UNDERSTANDING FIRST

then decide what the next steps should be.

On occasion, even this doesn't work. Then decisions need to be made about continuing to work together or not work together. The consequences vary for both people depending on the issue. The key point here is to

RESOLVE THE SITUATION IN A VALUING WAY.

Finding fault and pinning blame accomplishes absolutely nothing. Making a change to a more productive working climate helps all parties including the enterprise.

Finally, PERFORMANCE REVIEW and APPRAISAL culminates the best of managing on all our parts, whether we are supervisors of others or not. This face to face event where we share our honest thoughts, feelings and evaluation is worth every bit of our effort to make it a real opportunity to celebrate and enjoy.

GO IN PEACE AND SERVE EACH OTHER

The ***Working Agreement*** format and operating principles have a number of additional uses. We use the ***Working Agreement*** for writing PROPOSALS to our clients, as a means for doing special PROJECTS like writing this book, and as an ongoing FUNCTION like marketing and sales where similar work is done by many different people. Let's look at each of these three uses PROPOSAL, PROJECT, AND FUNCTION individually:

PROJECT WORKING AGREEMENT

- Project Working Agreements have a specific purpose involving other people in a direct reporting relationship to a project leader.

- The people on the project may already work for the leader, may be from a different department, may work part time under either condition.

- Each person must see their work in the overview of the project leader. The project leader's ***Working Agreement*** is the controlling document. All project work tracks back to this position.

- The project leader gains UAS with both the person working on the project and the person's supervisor. The results of the individual's work becomes a part of the supervisor's input during formal performance review and appraisal. The project leader provides a formal performance review and appraisal after the project is complete. There are times when a project is long and an interim review is necessary. This interm revies added to the person's annual review (or whatever the period may be).

- Each individual fills out a ***Working Agreement*** for this project just as indicated in the "Individual" ***Working Agreement***.

- The ***Working Agreements*** are shared throughout the project and with key interface people. Gaining UAS increases the possibilities for success and minimizes the we/they behavior that so often develops with "special project" work.

PROPOSAL WORKING AGREEMENTS

Proposal Working Agreements:

- Have the same format as the other ***Working Agreements*** and are filled out by an individual, team, or it could be as we use it by our company to the client.

- Are generally a discussion draft that recognizes the real need for "thinking out loud" during the initial stages of UAS. The clearer the beginning the more probable the opportunity to succeed.

- Differ from a project ***Working Agreements*** in their starting point. Internal discussion on work generally becomes a project, where people external to a unit needing the help make recommendations via a proposal which then becomes part of the project.

FUNCTIONAL WORKING AGREEMENTS

Functional Working Agreements use the same format as the others and have:

- A focus on like work among others. eg. sales
- Generally are developed in plenary working sessions where all participants give their input and gain UAS.
- Individuality in geographic area, quotas, products, and their own visions and beliefs.
- Are supported by additional detail work documents like routings, policies, technical project direction, and procedures.

Keep in mind that the principles of the ***Working Agreement*** are the critical elements, **not the format.** Wherever these principles are followed with discipline, integrity and hard work the individual gains, the team is successful and the enterprise grows, is profitable and prospers.

Part III

CHANGE

A Personal & Organizational Challenge

Part III

CHANGE: A Personal and Organizational Challenge

"For I am the Lord, I change not...."
—Malachi 3:6

One way at looking at successful change is to view it as based on implementing our good decisions, overcoming our poor ones, and establishing a reserve (financial-psychic) from our good ones in order to feed more good opportunities for change. Under no circumstances should we feed a poor decision from the good reserve bucket. That would be like eating the seed corn instead of planting it.

Chapter 13 focuses on "Managing Change is Everybody's Business." It provides a common format for understanding some major opportunities and barriers to individual and organizational change. It takes a look at:

- **How our past, present, and future contribute to helping or hurting us as interdependent phases of our life**
- **How labeling people affects productivity**
- **How habits, help us, or get in the way of our effectiveness**
- **How we are in charge of our memories, our own private mental computer storage system where random access to useful information is really our choice.**
- **How beliefs, both organizational and personal, affect getting the job done to everyone's advantage or disadvantage depending on our own choice**
- **How positive visions, provide hope, excitement and energy but, negative visions eat up most of the available energy**
- **How creative tension, acts as an approach toward ensuring change.**
- **Why dysfunctional tension, is the environment where most of the people are living today.**

Chapter 14 focuses on *"Work/Life* Approaches To Managing Change." One of the underlying principles is the importance of GATHERING USEFUL INFORMATION for implementing meaningful change.

We believe that the cost and effort for change must be less than the benefit for the change to be worthwhile. Useful information minimizes uncertainty. Uncertainty feeds resistance, but we believe people resist changing primarily because they lack enough useful information from which they can make a reasonable decision.

There are six elements in the information gathering cycle:

- **Determine the situation**
- **Gather information**
- **Diagnose the situation**
- **Gain UAS on the plan**
- **Implement the plan**
- **Evaluate the plan**

Each of these areas requires discipline and attention to detail for maximum effectiveness. When people "skim" through these six areas, they set others up for failure. Many top executives fail because they SKIM through complicated reports requiring their best judgement. That's like deciding to do heart surgery after taking someone's pulse and feeling under their arm pits to see if they are sweating.

The executive problem is compounded because in all probability their vice presidents do the same thing (with the exception that they probably put a stethoscope near the heart to hear any irregularities.) Just think of all the time, money, and "canned" executives wasted because these six areas weren't covered in sequence.

The techniques for gathering information have an important role in the success of implementing and evaluating change. We also include some guidelines for analyzing and giving feedback based on the information gathering techniques.

We all live with our own "change activities" and those of others. We also live with some things that are not what we'd like to see, but aren't worth moving in on. For some of us we have to "roll" with whatever is "coming down" or get a different job. The point here is we do something about those things where we have influence and control.

We cover gathering information through:

- Committee, where practicing the working guidelines gets a real workout

- Questionnaires, where confidentiality and anonymity are sometimes crucial and the results can be measured over time. Sometimes we state up front that the results will not be held confidential

- Interviews, how to do them, and avoid doing someone else's agenda

- Document reviews, hard labor or astute detective work for good or bad.

Chapter 13

Managing Change is Everbody's Business

Chapter 13

Managing Change is Everbody's Business

If you really change your ways and your actions and deal with each other justly....
–Jeremiah 7:5

Change is inevitable! We shouldn't fear change. It is with us every day The extent to which each of us becomes involved in or is impacted by external changes in society or changes in our personal/work lives depends on how we view

1) the past
2) the future
3) our present situation.

In this chapter we focus on all three. Our primary emphasis will be on the work situation, although we also recognize that separating work life from private life is nearly impossible.

When we go to work, we take our private self with us. If there are good happenings at home this will have a more positive influence on our work efforts. The reverse is also true. There have been times when the work situation was so hectic that we needed to declare some "down time" to the family before we could pick up our part of that responsibility. We feel that acknowledging the fact that **one part of our life is impacting the other,** without dumping or supplying information that was not useful to others, is a mature way of managing the interdependence of private and work life.

Change at work does impact our private lives. Let's not ignore it. The ideas we will be sharing here are readily translated into' the private life arena.

In most work situations, the process of change is accelerating, jobs are changing, and the basic processes or ways of doing business are in a dynamic state of flux. Most people, when pressed, will acknowledge the need for changing some of the ways that they manage or carry out their work. In this context, we have some choices about how to view change:

- We can see change as the "enemy." It is defeating us.

- We can accept that change is necessary, but "not during our tour of duty."

- We can acquiesce to change and try to ignore or deny its impact.

- We can see change as being full of possibilities; we can deal with it, influence it, and manage it.

We believe that in order for organizations to effectively manage change, the people involved must have a commonly held framework of the change process. This chapter offers a useful framework for change and provides some specific suggestions for how to overcome obstacles to change and for managing the kinds of changes we want in our organization.

The change framework is based on the following idea:

CHANGE IS MAINTAINING CONTINUITY WITH THE PAST AS WE MOVE INTO THE FUTURE.

This view is based on several assumptions and principles to which we are committed :

- Social, political, technological, and economic factors that affect an enterprise and its ability to conduct its business are all constantly changing, making it necessary to continually evaluate the appropriateness and effectiveness of our current methods of doing things.

- Of all the ways that an organization has conducted business up to the present (e. g., policies, practices, procedures, production methods, plans, tools, equipment, ways of organizing, attitudes, behaviors, management philosophies, and so forth) there are those elements that:

    a. No longer serve the business in light of changing circumstances and should be dropped

    b. Are no longer effective as practiced (or may never have been) and need to be done differently; or

    c. Have been effective and will probably continue to be effective in the foreseeable future. These are the things to continue doing.

- There are new challenges facing any organization which require dropping some existing practices in order to make room for new ways of meeting those challenges.

- Things happen only in the present. The past is already gone, and the future never comes. Therefore, in order to be useful, any reference to the past or to the future must be couched in terms of its relevance to the present. Brooding about some event that happened in the past usually results in getting stuck and seldom produces any valuable outcomes. Similarly, idle fantasizing about the future can be at best a waste of time and at worst a source of frustration.

    Does this mean that we should ignore the past, eliminate planning for the future, and live wholly for the present? Quite the contrary, an orientation to the past and to the future can be very useful in determining how to function most effectively in the present.

- **By committing specific time in the present to establishing direction for the future, we manage change as opposed to having it happen to us!**

    In fact, this entire book is about effectively managing change. We will find people to whom some of these ideas are familiar, others less so, and some new. In the past ten years we have had a lot of feedback that said the way we have introduced the familiar, less familiar and new is unique and very helpful.

Take time to review all the chapters. Based on the reactions of many satisfied customers, we believe this will be a very valuable tool for influencing change in peoples lives.

FIVE RESIDUES OF THE PAST AND HOW THEY AFFECT CHANGE: HABITS, MEMORIES, LABELS, VISIONS AND BELIEFS

Among the many things that affect change, we have found five critical elements that affect people's ability to make change in their work or personal situations: habits, memory, labels, visions and beliefs. We'll discuss each of these and how they can affect change both positively and negatively.

HABITS

Habits are ways of behaving or doing things that were chosen at first, but through repetition and practice have become almost "automatic." For many of our habits, we are frequently not even aware of doing them. For example, if you wear trousers, which leg is put on first when getting dressed? Do we always sit in the same place at the dinner table? Why? Here are a couple of other examples of habits:

- A number of years ago we repeatedly used the words "you know" in conversation. One of our peers called it to our attention as being unnecessary when talking to him. He agreed to help us by calling it to our attention when he heard it. We asked others to also help, and within a few months, we had broken the habit.

- When dealing with people in tough situations, we have a habit of using an easel, or at least a sheet of paper to write down the critical elements and to keep checking out our data, perceptions, interpretations, and evaluations. This is a very useful habit to us , and we intend to continue using it. Writing information down helps us improve our communications and achieve commitment from others that lasts.

- Eating is a habit we love; it is also a habit that has many negative aspects for us. When we are in a hurry, eating is not an issue for us. But when we slow down, a peanut butter sandwich and a half dozen cookies disappear like butter on a hot griddle.

This kind of habit has made millions of dollars for people in the diet and weight loss business.

Habits are not necessarily bad. In fact, as illustrated above, many habits are very positive and serve us well. WHAT ARE SOME EXAMPLES OF POSITIVE AND NEGATIVE HABITS? As a first cut, we suggest the following steps to begin to identify what habits are and decide which, if any, should be changed. Later in the chapter, we offer some more specific, practical steps for changing undesirable or unwanted habits or ways of doing things.

1. Make a written inventory of those habits you have that affect health (physical, mental, emotional, spiritual) or the ways people work and/or play with others.

2. Enlist the help of one or more people to check out their perceptions of those habits (particularly those that affect them).

3 Decide what can be done to build on your good habits and/or change the more important "negative" ones.

4. Decide where help is needed from others and ask for that help.

Habits can be real obstacles to an effective change process. First, they are not that easy to change. Some of us spend many years practicing and using our habits. It takes discipline to change the more entrenched ones.

Second, even though we may have excellent intentions and be making progress in changing some negative habits, when the going gets tough, we tend to fall back on our habitual ways of responding.

For example, members of a management team were working to change the typically negative ways they worked with each other in team meetings (put-downs, ignoring each other, interrupting the speaker, ridiculing others' ideas, etc.). Things went along fine until they came to a difficult discussion about allocating scarce budget dollars. At this point, they slipped back into their old habitual ways of dealing with one another.

MEMORIES

By "memories" we mean those experiences we've had in the past that:

- We still "remember."
- Still influence our actions.

We put "remember" in quotes, because what we remember is almost always wrong, that is, it bears little resemblance to the actual events that occurred. We distort and construct our memories to justify or rationalize our behavior in the present. For example:

Years ago it was the custom to make a major purchase of a piece of property with only a handshake. Now many states have enacted a law that allows a three day waiting period for the buyer to reject the deal. This was done to offset the skills of "high pressure sales" and to make sure the person knows what the deal is about. The deal must be in writing. Any unsigned changes void the deal. The "in writing" was to help people remember what the agreement was. Even today people will sue based on their own perception, interpretation, and evaluation of what is written. Where money is involved, get it in writing because there is overwhelming evidence of MEMORY FAILURE if the deal goes sour.

Just as for habits, memories can be positive or negative. Many of our negative memories come from situations in which we have felt hurt, rejected, deceived, defeated, or otherwise mistreated by others. When, in our work, we find people who are at odds with one another, we gather information to find out what is behind their differences. Many times, the real cause goes back to something that happened 1 year, 5 years, even 10 years ago. The current memory of that past situation maintains distrust and causes people to conclude, "get me once, shame on you; get me twice, shame on me!" The desire then is to get revenge or retribution, and people behave in defensive or even combative ways.

Here are some more examples of how memories affect our actions:

- Forty-five years ago, I sat behind a student in grade school who had an offensive body odor. For nine months, I felt like I was suffocating. Even today, I'm very sensitive to negative body odors. Based on this memory, I have developed some worthwhile personal hygiene habits. Furthermore, when we run into managers who have to deal with people with body odor problems (it happens more frequently than one might expect!), we encourage them to deal with it using "criticism without blame," which is described in this book.

- A group of executives was reviewing candidates for a top level job which involved a good deal of exposure to the public. One of the candidates came close to losing out because one of the executives in the group had had a bad experience with the candidate's wife, who sold real estate and was very aggressive. When asked how long ago this had occurred, the answer was 7 years. Further analysis showed that the wife had been out of real estate for at least 5 years and that the candidate no longer lived in the same area.

- Sometimes so called "good" memories can backfire on us. For example, some people are selected for jobs because they remind the boss of someone else who was a top performer in the same job. In all too many cases, the new person doesn't meet expectations.

The essence of the memory phenomenon is captured in the one-liner, "you never get a second chance at a first impression." Think about that. If our experience with you has been great the first time, in all likelihood, we will at least be open to you the next time we get together. If our experience with you hasn't been great the first time, how open will we be next time? This premature closure on people has caused us a lot of unnecessary sadness and loss of effectiveness in our work.

So, what can be done about memories that are getting in the way? Here are some ideas:

- Once again, take an inventory of those situations where conflict exists and ask why. Be tough on yourself and continue asking why. If it is still unclear, think back about similar people or situations. Are there continuing unfavorable memories about this or a similar person or situation that get in the way of seeing how things are now? It's surprising how many "ah-hah's" occur.

- Invite someone to listen and ask questions. Often, another person can challenge us when we are not being totally honest with ourselves.

- Write down the significant incidents or situations.

- Keep this search simple. We're not engaged in psychoanalysis here!

- Where we find that memories of the past are preventing us from working with someone or some situation, ask ourselves, "what the risk if we set this memory aside and look at the person or situation with a new openness?" Remember, the memories that we still carry can become self-fulfilling prophesies.

- Be prepared for some surprises when we set our negative memories aside.

LABELS

Labels are words or phrases that are used to describe people and their actions. Since labels are usually placed on boxes, we have found that people like to place themselves as well as others in boxes and label them as a convenient way to sort out what is good and not so good about themselves or others. Labeling is a strong part of our culture. We use labels for many reasons, some of which are helpful in a true sense, but many of which actually prevent us from working effectively with other people. Here are some of the ways labels are used:

1. To distinguish people by virtue of their race, ethnic group, creed, religion, political persuasion, or other characteristics. These labels are usually used to maintain stereotypes (generally untrue pictures of what people in a particular category are like), that we use to justify or rationalize our behavior toward them. Doing so blocks our ability to see and value the uniqueness of each individual.

2. To express humor (usually put-down), rumor, innuendo, or anger and therefore to avoid taking responsibility for clear communication. For example, "He's an engineer, and we all know what kind of people they are."

3. To save time in dealing with people. For example, we know an executive who classifies people into three categories:

a) "Top Dogs"—those people who are the real winners, like us.

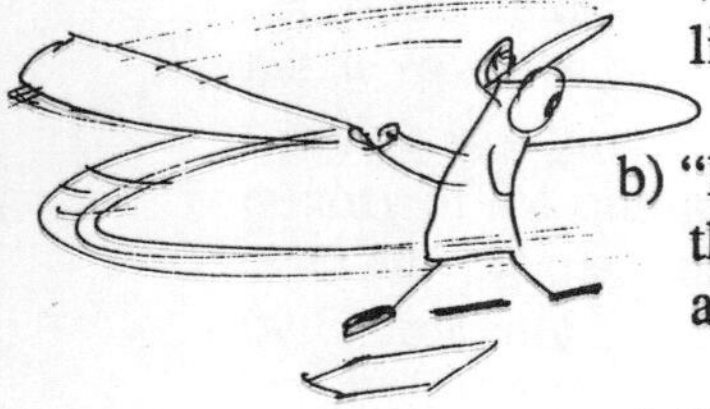

b) "Hard Hitters"—those who get things done, but make a few mistakes.

c) "Weak-Kneed Suckers" —those who are there to do the bidding of others, but who could not manage their own way out of a brown paper bag!

With very little information, he classifies people into one of these categories. How would we like to live with and/or work around a person who puts people into these boxes?

4. To aid in working more effectively with people. This approach has even been formalized and legitimized "scientifically." Today there are many standardized instruments on the market that profess to measuring traits or behavior patterns for individuals. A typical process for a company is to have each employee complete one of the standardized forms and produce a "profile" that defines his or her type. Then, people who work together learn one another's types and how to deal with people who are of each type. To the extent that this process helps people understand themselves and others, it can be useful. However, all too often, the types become labels with which people keep one another in boxes and provide excuses for ineffective behavior.

5. For venting. This process usually produces labels that focus on one's intelligence, family, physical characteristics, attitudes, and behavior (e.g., "what a jerk!"; "only a nerd would do something like that"; "she's really a porker.")

Think about the many different people that we must face each day in our personal and work life. What labels have we placed on our associates? In what type of box do we have each of them? If it is a "good" box, how willing are we to let them make a mistake and grow?

What about the people we have placed in "not so good" boxes? What chance do they have of improving in our eyes? Years ago, someone gave us the following formula for making up for a past mistake:

IT TAKES FIVE "ATTA-BOYS"
TO MAKE UP FOR ONE "AW-SHUCKS"

Based on this, we visualize people carrying tally sheets around to keep track of the atta-boy/awe-shucks ratios on all the boxes. What a terrible waste of time.

The real challenge is to clean out our storage bins and be open to the precious new information that will help people succeed at changing themselves and their work.

One more thing about labels: One of the most pervasive and destructive labels is the use of negative self-labels. These can have a significant impact on our own level of success and how we work with others.

We have found many people in management positions who say, "I'm not a manager; I'm here because it's the best way to get promoted." Others say things like, "I'm only an accountant, not a manager," or, "I'm only a secretary." These "I'm only" and "I am not" labels become self-fulfilling prophesies and real barriers to change.

Let's take a look at how personal labeling can affect success in keeping weight off, which seems to occupy a lot of time in our society:

> Like many people, we work at keeping extra weight off our frame. Our early attempts included the pig on the refrigerator. That didn't work, so we added heavy people cartoons. When that failed, we tried some of the well known group plans. We travel a lot, so we didn't make the meetings, and they didn't work. Finally, we decided that what we really needed was to have some successes.
>
> The answer was to keep it simple. Every time we talked ourselves out of those extra helpings and deserts, we celebrated a success, and the process has worked. When we labeled ourselves with the refrigerator pig, the fat cartoons, and special diet groups, we had a negative self-image and a corresponding failure at losing weight. By celebrating our specific, small, do-able successes, we saw ourselves as in charge and heading in a positive direction.

What can we do about labeling ourselves and others? Consider the following:

- Inventory our stock of labels for ourself and for the people who we most frequently label. How much overlap is there?

- Be aware of the "impossible task" syndrome, which is characterized by labels such as, "We are only a ________," or, "she can't possibly do that; she's not ________." Look instead for opportunities for manageable successes and celebrate them.

- Routinely ask those with whom we associate for help. When we slip, be open to a gentle reminder from them.

HABITS, MEMORIES, and LABELS are three residues of the past that affect our efforts to look into the future, and have a strong impact on how we go about doing our work today. While they can certainly be helpful to us, we all too often use them destructively. Here is something to keep in mind: THE ONLY WAY THE PAST CAN LIVE IN THE PRESENT IS IF YOU KEEP IT ALIVE. ***Decide which habits, memories and labels serve us and others and use them.*** For those that get in the way of our being as effective as we would like to be, do what we can to change them. It's worth the investment.

THE POWER OF VISION IN BRINGING ABOUT CHANGE

We've talked about some residues of the past that affect our ability to be effective, and now we turn to the future. Just as for the past, our orientation to the future profoundly affects our current experiences and accomplishments. In organizations, we find many instances where there is very little hope, excitement, and energy on the part of employees at all levels. Motivation in these cases is reduced to the extrinsic level of showing up and doing what one needs to do in order to assure continuing employment and a corresponding paycheck. Inspiration and creativity are at a minimum.

Missing in most of these cases are VISIONS for the future. Visions are pictures, images, or descriptions of preferred futures that

1) are rooted in our beliefs and values
2) build energy, hope, excitement, and inspiration.

A notable public example of the inspirational power of vision is President John F. Kennedy's speech to the nation about landing a man on the moon and returning him home safely by the end of the 1960's decade . This vision galvanized the creative energy of the nation and inspired the program that led to the Apollo explorations.

Most people go through life riding on the visions of other people. Many times, they are saddled to visions that they really don't understand, or if they do, they have very little commitment to them. When we interview people in our work, we frequently ask people to share their visions for themselves and for the organization. For many people, this is a very difficult question; they don't have an answer. One executive said it in a sadly profound way, "I've been following so long, I don't have visions for myself or for the company."

Check out our own commitment to our visions. Ask ourself,

- When was the last time we really got excited about our work?
- Why were we excited?
- What can we do to make sure it stays that way?"

We will probably discover some opportunities to change either what you are doing, how we do what we are doing, or how we think or feel about what we are doing.

The Bible says, "without vision, the people perish." We know that this is ultimately true for business as well. We have seen many individuals who are working at jobs which challenge only 10 to 15 percent of their capabilities, let alone their potential. Their very physical beings reflect this loss of power. While listening to them, we find disgruntlement, anger, hopelessness, and apathy.

- What is the cost to their employer?
- to their family?
- to themselves?
- What is the cost to us as a part of that group?

Remember, these are good people who want something different. Without a vision, what chance do they have? The first and most important value of visions is that they give us hope for the future. This hope may be just beyond reach, yet we have every chance of achieving it. By contrast, idle fantasizing or fearful projecting of the future can lead to despair and hopelessness. Taken to the extreme, these can manifest themselves as mental illness, alcoholism, degenerative disease, or, in the case of total hopelessness, suicide.

Hope for the future is a driving motivation to continue working at improving our individual, family, or work situations. We have seen and experienced many instances in which "miraculous" solutions to difficult or seemingly impossible situations have emerged when the people involved had the wisdom and courage to **spin the vision.**

One of the most useful ways of thinking about the future is to "spin the vision." Again, visions are pictures or statements of our preferred future that are rooted in our values. We can spin visions for ourselves as individuals and for the enterprises of which we are a part. It is helpful to recognize that visions occur in varying degrees of clarity, some being very clear and others being less clear and not completely formed. We conceptualize visions as falling into four phases of clarity:

- Misty Outlines—Something is there, a notion, a sense, a feeling worth following up

- Foggy—We know what it is, but the details are unclear. We're getting excited about it; it's becoming a high priority for us to put some real energy into it

- Partly Cloudy—The vision is pretty well formed, and we are excited about it. We can move the idea into strategic planning to test for feasibility, and it is time to touch base with others to make sure their input is considered

- Clear—We know what to do, what resources are needed, the benefits, who could do it, and how much it could cost. We're ready to select this vision and develop strategic goals that express our intent to move toward fulfilling the vision.

An important caution is in order here: Visions do build excitement, energy, and hope. In the excitement of developing visions, it is tempting to make commitments of personal or organizational resources prematurely, before the necessary staff work is done to ensure that the new direction is consistent with other activities and that it is feasible within the limits of available resources.

Over and over in our business we have heard people at the closest point of action comment on how they must take the executive's irons out of the fire because they made decisions without reasonable operational data. Generally this extra work is at the expense of the profits of the company.

Focusing on the future is healthy and effective to the extent that it has relevance to the present. Many individuals (and organizations) get into an unhealthy preoccupation with the future. A very important example of preoccupation with the future shows up in the planning activities of some organizations.

Many large enterprises have developed full-time positions for planners. A danger in doing this is that the role of planner is often misunderstood and managers abdicate their legitimate planning roles to the planners, who in turn devote all of their time to developing plans. A problem with plans, of course, is that as soon as they are committed to paper, some significant aspects of the situation change in unanticipated ways, necessitating a change in the plans. While this can be frustrating to the organizations, it does represent the possibility of continued employment for the planner!

A related danger in this type of planning process has been evident in several of our client organizations. The planning responsibility is entrusted to planners, who have lots of responsibility and little authority.

Meanwhile, line managers, who are relieved of their planning responsibilities take little ownership in the planning process and the resulting plans. Frequently they see the planning activity as an unnecessary overhead burden that could be more appropriately devoted to the direct work of the enterprise. These managers grudgingly and reluctantly supply the planners with information they need for planning and complain about it taking them away from their "real" work.

We have also experienced people's reluctance to visualize the future much beyond their present work assignments or their immediate promotion. It is threatening to some people to have several visions in various stages of clarity. Visions seem threatening for a variety of reasons, including past disappointments, low self-esteem, low levels of skill, or being surrounded by people with a "can't do" attitude. As we stated before, **most people go through life riding on other people's visions!**

We see one of our challenges as giving people tools and perspectives to help them lift their sights, aim at more meaningful work/life situations, and go for it. One of those tools is the use of **MISTY, FOGGY, PARTLY CLOUDY,** AND **CLEAR** phases of a vision. Take time right now to:

1. **List those personal visions** which fit in any of the four categories. How difficult was it? For those who are excited about their life and look forward to each day as a great opportunity this takes a half hour. For others, this may take a great deal longer.

2. **Pick the vital few visions** out of each category and set up a plan to move them through to the clear status. Note that some may take from days to years to accomplish. We have been in business for ten years and are still working on some of the visions we had before we set up the company.

3. When getting ready to do some "for real" strategic planning on the most clear vital few visions **stay open to new information** about the actual situation happening today. Visions make it when they are realistically tied into the vital few needs of the NOW.

4. **CONSTANTLY KEEP UPDATING OUR VISIONS** IN ALL CATEGORIES AGAINST THE TEST FOR HOPE, EXCITEMENT, AND ENERGY. Do this by simply asking ourselves "How do we FEEL about this vision now? Why?" The why question will either help us continue with this vision or drop it. There are times when we may want to include others in this process, both because it may be a work situation, or we may want some personal help.

The Power of Vision in Bringing About Change has been shared. Like many good ideas this doesn't stand alone. The way we work in the PRESENT has a lot to do with merging visions into reality.

CREATIVE TENSION AND HOW IT AFFECTS CHANGE

It is in the present that the very processes of change occur, where we have the opportunities to maintain appropriate continuity with the past as we move into the future.

One of the central concepts of the Work/Life Management System is the idea that tension is required in the present in order for the system to operate either in a creative, sustaining fashion or in a destructive fashion. It is like a rubber band; with no tension, the system is useless; with too much tension, it breaks. With the right amount of tension it functions effectively.

We distinguish two types of tension that can and do occur in any human enterprise: **creative tension and dysfunctional tension.**

Creative Tension

Creative tension is based in the difference between what is and what we would like to be. It inspires us to take necessary action to achieve something worthwhile. Perhaps we can illustrate the concept by citing several examples of behaviors or situations that foster creative tension:

- Having mutually understood, accepted, and supported goals that are beatable/achievable and that stretch the enterprise by challenging its resources and capabilities and stimulating its creativity

- Encouraging people to take knowledgeable risks and being willing to support them when they "fail"

- Recognizing "failures" as opportunities for growth, development, and creative problem-solving

- Matching people and work for challenging opportunities with a commitment for ongoing performance assessment and review

- Being willing to value diversity of skills and ideas as a valuable resource, and managing in such a way as to capitalize on those differences

- When appropriate, giving criticism without blame

- Providing positive feedback (validation) for well-dones.

When asked to identify those things that can or do lead to creative tension in their organizations, our clients typically come up with lengthy lists of possibilities.

Try it for your own family or work situation. What are some specific ways to build creative tension in the enterprises of which we are a part? Make a list, see how we are doing, and discover possibilities of doing an even better job of fostering a situation of creative tension.

The other type of tension that can seriously impact change is DYSFUNCTIONAL TENSION.

Dysfunctional Tension

Dysfunctional Tension, in many ways, is the opposite of CREATIVE TENSION. We have seen many examples of tremendous resources being wasted when individuals, groups, and the enterprise engage in operating predominately under dysfunctional tension. Situations of dysfunctional tension draw resources away from an enterprise's mission and purpose and can literally eat the heart out of the it. Here are some examples:

- Hiring relatives, girl friends, or cronies at the expense of current employees and the company's pocketbook.

- Psyching out the boss to make sure that the "800 pound gorilla" gets the expected results, not necessarily the results that are best for the company:

    - Telling people what they want to hear, not what they need to know

    - Setting goals that are so unrealistically high that the enterprise is doomed to failure before it starts

    - Parceling out work to people, but keeping the overall strategy a secret

    - Routinely focusing on what is wrong and finding fault, pinning blame, and punishing the guilty;

    - Abusive use of alcohol or other drugs, with negative consequences at home, at work, and in other situations.

A key to creating a climate of creative or dysfunctional tension lies in the behavior of the people who are part of the system. Creative tension is fostered by what we call "valuing behavior," which is behavior that is positive and supportive of other people.

To value other people means to support their wholeness, their health, their well-being, their positive self-concept, their contributions, and their dignity.

This does not necessarily mean that valuing behavior is soft. Sometimes the most caring and valuing thing we can do for another person is to forthrightly confront them about their own behavior or situation.

For example, we recently had an "opportunity" to confront an assistant pastor of a church about his chronic body odor problem. Neither the senior pastor nor any other member of the congregation had been willing to speak to the young man about his body odor for fear of embarrassing or humiliating him. So instead, everyone had talked about it behind the man's back. Was this valuing behavior? We think not.

When we confronted him about his body odor, several things happened. His initial reaction was to be self-conscious and ashamed. As is true for most people with unpleasant body odors, he was not aware of it.

We ultimately discovered that he bathed regularly and that he laundered his clothes but he had not learned about dry cleaning the only wool sweater he owned! The solution to his problem was quick and easy, and he has expressed gratitude to me for being honest with him.

We describe the other end of the behavior spectrum as "devaluing behavior," which is behavior that is negative toward other people. Devaluing behavior lies behind most dysfunctional tension in families and organizations. The result is that people waste a lot of time and energy protecting themselves from the effects of devaluing behavior. You will note that dysfunctional tension and devaluing behavior are directly related to each other. Here is the relationship we have been describing:

DEVALUING BEHAVIOR<——>DYSFUNCTIONAL TENSION
VALUING BEHAVIOR<————————>CREATIVE TENSION

We have offered specific "how-to's" for increasing valuing behavior and building creative tension.

What conclusions should we draw about how creative tension affects change? Yes, change also will occur in a climate of dysfunctional tension. Sometimes the cost includes losing good people, unnecessary delays, excessive scrap and rework, ulcers, heart attacks, and withholding new ideas and useful information.

Take the time right now to analyze our own situations. What opportunities do we have to increase valuing behavior and change the situation from one of dysfunctional tension to creative tension?

Involve other people with whom we work in this activity. Be prepared for some creative and exciting possibilities!

Why Beliefs are Critical Elements in the Process of Change

Beliefs about such things as managing, communication, human behavior, organization, work, and conditions for success have been sources for success and/or failure for all of us. We all have them. Sometimes we follow them and sometimes we don't. They are our beliefs and we have a choice to use them, ignore them, or change them.

Here are samples of beliefs expressed to us by hundreds of people:

What I permit I promote.
If it ain't broke don't fix it.
Most people want to do a good job.
I must inspect what I expect.
What goes around comes around.
What I don't chart I won't improve.
I can't create the energy for change.
If I want it done right I do it myself.
I never squelch a generous impulse.
Treat everyone as my customer.
Golden rule —those who have the gold, rule.
We can't separate our work lives from our private lives.

CAUTION: Remember that beliefs are a part of each person's fiber. There are a number of the beliefs listed above that don't fit us. The same may be for others. If we know your beliefs, then we have good information about "what makes you tick". For example :

- One of our beliefs is that we cannot create the energy for change. When people who work with us know that, they realize that we will provide opportunities for them to be a part of a project. The extent to which they really get involved is directly related to the hope, excitement, and energy they bring to the party. This belief has stood us in good stead over and over again.

- Another of our beliefs is that what "**we permit, we promote**" (as stated before). This means if I see something going on that needs correcting and don't make an effort to see that it is handled, then we own part of that situation. Even if we are on the periphery, we still have a responsibility to declare our position. Do we do this all the time? No, but I work hard at following up on the VITAL FEW. We have had hundreds of people in supervisory and non-supervisory positions list their beliefs about managing. Over and over again they were surprised at their own beliefs and those of others.

Differing beliefs can be a root cause for many problems at work and at home. For example:

We may have a belief that we should treat everyone as our customer (since customers are important to us , so is everyone else). We work with someone who believes that "put down" humor is okay in the work place. Put down humor is devaluing behavior, treating everyone as our customer is valuing behavior. It seems to us that we could be at odds with each other. We find this particular set of beliefs very often in the businesses with which we have contact.

We have divided beliefs into two groups—Corporate Beliefs and Personal Beliefs.

CORPORATE BELIEFS are those beliefs that are commonly subscribed to by at least a critical mass of the people employed by that enterprise. There are formally written corporate beliefs and unwritten ones. Whether written or unwritten, they both greatly affect change. Some formally written corporate beliefs are:

- We believe in the respect for the integrity of the individual.

- We believe in striving for excellence in the quality of our products.

•We believe in providing the best possible service to our customers.*

* 3 Basic IBM beliefs

Some unwritten corporate beliefs which some people subscribe to are:

•A belief in budgeting high on expense and low on income. Positive belief

•A belief that what our customers don't know won't hurt them. Negative belief

•A belief that a budget is the price of our plan not a license to spend. Positive belief

•A belief in keeping our cash flow healthy even if it is at the expense of our suppliers. Negative belief

Once again these are beliefs we've run into with various enterprises. Some we concur with and others we don't. Maybe it is just as well that some of the above aren't written down. If we were a supplier to the company that believed in operating at our expense, we would have to make it worth our while to do business with them.

One of our corporate written beliefs is **"The most prevalent form of organizational theft is the withholding of useful information"**.

Here are some things that we can do to check out our beliefs:

CORPORATE BELIEFS:

Check the corporate employee manual and public relations literature for written beliefs. In many cases they say "Corporate Beliefs."

List the common working beliefs that people adhere to that are not written down. Check out their understanding about how those beliefs impact work situation the most. Be ready for a lot of blank faces. Persist! The payoff will be directly related to increasing the flow of useful information which will help increase your effectiveness. If we are unable to find any — CALL W/LSI, BECAUSE THE COMPANY COULD USE OUR HELP.

PERSONAL BELIEFS:

List those beliefs that should be shared with others. (Make a separate list of those to be kept private.)

Share these beliefs with the various individuals and groups with whom we work most closely. Ask for feedback regarding how close our behavior matches their beliefs, as they see it.

If some of our feedback is that we say one thing and do another, ask them for specifics and to let us know when that happens the next time. If it is really negative, ask them to do it privately. Now we have a choice—to do something or not to do something. We may want to get help from someone who is not directly associated with our everyday work. Take this suggestion seriously. We know people who have lost good jobs because they got into sloppy habits of not following what they believed.

Our beliefs can be very difficult barriers in the process of change. We all have cultivated our beliefs over long periods of time, and with a great deal of ownership. Even following the ones we like is difficult if the people around us operate differently. **Making changes of significant worth in an enterprise will invariably run up against someone's beliefs.**

How they are dealt with is the critical issue. In a valuing way? Devaluing Way?

We intend to keep operating— in a valuing way with all our warts and sharp edges. That's why Managing Change is Everybody's Business.

We have covered a lot of ground tilling the fertile soil of managing change. We've planted some seeds about how HABITS, MEMORIES, LABELS, VISIONS, TENSION, AND MANAGING BELIEFS affect all of us as we go about doing the work we are hired to do. The moisture is provided by our growing interest. As our interest has grown, so have the seeds. It is time now to cultivate those crops and prepare for the harvest.

As we do this let us keep in mind what the Bible has to say:

To every thing there is a season,
and a time to every purpose under Heaven.
—Ecclesiastes 3:1

Having visited the past, looked at the future, and explored the present, we now revisit our concept of change. We see change as the **process in the present of maintaining appropriate continuity with the past as we move into the future.**

CHANGE MODEL

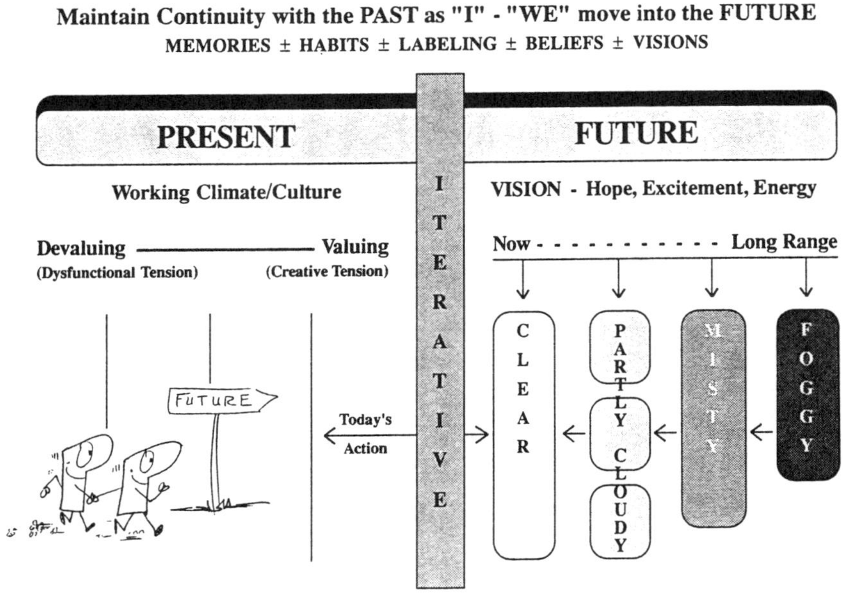

The idea of "appropriate continuity" suggests that there are some things from the past that are still of value to us and are still useful in light of current or anticipated situations, which we want to carry with us into the future. At the same time, there are other things from the past that may or may not have served us well then, but which are no longer helpful or of value to us, and that we want to leave behind.

This is illustrated nicely in a recent communication from the Chief of the U.S. Forest Service to his employees. The Chief's message was that as an organization, their desire was to hang on to many of the traditional values upon which the organization was founded, but to be willing to abandon traditional methods of doing business in favor of new methods that are more appropriate to this day and age.

SOME CHANGE IS NOT ORDERLY

Even in our own description of change as maintaining **continuity with the past as we move into the future**, we run the risk of implying that all change is an orderly, linear, and predictable step-by-step process.

While this is true of some managed change, many types of change are far from orderly. Often, events from outside or inside the business/family throw the system into chaos or disorder that threatens the status quo. The business/family responds in one of three ways:

1. ***It successfully nullifies the effects of the events and returns to its original state*** (e.g., companies getting rid of employees who are union organizers, families go back to find fault and pinning blame)

2. ***It becomes overwhelmed by the event and dies*** (e.g., goes out of business; a marriage breaks up); or

3. ***It reaches a crisis point and breaks through to a new, higher level of functioning as a system.*** This higher level of functioning represents a creative act on the part of the business and family members.

An important thing to recognize here is that the events that bring about the kinds of discontinuous change described here are often small in relation to the size and scope of the organizations they affect. For example, there are many documented cases in which product safety lawsuits have toppled large companies.

As another example, legal action by an environmental coalition stemming from their concern for the maintenance of suitable habitat for the Spotted Owl is likely to have far-reaching consequences for the ways in which the U.S. Forest Service and other federal and state agencies manage millions of acres of public lands. As of this writing, this drama is still being played out, and the outcomes are not yet clear. (Note: this comment was made 5 years ago as I began writing this book. Today the whole logging industry in Washington and Oregon are significantly impacted by the "locking up to timber land". To protect the Spotted Owl. Some still question the need to take such drastic steps to protect the Spotted Owl.

For all of us, this type of discontinuous change poses a dilemma. First, the events that stimulate these changes represent tremendous opportunities for organizations to be creative and achieve marvelous breakthroughs in their own growth. Thus, we all are challenged to create and nurture a working situation in which people can respond creatively and take the risks necessary to bring about effective change.

At the same time, we all have a responsibility to manage the current system efficiently and effectively. While these two directions may appear contradictory, it is possible, and necessary that managers take a "both-and" perspective. They must strengthen, work with, and give the current system every opportunity to succeed, and at the same time, be willing to let go and break through to new approaches as the situation demands.

SUMMARY

In summary, we recognize change as a process in the present for maintaining appropriate continuity with the past as we move into the future. Change is a way of life; it is always with us whether we want it or not. The question is not whether or not to change, but rather how and in what ways we want to change to benefit ourselves individually and collectively. Each of us has responsibility for harvesting and making use of these ideas. We need to begin to use them to our advantage now.

Chapter 14

Work/Life Approaches to Managing Change

Chapter 14

Work/Life Approaches to Managing Change

In a moment, in the twinkling of an eye, at the last trump:
for the trumpet shall sound,
and the dead shall be raise incorruptible,
and we shall be changed.
—I Corinthians 15:52

Don't confuse me with the facts! My mind's made up!

Making change is for people who have money, we're getting along well as it is.

If it ain't broke don't fix it.

Why do we need this book to lay out for us what to do? We've heard all that stuff before.

I don't want to waste your time. We're just not ready yet.

The timing isn't quite right. Let's hold off for about six months.

Keep me informed of your new approaches. Maybe we can get together sometime and reconsider.

We really just have too many other things to do right now."

We hear these comments and many like this when people are face to face with the prospect of deciding to CONSIDER doing something different.

How does any one of us cause people to really want to change?

ANSWER—We don't. Change individually and/or collectively comes from within. We can explain what must be done and hold people to it as long as we have high influence and control. For some people, getting started at doing something, even against their own desires, eventually gives them enough exposure to the new idea that they see something in it for themselves AND THEN CHANGE.

For example when word processors first appeared on the market, a number of our clients had difficulty introducing them to top typists. One lady was adamant, and said, "I wasn't hired to work on a computer. I'm too old to start something new now. I can get MY work done just as well without it. After all I've been doing it this way for the past thirty years. Why I even remember when they first came out with electric typewriters twenty five years ago." The person she was talking to responded with the question, "How did you feel about having to change to an electric typewriter?" To which she responded, "I didn't like that either."

When change is viewed only from the "I" position, it is often difficult to see value and commit to making a change. The ***Work/Life Systems*** focus emphasizes the need to see beyond our own individual sphere to that of interdependently working with others.

Let's go back to the interdependent need for using a word processor. The woman was involved in typing technical documents and reports that had a number of repetitive bits of information from project to project and month to month. Others added information along the way.

When changes were made a lot more time was necessary to update the work. Word processing was going to speed up the process, even allow less skilled typists like technicians to input their minimal information and feel good about keeping the flow going to meet their targets (particularly after they had made a mistake).

This was explained to the woman. She reluctantly went to training class, swore that the colored screen was ruining her eyes, and knew that this new job just had too much stress attached to it. "I'm sorry," she said, "I just can't possibly do this job." Well, now what do we do? Up to this time we had a very productive employee, who is on the verge of being TECHNICALLY obsolete. Labor cost what they are, we just need to make the transition to word processing.

ONE ANSWER IS: Let's dump her! WRONG ANSWER! Well, then, we'll just TELL her she has to do it! WRONG ANSWER! Well, then we'll soften it a little and persuade her to do it. WRONG ANSWER! So what is the right answer? IT DEPENDS. Here is something we might consider doing:

1. **Determining the situation.** Take time out to reaffirm the good work she has been doing. Follow the VALIDATION Process. Describe the situation to her by showing how what IS GOING ON with her current skill and equipment is not matching up with what SHOULD BE GOING ON based on the needs of others in relation to the new drive for cost reduction, improved time schedules, and the need for flexibility.

2. **Gathering information.** For many of us, new ideas need a warming up period. The concept of VALUING people asks us to take time out for listening to their whole story. Asking questions like: How do you see this piece of equipment helping you? Give her a chance to think this through. Suggest some ways. Discuss some possibilities. Always start with these positive opportunities. Remember the OPPORTUNITY/ THREAT concept. We may even share it with her as a review. How do you see this equipment getting in the way of your effectiveness? These real negatives are valuable to her. Follow the WORKING GUIDELINES. Provide time for her to release her information until she FEELS that she has been listened to. Make sure she knows this is an information gathering phase not a decision making one. Constantly check for a mutual understanding of her information.

3. **Diagnosing the situation and information.** There are some decisions that are "boss" decisions and the best opportunity we have is to help make them work even if we don't agree, but have been heard. At the same time, this type of decision requires management to set up a process for gaining the UNDERSTANDING, ACCEPTANCE, AND SUPPORT OF THOSE PEOPLE AFFECTED BY THE DECISION. When looking at the whole package we find she is really afraid that she won't be given enough time to become competent at using the word processor. Furthermore, others have already told her horror stories about losing information, power failures, and "floppy" discs. She feels bad because she wants to always be an outstanding employee and she has read "that book about

people being promoted to their highest level of incompetency." The reasons for making a technology change were left up to a vague overview for a few minutes in a department where the manager asked for questions, then waited ten nano seconds for people to respond, and went on to another subject. She is going to retire in eighteen months and had already began the process right after her last review six months ago. She was peddling down hill and didn't think it was right of them to make her change gears on her two speed bike. She sees the word processor as a long haul all up hill, with no rest stops along the way. Even old horses are given the lighter loads before they are turned out to pasture. **Thou good and faithful servant you have done well, go and retire gracefully**. There you have it. **Now what do we do?**

4. **Settle on mutually understood, accepted, and supported expectations for the period**—from now to retirement in 18 months—and how to go about getting them done. In other words THE PLAN. Many people are afraid of change because they lack the skill at VISUALIZING the outcomes in a way that has value for them. For this visualizing to be meaningful she needs:

- In depth information about the word processor, what it does, how it works, what it looks and feels like, and why it is of such value to the enterprise.

- Assurance that she is scheduled for training at a pace that will ensure her success.

- Opportunity to visualize how this new skill may or may not be of help to her during he retirement.

- CWB (criticism without blame) regarding her obligation to perform a fair day's work for a fair day's pay up to her retirement date. There are times during transition from one technology to another that overlapping skills are needed. This consideration may be a win/win solution . She becomes willing to fill in for the next 18 months in those areas that still require a typist and not obligate her to word processing training. Where the SPIRIT OF INTENT is an openness to value both the person and the enterprise, people find ways to help change occur.

5. Implementing the plan. As it worked out, she elected to be the roving typist and accommodate those areas that needed her skill during this time:

- She attended the word processing training to become familiar with its possibilities and give her an opportunity to become skilled for her own awareness and possible suggestions for further use as she continued to do typing.

- A special effort was made to keep informed about how she felt towards moving to various areas.

- All the people she worked for contributed to her ongoing performance review and each included her as part of their particular department.

- She was included in the status reports regarding the implementation of word processing and saw the important part she played as general typist work decreased. The excitement of younger people being trained earlier for word processing added to her self worth.

6. Evaluation is an ongoing part of change. None of us are wise enough to set plans and have them work out perfectly. Evaluation continues to be a part of the control function in the managing system matrix that are discussed in detail throughout the remainder of this book.

The unique feature of the Work/Life System is a direct tie in of the hard, bottom line targets of an enterprise with the soft, intangible targets of how people go about working together in ways that both the enterprise and the person grow and prosper.

The six elements for affecting change as listed above are:

1. Determining the situation.
2. Gathering information.
3. Diagnosing the situation and information.
4. Having a mutually understood, accepted, and supported plan.
5. Implementing the plan.
6. Evaluating the change.

These six elements are as universal when considering change as planning, organizing, directing, leading, and controlling are in the managing system as discussed in this book.

There is an old saw that says "familiarity breeds contempt." We find people in many tough situations that have ignored these basic elements during their attempts at individual and organizational change.

We continue to stress the importance of useful information (relevant, valid, timely and reliably). Our approach to change recognizes the discipline of gathering USEFUL information. We believe that having a broad understanding of the general techniques for gathering useful information will increase the possibilities for success in many change ventures. These techniques are:

1. Committee Option
2. Questionnaire
3. Interviews.
4. Document Reviews.
5. Guidelines for Analysis and Feedback.

Our intent is to describe each of these techniques in a manner that helps us gather useful information as we go about managing change. We strongly recommend that a combination of techniques be used. Any one technique has its particular strengths as well as its unique weaknesses or limitations. The limitations of one technique can usually be offset by the strengths of one or the other methods.

Furthermore, interpretation of information (meanings we ascribe to it) is strengthened / validated by information of a similar nature from two or more additional sources.

It is very common to find the same strengths and weaknesses in an organization or individual from different sources.

1. COMMITTEE OPTION

Here we are talking about a needs assessment committee consisting of people from various levels and units of the organization. This information gathering committee can:

- Help to legitimize and add credibility to the information gathering effort throughout the organization.
- Provide valuable assistance in tailoring the collection effort to that particular organization.
- Participate in selecting the most relevant information to collect.
- Provide logistical support in the actual collection of information.
- Facilitate interpretation of results.

Whether or not a committee is used depends on several factors, including:

- Size and scope of project
- Previous information gathering experience in the organization. Think about the complexities of gathering information from 100 people—500—8000. It takes knowledge and skill based on experience. A lot of expectations are raised when formal information gathering is placed into motion.
- Attitudes in the organization about information gathering. Sometimes people are disenchanted because they have been through this before and nothing happened. In other cases information was distorted and people were sent into a turmoil.
- The credibility of the person(s) in charge of information gathering. Trust and confidence go hand in hand. The W/LS builds on the valuing of people by including them in the information gathering phase of change. Who knows what's going on better than the people involved when there is a

climate of openness and trust. Checking for things that are going well is as critical as finding those things that are not going well.

We all have probably heard the comment that a camel is a horse built by a committee. We may also have heard that where ever two or three are gathered together someone needs to be in charge. Perhaps the most accurate statement should be

WHENEVER MORE THAN ONE PERSON IS GETTING TOGETHER, MAKE SURE THERE IS UAS ON WHY?

Working with others is fun, productive, and increases the possibility for gathering useful information exponentially.

2. QUESTIONNAIRE

Many of us have experienced the questionnaire as a negative, misused tool for gathering information. We worked with one organization where a questionnaire was eight pages long and generated so many questionable conclusions that the management team was inundated with irreverent comments about what should happen to this FOUR INCH reference material. As a matter of fact some of those suggestions were implemented a year later.

A questionnaire, done properly, is an excellent method of gathering organizational information. Questionnaires can be used to:

- get indicator information that highlights areas for more in-depth study by other methods.

- get specific information in situations where the issues are clearly defined in advance.

We find the following guidelines helpful in conducting a successful questionnaire project:

- Always pretest a newly-developed questionnaire. One of the tragedies of life is the *murder of a beautiful questionnaire by a brutal gang of respondents*.

- Keep it brief. The return rate for a questionnaire is usually inversely proportional to the weight of the questionnaire. In other words the heavier it is, the fewer returned.

- Include only the most important key questions.

- Be sure that questions and the choices people are to respond to are:

1. MEANINGFUL
2. RELEVANT
3. UNDERSTANDABLE TO THOSE BEING SURVEYED.

- Make it easy to fill out. People are more likely to give checkmarks than handwritten long answers.

- Be sure the instructions must be clear.

- Assure anonymity (no one will know) and confidentiality of the responses.– There are times when the opposite is necessary, this must be UAS up front.

- Have a credible individual (i. e. the boss) endorse the questionnaire project and encourage participation.

- Make it easy to return completed questionnaires.

- Know how we will analyze and use the information before we collect it.

The majority of our Work/Life System questionnaire work is with a one page "core" questionnaire. In some instances we expand the core questionnaire to include items that pertain to a particular organization.

Be wary of any questionnaire more than four pages.

Let's look at the advantages and disadvantages of gathering information with questionnaires:

Advantages:

- relatively inexpensive
- can get information from lots of people quickly
- can be done anonymously
- consistent format and wording of questions to minimize bias
- relatively easy to tabulate and summarize
- allows easy comparisons among groups or over time.

Disadvantages:

- lack of control of the process of responding
- no opportunity to "probe" or clarify responses
- obtrusive—the questioning process may create the answers
- can result in more data than can be used or managed
- it is a snap shot in time and needs added follow-up

Why give us all this information on questionnaires? All walks of life are affected by questionnaires. The shopping malls have become a haven for questionnaire addicts.

Market research people live, breath, and masticate questionnaire information. Where does the information come from? All of us. Let's be knowledgeable about the vital ingredients for "good" questionnaires and recognize their limitations.

Questionnaires must always include a defined process for giving feedback to the people taking their time to fill it out. The best way to do this in a company is through the normal channels of management.

This means that supervisors must have the skill to listen to their peoples' view of the summary information and be open to CRITICISM WITHOUT BLAME. After all the reason for gathering information is usually to "dip stick" the temperature of the water and celebrate what's going well, and correct what isn't.

3. INTERVIEWS

Be not deceived:
evil communications corrupt good manners.
—I Corinthians 15:32

Interviewing is something all of us do. It is a way of gathering information with the primary purpose of understanding another person(s') point of view, position, knowledge of an issue, situation, or task, products, service etc.

The most general tool used for interviewing is the OPEN-ENDED QUESTION. An open ended question allows an unlimited number of responses from the person being interviewed.

Open-ended questions frequently begin with words like "what," "why," or "how." They enable the interviewer to get in-depth information from the person(s) being interviewed.

Closed questions allow only "yes-no" or limited, predetermined alternatives. Example: Do you want to drive or do you want me to drive? Do you want to go along?

Interviews can be:

- Formal or informal

- Structured, which means having predetermined questions with limited possible answers

- Unstructured, which means the questioning is guided by the responses to the previous questions. *Example.* What is your position on the recent organization change in the sales department? How do you reconcile your comments on sales with your responsibilities as the vice president of marketing?

- With one person or a number of people if the level of trust will allow them to be candid

- In person or by telephone

- Brief to lengthy

The interviewer has the option of recording the responses to interview questions by:

- Trying to remember them
- Writing complete (verbatim) or abbreviated answers
- Audio-or video taping answers
- Charting answers on chartboards, particularly in group sessions.

When gathering initial information, consider coupling individual and group interviews with a brief questionnaire. We are able to use the interview process to probe questionnaire responses and identify relevant issues.

There are times when people try to put interviewers in unintended roles, which can affect the quality and quantity of interview information. Here are some examples:

Counselor—can help me with all my problems, both personal and work related

Omniscient expert—already knows this, so I don't have to tell what I know

Go-between—to handle all my problems with upper management and take me off the hook

Shill—working at the bidding of someone else, where the information will be used to someone else's advantage and my disadvantage

Sponge —at last, someone who will listen while I dump everything that has been bothering me lately

Sympathetic—someone I can enlist to champion my cause

Academic—a person who has a lot of "book learning" but couldn't manage his/her way out of a paper bag

Shrink—if I'm not careful, she/he may discover the real me

There are also advantages and disadvantages with the interview process: Here are some things to consider:

Advantages

- Can probe and get in-depth answers
- Can check out unclear responses
- Can follow important leads with following questions
- Can encourage candor by developing rapport
- Can uncover important information in situations where the issues are not clear beforehand

Disadvantages

- Costly
- Time-consuming
- Lack of anonymity may limit candor
- Characteristics of the interviewer can affect answers (body language, the way things are said, appearance)
- Obtrusive—the questioning process may create the answers. (the person may respond with "Gee, I hadn't thought of that"
- Difficult to analyze and summarize results
- Subject to interviewer bias

Interviewing takes a lot of personal discipline and skill at listening to a person's responses long enough to ensure the accuracy of the information received. As interviewers we know that we are not perfect listeners. So we continuously check out our understanding of what is being said until the interviewee confirms our "getting it right."

There are times when asking questions that we must continuously check out peoples understanding of our question. Not because they are poor listeners, rather we are not perfect communicators. This is very important and must be adhered to!

4. DOCUMENT REVIEWS

Organizational documents and records are valuable sources of information about how the enterprise is functioning. In fact, what is not available in writing can be as important as what is in writing.

For example: if an enterprise is without written work plans, it is quite possible that important work is not getting done. The lack of written and up to date performance reviews and appraisals reflects a behavior that "the bottom line is all we are really after." The facts are that the bottom line suffers when people don't know where they are stored. We have some specific examples of this in the performance review section of chapter 12.

Some of the documents to consider reviewing are:

- Organization charts. (Changes in the past three years?)
- Planning documents (individual and corporate)
- Budgets
- Position descriptions
- Policy and procedure manuals
- Minutes of meetings from special groups, major happenings
- Financial statements (overview past three years, current year to date)
- Performance appraisals, work flow paper tracks, (officers and cross section of the rest of the enterprise)
- Annual reports and sample of correspondence files with suppliers, customers, and key internal functions
- Sampling of policies, practices, and procedures

When reviewing documents we treat them like a person being interviewed. Know what the purpose is, raise questions for future follow-up, and be aware of the "not

invented here" syndrome. That's where people rationalize not keeping track of information that is recorded normally in other enterprises and feel if it was worthwhile they would have thought of it.

Let's look at some advantages and disadvantages of document reviews.

Advantages

- Unobtrusive, not biased by the information collection process
- Can show glaring weaknesses in practices
- Can validate findings from questionnaires or interviews
- Can provide topics for interview questioning

Disadvantages

- Time consuming
- Information usually limited to the "formal" system
- Low yield, have to sort through lots of irrelevant information to get useful information
- Many documents are written to present the enterprise in the best possible light and little regard to actual practice (annual meetings, policies, and procedures that are needed to meet outsider requirements)

Document review must be selective in light of the overall reasons for gathering information. The focus is on sensing the formal information system and the extent to which people are actually doing what they say they are doing.

The formal information system has the reputation of being a "protection device" for covering various "holes" in the enterprise. If it isn't in writing people can say "I didn't know that, "or" Gee I forgot." If it is in writing, but was wrong people can say, "Well I did what it said."

It is prudent to have a continuing sense about formal documentation and its impact on future decisions.

5. GUIDELINES FOR ANALYSIS AND FEEDBACK

Information that has been collected has value only to the extent that it can be analyzed, interpreted, and presented in a meaningful and understandable way and used. Here are some guidelines:

- Plan ahead. Know how the information will be analyzed and used before collecting it. This will insure that the right information is collected in the right format.

- Questionnaire information can be completed for the organization as a whole as well as for individual divisions, departments, or other subunits. We never tabulate responses where there are less than five people in a group.

- A picture is worth a thousand words—questionnaire data in graphic form quickly conveys what it means to convey without a lot of explanation.

- Interview information can be classified into categories or themes. This process requires considerable judgement, and care must be taken to avoid bias. One way to minimize bias is to be open to additional information from others after the information is compiled.

- Involve people from the organization in the process of interpreting the results. Interpretation here is identified as the "meanings we ascribe to things." Some questions to ask people both individually and in groups for clarification are:

What do these results mean to you?
Why do you think —?
As you see it, what are some specific causes—?
How do you feel about——?

By involving people in the interpretation process, they are more likely to take ownership of the findings. Furthermore, have one of their people record the ultimate findings— those findings that have been presented and where there is mutual UAS.

- MAKE ABSOLUTELY CERTAIN that information from individuals is kept strictly confidential. It is better not to present a particular set of results when there is a risk of exposure of the answers of one or more persons. A violation of confidentiality can result in a severe setback in the process of collecting human resource data in the enterprise.

- Where possible, show specific conclusions from several sources of information. For example: a document review shows that there is no work planning system— questionnaire data reveals that many people are confused about specifically what they are hired to do—interviews reveal several specific examples of situations in which important work got overlooked and different individuals were working in conflicting directions. Conclusion—effectiveness could be increased by implementing a formal work planning system designed to focus on the vital few work.

- Keep it simple. Pages and pages of statistical tables tend to be a sleeping potion and overwhelming to those who make decisions. The bottom line is they don't get used. A simple, clear, straightforward presentation of the vital few, key findings facilitates the planning and decision making process.

Remember the reason we share this information on the general techniques for gathering useful information is: OUR FIRM BELIEF THAT GATHERING USEFUL INFORMATION REQUIRES DISCIPLINE, PLANNING, ADHERENCE TO VALUING PEOPLE, AND ENDS UP IN USEFUL RESULTS. We know that when useful information gathering is part of the culture of an enterprise that the climate for change is warm, sunny, and has just enough moisture to make sure that the vitals all grow and prosper.

We don't kid ourselves about people's ability to change. We know of a fellow who smoked for forty years, had a heart attack, recovered and never smoked again. The motivation was self evident.

Where there is a will there is a way. The best many of us can do is make sure that we share the most useful information possible, in a manner that values people and gets the job done to the satisfaction of the stockholders who have intrusted their wealth in the hands of all of us who do work for them.

We know that if we just talk to people and they listen without interacting that the retention of the shared ideas is 70% for 3 hours, 10% retention in 24 hours and 2% retention in 72 hours. Is there any wonder that parents, pastors, and many teachers have problems getting people to change?

On the other hand, when people actively express their understanding acceptance and support for a change whether it is personal or organizational, then go about practicing their commitment, we SEE EVIDENCE OF CHANGE.

Keep in mind that wherever two or more get together to do something there is a better chance for sustained change. In truth only the individual, evidence of action available for others to observe, and time will make the final judgement on lasting change.

There is much wisdom in print regarding processes for getting people together, resolving problems, making decisions, taking action, evaluating results, etc. There is an old saying "ya gotta have a dollar to make change." THERE JUST HAS TO BE SOMETHING THERE FOR CHANGE TO OCCUR.

Change is greatly influenced by our habits, memories, beliefs, labeling of people, and visions. There are both positive and negative aspects to these elements of change. None of us are omniscient (knows everything), omnipresent (all places at all times) omnipotent (all powerful) or without opportunities to change.

The last book of the old testament in the BIBLE is MALACHI. In chapter 3 vs. 6 it reads "For I am the LORD, I change not." We take HIM at HIS WORD. Everyone else is fair game.

The ***Work/Life Systems*** tools are there to be used as a betterment for man's human condition. We see ourselves as instruments to share ideas that have already impacted many people in their search for improvement in their physical, emotional and spiritual nature. For us the BIBLE provides that guidance.

DECIDING TO CHANGE, MAKING THE CHANGE, AND ENJOYING THE CHANGE ARE ALL PART OF THE SAME PACKAGE.

Have some fun, when things are tough, stay around long enough to "last" through it by keeping our eye and heart on the visions for the future. Make sure those visions are documented, continuously rerun in technicolor, and "sashay" on into success. Look at it this way. It is a lot better than the alternatives of "Woe is me, ain't it awful, there is nothing I can do, this is my lot in life."

Let's not dwell on missed opportunities and let them get in our way of changing. Missed opportunities are like last year's taxes, paid for but not of much value, unless the opportunity to refigger becomes real.

So what if others don't notice our efforts to change. Stand in front of a mirror, walk through that mirror and look at the real Mr.. Nice isn't it. Keep gathering useful information about you in ways that value our gifts, and visions for the future. Remember joy adds to our reserves in tough times. Heap up our joy bucket then there will always be enough to go around for others. Many times change comes first as a result of helping others, not trying to help ourselves.

Then there are times when we must take the beam out of our own eye before we can help others. The W/LS concepts are designed to help that process. Go in Peace.CHANGE A LITTLE!

Once again, the importance of change is tied into how we increase valuing behavior and the flow of useful information as a direct means of building trust. Trust makes change less frightening.

For we are saved by Hope, but Hope that is seen is not hope.
—Romans 8:24